War of the Angels

by

Michael Mullen

1663 LIBERTY DRIVE, SUITE 200
BLOOMINGTON, INDIANA 47403
(800) 839-8640
WWW.AUTHORHOUSE.COM

On the front cover you will see an actual drawing of SATAN as seen by Michael Mullen, author of *War of the Angels*. Satan is a real being and not a myth or a cartoon character in a red suit, carrying a pitch fork. The top of his face is that of a wolf, and the "horns" are actually his ears. The lower half of his face is "fishy." His mouth is similar to a large mouth bass, and it puckers like a fish when he breathes. In the middle of his face is a large welt in the shape of a cross, as if some other being stamped him with a hot branding iron as a sign of banishment. His torso is reptilian with scales, and the midriff looks like the underbelly of a serpent. His arms are long and lean. His legs are heavy, much like that of a dinosaur, while his tail is similar to a crocodile. In reality, Satan is part wolf, part fish, part dragon, and part serpent, all accurate descriptions portrayed in Biblical Prophecy and witnessed by the author of this book.

The picture of Satan was drawn by Stephen Mendez, Director of the WOTA Center for Exorcisms and Demonic Healings. The drawing of Satan was based upon numerous composite sketches as described by Author Michael Mullen, much in the same manner as a witness would describe a suspect to a police sketch artist.

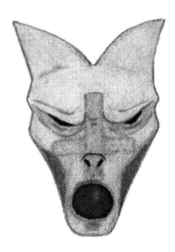

The back cover contains a computer enhanced picture of the man whose image is embedded on the controversial *Shroud of Turin*, the proclaimed burial cloth of Jesus Christ. This is the man who commanded that Michael Mullen write this book. This is also the man who branded Satan's face with a cross. The two of them are at war. This book is an eyewitness account of that war.

www.WaroftheAngels.com

War of the Angels

by

Michael Mullen

© 1981, 2001, 2005 Michael Mullen. All Rights Reserved.

No part of this book may be reproduced, stored in a retrieval system, or transmitted by any means without the written permission of the author.

First published by AuthorHouse 05/12/05

ISBN: 1-4208-4896-8 (sc)
ISBN: 1-4208-5370-8 (dj)

Printed in the United States of America
Bloomington, Indiana

This book is printed on acid-free paper.

Front cover by Stephen Mendez. Copyright © 2005. All rights reserved. May not be reproduced in any form or manner, including but not limited to: photocopying, emailing, internet posting or downloading, or digital reproductions of any type without written permission from the artist or publisher.

First Printing October, 1981 by USA Publishing
Second Printing August, 2001 by Booklocker
Third Printing April, 2005 by AuthorHouse

Visit the most unique web site on the internet
www.WaroftheAngels.com

What Readers are Saying about *War Of The Angels*

WRITER'S DIGEST BOOK REVIEW
"The thing that I found most impressive about War of the Angels is how incredibly believable it is. I found myself unable to put the book down once I began reading. I think that the author merged the stories of the U.S.S. Indianapolis and War of the Angels very successfully."

FIVE STARS! TWO THUMBS UP! I knew the author a quarter-century ago when he was writing this book. I can attest to the fact it was originally written a long time ago, yet it seems like today's headlines. It is already coming true; everything in it. How can anyone read this book, watch the daily news and not believe it? This book will make a lot of enemies of non-Christians. The author makes it quite clear that you are on one side of the fence or the other. Hence, I think readers will rate this book either 5 Stars or 1 Star with nothing in between. I give it 5 Stars because I see it happening all around me. I already know a lot of people who are getting into heated arguments after reading this. Non-Believers will try extremely hard to prevent you from reading this book. And so will Satan.
John Z., Retired Judge, Texas

"As an enlisted soldier I feel that this book can give me a further understanding and insight to the truths of our present day positioning in the war, and can be used as a valuable tool to recruit new soldiers."
Materi

"You really have a message to tell! I don't read that many books because they don't keep my interest, but yours I read almost cover-to-cover as soon as I picked it up from the mail. You have helped make sense of what is REALLY going on in the world today! I know a lot that I can't talk about because of what I do, and your book is right on target."
(STAFF SARGENT Combat Arms/Security Specialist)

"I read War of the Angels straight thru. I could not sleep afterwards. I heard a voice in my stomach say, 'Believe,' clear as day."
Jason

"It was great! I saw an angel too and it was huge."
Aaron at AOL

"Worth its weight in Gold! This book has changed my life! This book is truly inspired by the Holy Ghost! I can confirm that this book was written before any of the prophesies manifested. You can find evidence of the latest terror attacks on Spain and a warning before Sept. 11th! The FBI has a copy of this book... its too bad they didn't find the book earlier."
Amazon Review

"War of the Angels reads like a story and not just telling facts. The characters make me want to see the movie. And it is very, very convincing."
Tony D., St. Petersburg, FL

"My mother read your book and she can't stop laughing about the scene with the cows."
Fritz P., Indianapolis, IN

"It is the best book I have ever read in my life. It is wonderful."
Sue C., St. Petersburg, FL

"Oh, wow. I'm so nervous. It's really going to happen. I can already see it in the news."
Trivonda R., Jacksonville, FL

"I believe you (the author) are really blessed. Can you say a prayer for me?"
Carol, St. Louis, MO

"I drove to a bookstore looking for a copy (of War of the Angels) just to see what all these wild claims of angels were about. I found your book interesting and moving, if not unsettling and terrifying. The strangest thing for me was the feeling that i

knew and felt completely what you were saying, and more importantly that i believed you. Immediately i started to do research of my own on the topics you spoke of. The messages that i came across in War of the Angels have stayed with me to this day, especially when i follow the actions in the Middle East and the EU."
Michael

"The book is remarkably enthralling. The prophecies are shocking, and deeply disturbing. I just hope you're not right."
G.H., British Soldier in Iraq

"When I read your book, it just hit me as true. Then my skepticism kicked in, and I wondered, but something just felt right about it. I just FELT it was truth, if that makes sense. Suddenly, I heard a voice, an audible voice that I will never forget say "I AM." It came from the area of my chest, that's the only way I can describe it. It was loud without yelling, commanding, I just lay there stunned."
Linda C.

"I am extremely aware of my angels presence now, always to my right, in the back of me. It is so noticeable that I find myself turning around constantly to see if someone is standing there. I am really starting to understand much more about why these things are happening."
Wilson

"It had me hooked the entire way. The book is so gripping and intense, it's easy to say, "My God, that sounds so right, this HAS to be true!" But I'm not sure if God would allow a person on Earth to know this much if it is in fact true. The entire "Holy Mafia" information was spine-chilling. (The book) prevents me from seeing anything in this world the same way again after knowing all this, and this is really what gives the author so much credibility in my eyes. Regardless if this book is true or not, I thank Michael Mullen for spectacular new insight into the realm of the supernatural, and quite possibly, the Holy prophecies themselves."
Talisac

"Be aware of the Holy Spirit while you are reading War of the Angels. I must say that I did feel an overwhelming kind of spiritual harmony, and for the first time in my life, I truly did believe. The power of the book is so compelling, that I simply can't NOT believe it. Seriously mate, read the book. In my humble opinion, not only did it open my eyes, but it gave me a sense of "knowing." I knew I was being watched by something not so nice and I know it didn't like me reading the book, but it just cemented my belief in the revelations in the book."
Graham, British Paratrooper

"Reading the book felt like entering some kind of strange conflict, just by knowing. There was a feeling that I was reading something very serious with two sides pulling on me. Definite chills, as if it was important to read it, but there was some unsettling force that didn't enjoy me reading it. The message in the book is strong, very strong, more than just a good story."
Mars

"This book is ALIVE man!! My brain keeps talking to me that it's fake, and my insides are busting out to say it's real. But I can SEE it now. It's everyday on TV. I'm going to hand it to my friends and watch their look when angels or something start talking to them!!!"
Chad

"What can I say? Amazing!! I really believe that your story is from the Lord. And that you have a mission from Him."
G.B. (Sweden)

"I am really impressed. I can't wait to read it in French."
Nick (Quebec)

"Se presisarem da minha ajuda, estou a disposicao. E so dizer quem e o alvo!"
Lourenco Benedito Neto, Portugal

"Czy mozecie mi przyslac jakies info na wasz temat, bo bardzo mnie to zainteresowalo...Pozdrawiam! Szem ha-meforasz!!!"
Ewa, Poland

"Before I read (War of the Angels) I believed in the other world, sort of. I have become more aware of things. I was tested yesterday, when I did not do what it wanted me to do and it visited me last night. I just kept repeating `BY THE POWER OF HIS BLOOD.' This has helped me drive evil away. It keeps trying to get us, but you have helped."
Linda

"This would make the coolest movie I ever saw."
Allen

"I have read (War of the Angels) and a couple of my friends have also read (it). We find your book amazing and I also believe."
Fred M.

"Wonderful!!!! I believe God led me here for a reason. I loved reading (War of the Angels) about the spiritual world that exists out there."
H.S.

"I just finished War of the Angels in 1 day! It was a very powerful book and the Holy Spirit tells me its true."
James

"When I read (War of the Angels) it just hit me as true. Then my skepticism kicked in. But something just felt right about it. I just FELT it was truth. And I couldn't put it down, and when I was done with it, I started looking at the news, and War of the Angels popped into my mind. I have known Bible prophecy for quite awhile, but your book put a new perspective on it, brought it more into focus. War of the Angels had a powerful effect on me."
Linda S.

"I know that you speak the truth. I will tell others to listen."
Liz J.

"This book is very believable. Anyone that claims it is not believable is being stubborn and probably has an axe to grind

with the author or is close-minded to the topic in general. Of course, whether or not you believe it is up to you."
Bob F.

"This book was definitely written for the 'skeptics' at large. It has served as a great springboard in researching and examining current global events in a new light. A definite aid, in putting all the pieces together. A book that is guaranteed to generate a lot of controversial opinions and outlooks. Undeniably, this book has had an impact on my life in ways that are beyond words. It has opened my eyes to the 'unseen' world. It has given me an understanding as to the forces that surround us, and exactly what those forces are. After reading this book I have not been able to view the world the same. Written over 25 years ago, and yet it reads as today's headlines"
Amazon Reviewer

"I ran across this book on the Internet. The author made the first section of the book available online. I read the free section in one sitting, then I ordered the electronic version online, because that was the fastest available means of obtaining a copy, and I simply could not wait any longer to finish the book. Once I downloaded the book, I completely devoured it the same day. I have never read a book that captured my attention so forcefully. The story is true (despite comments made by skeptics to the contrary). The entire time I was reading the book, I kept checking to ensure that the book was indeed billed as non-fiction, because I couldn't believe what I was reading. I contacted the author via email, and he ensured me that everything in the book actually happened to him. Still skeptical, I even took the trouble to check-out some of the characters from the book, and everything I found confirmed what the book said. If you are interested in eschatology, then you will want to read this book. If you simply want to have the living daylights scared out of you, then you must read it. It will send chills down your spine."
Reviewer, Atlanta, GA

"This book was definitely interesting. The material is very controversial but entertaining. Anyone with even the slightest interest in Bible prophecy or scary stories should read this

book. If the content is even remotely true, then it is a must read!! I personally have not yet decided whether I believe it or not. However, true or not, this book is definitely unique and worth reading. The author makes no attempt to claim that those who don't believe or read his book will go to hell. He also does not say that you need to read the book to be "saved".
Barnes and Noble Reviewer

"The book reads almost like a journal. It's an account of the end times we are living in now. The information given to the author is proving to be accurate, which is convincing to me since it was written 25 years ago. It made me question everything about Christianity, to strive to be what GOD wants me to be as a Christian, not some 'collection plate church peoples' idea of Christianity. I also think a visit to the website of the same name would be EXTREMELY helpful along with reading the book. There is lots more information. You just have to look for it."
Amazon Reviewer

"Best book I've ever read! However, EVERYONE is going to be "passionate" about it. I rate it five stars, but many will hate this book because of its controversial nature and they will rate it much lower because of their disagreements. The author will make many friends and many enemies. He has drawn a line in the sand, and you are forced to stand on one side or the other. That said, you cannot deny that Mr. Mullen is an extraordinary writer. I read the entire book in one sitting. I've never done THAT before. Just could not stop turning the pages!"
Barnes and Noble Reviewer

"Just finished War of the Angels. It is full of conspiracy and things I've heard and read before. Some would say it is self serving to the author, a way to prey on fear and make him a buck. I say, if there is a modicum of truth to what he says, EVERYONE should read it and be prepared."
Barnes and Noble Reviewer

"This is the best book I have ever read. From page one I could not put it down until I had completely finished. Although it is

classified as non-fiction, it was written as a compelling story with memorable characters. I loved George the Kat, and the scenes with the cows were hilarious as a comic relief to a serious and frightful story. I would love to see it made into a movie. The supernatural events that Mullen claims to have endured are Biblically sound, and I believe him. Those who do not wish to believe simply have their heads in the sand and want to completely ignore the headline news and current events of Biblical Prophecy that is leaping right off the pages of War of the Angels. My life will never be the same. And the amount of research that Mullen put into this book supports vividly the supernatural ordeals. The facts are named, dated, and sources revealed. I found the footnotes from the family of Pope John Paul I to be dreadfully revealing in their beliefs that John Paul I was murdered. This book will definitely be controversial, for the author pulls no punches. God and angels are real. The devil is real. This book will challenge your faith if you do not believe in the Bible literally, for the author dramatically creates a solid foundation that demonstrates that all the characters in the Bible are very, very real, and that events are unfolding right before your very eyes. War of the Angels will change your life forever, as it has mine."
Amazon Reviewer

"Outstanding read! 'War of the Angels' is one of the best books I have read in a very long time...Tells of end time events, identity of the Anti Christ, Bible Prophesy of events to come in this world...This book has changed my life for the better and I thank the Author for writing this wonderful book"
Kathy, A TRUE BELIEVER!,

"Great Book, hard to stop reading. I thought this book was great. It is enthralling and suspenseful, and very believable. I enjoyed this book because I am interested in supernatural stuff and Bible prophecy. If you have even a remote interest in these topics, you will appreciate this book. Of course, whether you believe it or not is entirely up to you.. If this book is even remotely accurate in any way, then it is a must read. Serious topic and well written. Very believable. Makes you want to keep reading."
Fan of Supernatural Thrillers

To Patrick

In death, may you find the peace
you never knew in life.

You never chose to be gay.
But you surely chose the Lord.

Table of Contents

PART ONE
"THE CALL OF THE DARK WORLD"

PROLOGUE	*Bad Things in the Dark*	3
CHAPTER 1	*The Baby Beast*	12
CHAPTER 2	*Top Secret*	21
CHAPTER 3	*Beyond Human Help*	27
HCAPTER 4	*Holy Murder*	40
CHAPTER 5	*The Beast*	49
CHAPTER 6	*The Origin of Bad Things*	59
CHAPTER 7	*Sumpin's Not Right*	71
CHAPTER 8	*The Burial Shroud Man*	89

PART TWO
THE RULERS OF DARKNESS

CHAPTER 9	*Open Wide the Gates of Hell*	113
CHAPTER 10	*There's Something Scary in My Basement*	127
CHAPTER 11	*The Drive To Hell*	138
CHAPTER 12	*Demon Priests and Holy Evil*	143
CHAPTER 13	*The Pit and the Dark Assassin*	157
CHAPTER 14	*Christmas*	167
CHAPTER 15	*Ancient Secrets*	184

PART THREE
WAR OF THE ANGELS

CHAPTER 16	*Get Out of That House -- NOW!*	195
CHAPTER 17	*I Beat You! I Beat You!*	200
CHAPTER 18	*Michael and the Living Star*	206
CHAPTER 19	*It Ain't Over, 'Til It's Over*	210
EPILOGUE	*Bad Things in the Dark*	221

PART ONE

"THE CALL OF THE DARK WORLD"

"For we wrestle not against (humans) ... but against (the demonic orders), against powers, against the rulers of the darkness of this world, against spiritual wickedness in high places."

Ephesians 6:12

PROLOGUE
Bad Things in the Dark

August 2, 1945
The South Pacific Ocean

"Shark! Shark! Oh, God! Oh, God!"

Bad things happened in the dark and nineteen-year-old Hafford Sharp tried to drown out the piercing screams coming from beyond the waves. It was frightening listening to a man being eaten alive. Piece by piece. The terse yelps of "*Shaaaark!*" intensified in the otherwise silent night. They called them, *Loners*. A nameless, faceless comrade who'd drifted too far from the dwindling group of *U.S.S. Indianapolis* survivors. Sharks whet their appetites on *Loners*, especially at night. 'Twas better to be dead, than to be a *Loner*. Suddenly it was over. A final "Sha..." was abruptly cut short, and the severed scream from this *Loner* clung to the moon and the stars, and would not fade away. The eerie nothings which followed proved to be the most dreaded sounds of all.

The nightly terrors of being lost at sea in the South Pacific proved unbearable. By his fourth day adrift in a tattered life jacket, at the blackest hour before dawn, the boy contemplated suicide. He justified death; nearly everyone else from the *U.S.S. Indianapolis* had already died and decomposed. He'd *earned* eternal rest, reasoned a voice from within, and he deserved to die as an escape. Fear of the night caused others to drown themselves, but Hafford yearned to see his family once more, and he postponed drowning himself, for a little while, at least.

When bad things happened, young Hafford tried his best to ignore them. Finally, *Insanity* befriended him as a life-saving mechanism and made the horrors go away. His brain escaped. His mind wandered home safely to Decatur, Alabama.

His fears dissipated into fond memories of yesteryear, to those carefree times when Momma and Daddy chased the goblins and ghouls into hiding—to those innocent days when his greatest fears were childish nightmares of wetting-the-bed or of having broccoli for dinner.

Reminiscing was more than a pastime for the lanky farm boy; it was a lifesaving ritual—thinking of home, recalling childhood pleasantries—while bobbing like a popped cork in a storm-tossed, tropical sea.

His naked, six-foot frame saddled the bucking waves and rode out the latest rain squall, as he and the diminishing survivors of *U.S.S. Indianapolis* prayed for rescue.

What was he doing here? he thought. Hafford should not have been in the water; he should not have been in the Navy at all. He'd flunked his physical; he was color-blind and not fit for military duty. He should have been home working in the hosiery mills, as he'd done since age sixteen, helping Daddy financially until their cotton fields bloomed for harvest.

Instead, he'd deceived his way into the service. He tried to enlist in the Navy in Decatur, but he failed the eye examination and was turned away. Wanting to serve his country, he sauntered into a nearby town, into another recruitment center where he started anew, *hush-hush*, with his physical. But he failed the eye test again.

Determined to join the Navy, he journeyed to a third enlistment board, in yet another town, and took the eye test once more. He'd familiarized himself enough with the color-charts by this time, that he was able to bluff his way through for a passing grade. His parents had bid him a proud farewell when he reported to boot camp last November for a life at sea.

But now the sea demanded too much. The boy yearned for the simplicities of life on the farm, and for the childhood security of a blanket pulled over his head.

A wave scaled his life jacket and choked him. He was sinking, dreadfully slow, like a helium balloon after four frantic days of treading the ceiling to avoid the deadly floor. The kapok stuffing in his vest bore an efficiency rating of only forty-eight hours, wrongly judged adequate by equipment designers, since rescue operations rarely exceeded two days. But his time spent in the water now *doubled* the limit.

Many drowned when their heavy jackets plummeted below. The salty sea knotted the leather cords too taut to be released. The frantic victims were ironically trapped inside the faulty equipment designed to save them.

They kicked back to the surface for a gulp of air and to beg God for mercy. They pleaded with their buddies to hold them above the water. They screamed for someone to help untie the cursed knots that doomed them.

Hafford tried saving one shipmate, but he lacked strength to support him, and had to sadly let go. The frightful cries echoed in Hafford's mind as he, himself, inched lower to death, and rested his chin on the polluted surface in a nauseating pool of oil.

When *Indianapolis* sank Sunday night, she still maintained three-quarters of her fuel capacity, and it spewed into the Pacific. The resulting oil slick drifted with the survivors, never parting its own separate way.

Oil coated Hafford. He sipped a rancid breath of air from atop the petroleum spill, and an uninvited splash of diesel fuel purged his stomach once again. Blood erupted from the cracked pit of his guts. He vomited. Often, the rankness of the fumes alone sparked convulsions, as if he'd cupped his mouth over the exhaust pipe of an untuned city bus and drawn a deadly breath. And when his poisoned lung sacs defiantly gasped for fresh air, they were treated only to a torment of sludge gushing down his opened mouth.

But as dizzy and nauseated as Hafford was, the internal pain from the oil and its fumes was a mere bodily discomfort, compared to the agony of the fuel soaking his ever-swollen eyes, burning as if a careless service attendant had sprayed a tank of ethyl gasoline into his opened eyes.

The situation worsened as Tuesday blended into Wednesday, when the oil transformed chemically into a thick, gummy pitch. It stuck indelibly to everything. Hafford's eyes bonded shut and his lashes fused together; his nasal passages swelled; his ears clogged; his hair sealed to the scalp. Unruly waves slapped tar onto his face—already bared raw by the rugged environment—and cemented his burning agony beneath a permanent black masque.

Darkness hosted many Angels of Death, but one in particular overstayed its welcome and wouldn't depart until sunshine burned it away like daylight on Dracula. Pneumonia created less drama than did sharks devouring Loners, but its little coughs and sniffles instilled as much fear.

Unlike Loners in the distant waters, pneumonia victims were nearby and plentiful. They uttered no resounding cries for help, nor were their lives sharply terminated, as were those falling prey to sharks. Pneumonia lingered.

Pneumonia killed in an orderly manner, in cadence, by the numbers with no surprises: first came the *Wheezers*, who whistled with each drawn breath, signaling "Go!" to the earliest stages; next in rank and file, the *Rattlers*, recognizable by the phlegm pounding against their brittle chest cavities; and very finally, the *Garglers*, who choked on the fluids of Death.

Whistle, rattle, gargle, die.

One-two-three-die, one-two-three-die.

Pneumonia was dependable.

Hafford, too, feared pneumonia, especially whenever it stormed, as it did now (and which it did most evenings, usually two or three times). He wondered why the potent virus hadn't yet claimed dibs on him. He assumed Youthfulness shielded him from death, so it seemed, since pneumonia apparently killed in a descending, chronological order: (*thirty-six years and older, start Gargling; thirty-five years, your turn to Rattle; age thirty-four, commence Wheezing*).

Casualties mounted. Pneumonia victims encircled Hafford. He couldn't see them in the dark, at least not while the rain blotted out the moon, but he knew they were there (*whistle, rattle, gargle*). And there ... over there, too. Experience warned Hafford he'd soon be amidst a floating graveyard, and in search of another group. Not good to be a Loner.

The rain diminished, but Hafford's profusely running nostrils steadily dripped. Green mucous flowed down the insoluble pasting of tar on his face, and spilled over his parched and bleeding lips like mud slides from a broken dam. And only the approaching sunshine had the power to plug the dike.

The erratic environment tormented his body. He burned in the daytime and froze at night. Shivering, he awaited the new morning's thaw. Finally, the sun rose, majestically slow, ascending triumphantly to its throne over the South Pacific in one small, ceremonial step at a time. The blackness faded to gray; a teasing hint of orange peeped shyly above the horizon. It was Daylight, once more. Heaven sent.

Daylight eased his fears. The sun allied with Hafford against the evils of darkness, though like a hired mercenary, it wasn't his true friend, and it cost him dearly. For its toasty warmth, he swapped layers of skin, and drew blood from banks of exposed capillaries. And for its creature comforts, he paid tributes of pain, from wounds swathed in saltwater and diesel oil.

The sun had—and would soon again—hurt him. And unjustly, dehydration kept the boy from crying his deserved tears. But compared to the horrors of darkness, the usurious cost of daylight was a bargain at any price. A blue-light special (*Attention shoppers* ...).

But daytime failed to deliver its expected pleasantries. Instead, Morning flaunted its past, pre-dawn horrors like a retired bowler displaying his trophies on the mantle. Bodies strewn about the watery graveyard would neither sink nor drift away. Hafford shoved them aside, yet they came back to haunt him. They stayed ... stayed ... stayed.

He saw bodies and pieces of bodies. Arms. Legs. Heads. And they smelled. The remainders of what once were able-bodied men floated in the hot sun and swelled up with gas and turned blue. Occasionally, the pockets of gas burst open; the stench nauseated Hafford, but sharks sniffed the aroma as if Grandma had placed a hot apple pie on the window sill.

Bad Things in the Dark

An inquisitive shark snatched the arm of a ripened carcass like a beggar thieving a hot meal, and descended for some private dining. The body returned to the surface, minus a limb. Hafford's world was a bowl of bodies, a'la carrion, abound with feasting sharks. Waiting-to-be-next frightened him. He tried not to think of it, and he did not appreciate the floating reminders. He wished ever so hard for them to sink.

The number of bodies increased substantially with the new morning's waves, all bobbing hello. Blessed Morning. The merciful daylight enabled the strong to regroup their forces, to discourage the feeding sharks.

Generally, sharks nibbled on seasoned corpses to satisfy their appetites. They thrived on free lunches, another predator's kill ... leftovers. They savored Loners, a shark's pâté. But sharks abhorred having to work for a meal and avoided the resistance from men grouped together.

Henceforth, by dawn's first light Hafford swam off to work, begrudgingly, like a boy with an early morning paper route. He combed the area for survivors and closed ranks. By his fourth day on the job, the chore was excruciating. Few survived, widely scattered. And it was hard to distinguish the living from the dead.

A wave elevated Hafford and at its peak he tread circles, scouting the area for survivors: *dead; alive; dead; dead; dead; alive; dead.* He spied a questionable one. He swam to the person or body, whichever, to investigate. He examined closely. He couldn't distinguish rigor mortis from the stiffness of baked tar. He pried open its eyes with a crunch. It was dead. He could tell by its eyes. If the pupils were dead, the whole body was dead. Hafford moved on to the next one. His route serviced many customers.

Hafford swam past a lifeless body who startled him by begging for help. He towed the half-dead shipmate beyond several waves, to a place where the fittest gathered the weak into a crude, protective ring. *Circle the wagons, boys!*

Back to work, Hafford swam into a puzzling situation: was it a corpse or a live body, floating aimlessly in front of him? He tore open its eyes and examined them. They didn't dilate, but still, Hafford had a gut feeling about the body. He pressed his ear against the man's face, in a pitiful effort to detect breathing. He couldn't tell. He slipped a hand inside the vest, and felt the man's chest cavity expand.

Hafford slapped him in the face to keep him alive. "Hey!"

The would-be cadaver uttered a fragmented, "Goway."

"Hey! Stay alive!" Hafford slapped him again.

"Goway. Leave me 'lone."

"Just stay alive. Stay alive a little while longer. Help is on the way. It will be here any minute, now."

"Wanna die."

Hafford grabbed hold of the man's life jacket, and tugged him to the group. When Hafford released him, the man drowned himself.

Hafford located another desolate shipmate, and offered encouragement to keep him alive. "Help is on the way."

"Heard it before. Not true. Nobody's coming."

"Yes, they are. Yes, they are."

"No. Gonna die. All of us. No use." He closed his eyes to die.

Hafford shook him.

"Leave me be," the man protested. "Let me die."

Hafford smacked an open palm across his cheek. "Stay alive!"

The man's eyes shot open. "Do that again ... I'll kill ya."

Intimidated, Hafford swam away. There were others on his morning route, more responsive, more appreciative.

By mid-morning, Hafford rested. He'd expended precious energy helping to regroup seventy-five shipmates. Now he waited for the rescue he'd so freely promised as encouragement to those barely alive. Bobbing, floating, drifting, he scanned the horizons through tar-caked eyes. He pushed away bodies and pieces of bodies, thinking about home and postponing suicide. Somebody would come looking for them. He believed.

Hafford kept a vigilant guard, scouting for ships or planes. But something was amiss. *Train tracks* now scaled the waves. He hadn't noticed *them* before. An oversight? How could he have been so stupid? He hadn't thought to watch for a rescue by train. Had he missed it?

There it was! Rescue! Help arrived. The locomotive chugged down the track. Its light shined a ray of hope; its stack spouted a smoky welcome. Thoughts of Alabama and family filled his joyous mind. Momma would have a nice, hot meal for him and a warm, clean bed made up. *Sweet home Alabama*!

A new danger evolved, however. He'd floated directly into the train's path. The barreling locomotive was about to run him down. Its whistle shrieked an ominous warning: *MMoooooove*! *MMoooooove*! Hafford tried to swim clear of the track, but entranced, he couldn't move and ...

Luckily, a wave pushed the track aside.

Hafford gawked as the train pulled into the station. Oh, God! He didn't have a ticket. He tediously swam across and purchased one for Decatur.

He relished the sounds of this home-bound train: the bells clanked; the whistle shrieked; the steam hissed. Treading water, he waited for the conductor's blessed words for all to board. But the train didn't stop. Hafford sadly watched it roll past. He heard the rumble of the rails, felt the heavy vibrations. People waved to him out of the windows, and he waved back.

He sadly watched the caboose fade across the sea. In spite of his dehydration, the boy gathered enough moisture to shed a crocodile tear. He had missed the train home.

The farm would be pleasant this time of year. Nicer than floating in the ocean, oh yes. The upland cotton would be in flower. Daddy would need him soon, when the white puffs poked through their bushy green leaves. Gotta get home. Think hard!

Hafford retained enough sanity to reason: *Let's see: the Navy won't send a ship; the planes won't land; the trains won't stop at the station—Got it*! He inserted a coin into the pay phone and called for a taxi.

The considerable wait proved worthwhile when a cab arrived. He swam to it, but a heavyset lady in a purple dress also wanted a ride. It wouldn't be mannerly of him to take this nice lady's cab, he thought. He drifted back a couple of feet and let her have it. He'd catch another. He spoke to her. "You have a good day now, Maam."

She smiled and said, "Thank you." She was kind. He wished he had a hat like hers, to keep the sun off. He helped her into the car. He waved to her, when the cab sped away. "Goodbye!" he yelled.

"Bye-bye." She returned the parting gesture, then disappeared down the road.

Many more cabs drove by, but none stopped, no matter how stringently he hailed. The cabbies waved to him as they sped by, friendly enough, but they all had fares in back. Taxis did great business on the Pacific!

Hafford raised his thumb to hitch a ride. Nice day for it. Trees lined the beautiful highway, as did flowers of every color. Freshly cut grass scented the air, and the farm boy sniffed it appreciatively. All afternoon, he floated by the edge of the road, skimming the waves, waiting patiently for a ride to Decatur.

Oh, God! The sun faded. *Hurry, somebody!* Some of his buddies removed their life jackets and waved goodbye to Hafford. They refused to survive. It wasn't smart to be alive, not now, not when Ole Mister Sun went down. Bad things happened in the dark. And the sun was going ... going ... gone.

Bad Things!

CHAPTER 1
The Baby Beast

On Friday, January 9, 1981, Sharon packed a couple of light suitcases into her maroon Oldsmobile and departed Indianapolis, Indiana, for Lexington, Kentucky, where she would visit Michael for a few days. She hadn't wanted to see him anymore. She was frightened, not of Michael, but of the Dark Things that confronted her every time she came near. Still she felt compelled to see him. She had messages to deliver. Supernatural messages for Michael, from the Man on the Burial Shroud. It was a bitter struggle between the Dark Things and the Shroud Man on whether or not she should continue to see Michael. She'd already said goodbye-forever three or four times, the last being just yesterday. But Sharon had another message and she drove a steady sixty-miles-per-hour down I-65 South toward Louisville, where she would then get on I-64 East to Lexington. She never understood the supernatural messages, but Michael always did, and that was all that mattered. This time was different, though. She understood very well the meaning of this message, and it wasn't from the Shroud Man, either. It was a warning to Michael from the Beast. As afraid as she was, she had to make the trip. Go tell Michael.

The tires on her old car passed noisily over the protruding rows of tar that separated each concrete slab of highway. The tar served as road expansion absorbers during the hot months, but in the middle of winter the black lines sticking above the concrete sections had grown cold and hard. Instead of squashing in silence beneath the car, the road drummed a rhythmic *ka-bump-ka-boomp-ka-bump-ka-boomp.*

To drown out the monotonous sounds of the road, Sharon inserted a cassette and sang. But when she reached Columbus, Indiana, her head suddenly ached too much for the stereo. She turned off Barbra Streisand in the middle of a song. But even the silence (*ka-bump-ka-boomp*) was too loud for her. Her head pounded to the beat of the car and kept reminding her she was getting sick. She made an unscheduled pit stop, topped off her tank and bought some aspirin. She pulled away, listening to the car's dreadful chanting. Near the Indiana-Kentucky border her stomach threatened to erupt. She hated to vomit. After crossing the Ohio River she stopped again, this time for stomach medicine. She would have turned back, but it was too late. She pushed onward to Lexington. Gotta tell Michael.

***

In Lexington, I wanted every detail to be perfect for Sharon. I wanted her visit to develop into a permanent move-in with me. I checked the refrigerator for the umpteenth time. I'd stocked every shelf with her favorite champagne. "*Welcome Home Sharon*" banners stretched the length of the living room. "*I love you*" notes and cards littered the floors. And each stairstep contained one word of a happy message, like *Burma Shave* signs on a highway leading up to the bedroom. I'd finished the balloons and banners long ago, but as I waited, I kept adding more. I was still scattering love notes on the bedroom floor, when I heard a commotion downstairs. *That's Sharon! She has her arms full and is shuffling around on the porch and needs help.* I skipped down two steps at a time and thrust open the door.

"Sharon, you ..."

"Mich ... *baaarfff.* Help ... *barrff.* Help me." She vomited on my front steps, so much that she had nothing to heave up but green slime, spit, and blood.

I carried her upstairs, undressed her and positioned her atop a bedroll on the floor. I had no furniture. While she napped, I retrieved her luggage from the car. I sat on the floor

The Baby Beast

downstairs, sipping coffee at a cardboard box which served as my kitchen table. I looked dejectedly at the banners. Two cups later I put away my mug, then busied myself collecting (*debris*) unread love notes from off the floors.

By early evening I made some chicken soup for her and took it upstairs. She sat up, leaning against the wall that doubled as our headboard.

"You make good chicken soup," she said, sipping from a mug, no spoon.

"Yeah, I do, don't I? You're giving me a lot of practice, huh?"

"Uh-huh." She'd been sick every visit. "Got any crackers?"

"No. I'll go get some. There's a store right ..."

"No, wait." She grabbed my arm. "You would, wouldn't you? You'd go running down the street as fast as you could to get me a cracker. I've never met anyone who would do that for me. You're so good. You're a good person, and you're good to me. But, Michael, I can't stay with you."

"Things'll change, Sharon. I know they'll be different this time."

"No. I can't stay, Michael. Please listen."

Tears filled her eyes and her voice strengthened. "Michael, it's *killing* me!" She grabbed hold of my sleeve, hugged my arm, and lowered her voice to a whimper. "It's killing me." She cried, softly. "Killing me."

"It'll stop. I know it will."

"Please, Michael, understand. It *won't* stop. It's getting *worse*. Haven't you noticed I get sick every time I come to see you? Don't tell me you've forgotten all that's happened. Can't you see *they* don't want me here?"

"Yes. That's why you should stay. Don't let them win. Besides, I love you."

"I know." She no longer followed with an, "*I love you, too.*"

The Bad Things were *real*. The Dark World was *real*. The demons were *real*. The Shroud Man was *real*. The Beast was *real*. But our broken hearts were *UNreal*!

I cried myself to sleep. Sharon cried herself to sleep. And somewhere in the Dark World, something laughed.

***

In the evening while she slept, the Shroud Man came and took Sharon out of her body again for another journey. She went into a dark, spinning tunnel, and out the other side to ... The Deep Forest?

The forest was so thick with oak trees that she could not blaze her way through, until she came to a narrow, worn path. She followed it. And followed and followed, so deeply into the woods. The strangest part of the forest was that it made no sounds. No birds chirped. No squirrels chattered. No crickets clicked. No toads croaked. No wind rustled the leaves. The silence screamed at her.

Finally, Sharon came to a clearing in the endless woods, a circle, cutaway like the hole in a donut. There, while hiding in the dense brush of the perimeter, she saw a wild dog in labor. It was a lengthy, painful birth. And when the baby slithered out of the womb, the dog howled. It turned around and ...

Oh, God, it sees me. Sharon and the wild dog locked cautious stares at one another. Each waited for the other to make the first move, and Sharon was determined not to make it. The wild dog broke its stare when it turned to look at its newborn pup. Then the wild dog glanced back at Sharon, and ran, abandoning its baby.

Sharon observed.

Mr. Curiosity spoke to her and they debated in her mind: "Go ahead, Sharon. Look at the baby. Isn't it cute? Want to hold it?"

"No, it's evil. I know it's evil. A Bad Thing."

"Not babies. Not little, tiny, cuddly babies. Babies aren't Bad Things."

"Well, maybe not babies. That's right. Babies aren't Bad Things. I had a baby. Babies are Good Things."

She came out of hiding and discreetly entered the cleared area, into the ominous circle. She looked around for the momma—the wild dog—it was a Bad Thing, oh yes. Very bad. But it was gone. Closer. "Babies aren't Bad Things. Go on, Sharon. Babies are Good Things. Look at the baby."

Sharon walked up to that pup and ...

"You're not a puppy! Hey, you don't even have fur! This baby's not a mammal. It's a (reptile) something. You're a tadpole."

No, it was not a tadpole. It looked like a tadpole, sort of. It was greenish like a tadpole. Its head was round like a tadpole. Its face was like a tadpole. It was yucky and slimy like a tadpole. Its body tapered back into a tail like a tadpole. But it was not a tadpole.

"Wait a minute, Baby! Now I know what your are. You are a ..."

The Baby Beast lurched at Sharon. It latched onto her face, sealing her mouth and nostrils so she could not breathe. It was killing her! It pumped a thick, green gel down her windpipe. It stuck to her face and she could not free herself. It was suffocating her.

She pulled hard, but the Bad Thing had such a strong suction grip that her efforts were futile. It was killing her. She pulled harder. Desperately, dying.

She could not inhale. Her oxygen was depleted. And the carbon dioxide buildup from not exhaling was about to burst her lungs. No air in, no air out. She was out of time and had only one chance left. She changed tactics.

Instead of pulling from the top, she pried upward from beneath. She slithered a long fingernail beneath its belly. She pried as a lever beneath a big rock. She slipped a second finger under it and pried. Three fingers and pried. Four fingers. Five.

It made a slurping sound when it popped loose from Sharon's face. A wet, green slime splashed everywhere. Sharon vomited a sickly-green gel. Her windpipe cleared. She gulped air, then blew her nostrils free. She held the Bad Baby at arms length and squeezed it. "YOU SON OF A BITCH! YOU BASTARD!"

The Baby Bad Thing begged with its eyes. Then it talked. "Please, don't Sharon. Please, no."

Its voice startled Sharon. In her amazement, she loosened her grip. She tightened back up, just as it made another leap toward her face. She grabbed hold with both hands. "Squirm, you little bastard!" She squeezed it. She squeezed for her life, and squeezed for its death.

"Noooo!" the Baby Bad Thing changed its meek tone and yelped a loud and final, "Please no, Sharon! Plleeaasssee, NooOO!" Then its head splattered as a green volcano erupting.

Green gel splashed Sharon's face: It oozed down her arms, dripped down her chest. "I crushed you!" yelled Sharon. "I finally crushed you!" She tossed its remains to the ground and the forest once again fell asleep, but only for a few surreal moments.

"HHowwwLL!" The mother beast wailed in grief. It crept out of the woods and into the clearing with Sharon. Its red eyes glared in anger at Sharon for having crushed its offspring. Unlike its baby, the momma dog did not talk. But its eyes threatened, "You killed my baby, you bitch!"

Sharon back pedaled on her tippy-toes.

It closed ground. You killed my baby, you bitch! It charged.

"Noooo!" Sharon blurted angrily. She stopped her retreat and attacked, to the surprise of the dog. She was fed up with beasts! Tired of Dark Things! Enough-was-Enough! If one of them was to die, then let it be NOW! Sharon screamed, clawed, scratched, kicked, punched.

The wild dog ripped at her left breast, then fled, wanting no more of her viciousness.

"Noooo!" screamed Sharon, awakening to the black of morning, the tenth of January.

I recoiled from my spot next to her on our makeshift bed. I instinctively reached to hold her, to calm her. At my touch, Sharon hit me. "You Bitch!" She unknowingly battered me. She thought only of the *Creature* that had lunged at her seconds ago; she believed she was still in the *Oak Forest*, clawing and scratching for her life.

I gently pinned her arms to her sides, snuggled tightly, and whispered an assuring, "It's okay, Sharon. It's me. It's me." I relaxed my hold on her long enough to roll across the width of the bedroll and reach for the table lamp that set on the floor.

Her startled, brown eyes scanned the lighted room like a computer reading its monitor, seeking input she could race to her brain for emergency computation. When convinced she had left the *Oak Forest*—when assured the *Creature* was gone—she recognized me and ceased fighting. She slowly gained control of her breathing. Out with the bad air, in with the good. Okay. It was safe to break down and cry.

I knew better than to nurture her with comforting words meant to diminish the realities of what she had been through, so I said nothing.

Suddenly, Sharon leaped off the piles of blankets that served as our bed. She rushed to the walk-in closet and flipped on the light. In one motion, she yanked her two suitcases off the rack, crashed them to the floor and popped them open. "I gotta go."

"Go where?"

"Outta here." She haphazardly packed her clothes, and paused only long enough to turn to me and say, "No more, Michael. They're *KILLING* me!" She emphasized the last part with gritted determination and in fear. And her adamant body language when she commanded, "No more," finalized her decision to leave. Right now. This minute. Not waiting for daylight. Adios, amigo.

I dared not argue. Petite as Sharon was, she would have struck me down. But more than that, I agreed. They *were* killing her. They were after *me*, but they vented their anger on the one person I loved most. Sharon was dead if she stayed. Both of us realized, no doubt. So while Sharon dressed and packed, I crept downstairs, out of her way.

In the far corner of the barren living room, I crouched despondently on the floor. I clutched Sharon's green bathrobe, caressing the terry cloth against my wet face.

Upstairs, Sharon finished with her suitcase. But she couldn't leave. Not yet. *Write it down*, she thought uncontrollably. *Warn Michael. Tell him to get the hell out before it's too late!* Faster and faster, words flooded the paper. The *Voice* directed her to write them down and give them to Michael. (*Hurry hurry done.*)

She fled downstairs, skipping steps and banging her suitcases alternately against the wall and stair railing. She slowed her exit and approached me in the corner. She brushed away one of many tears on my cheeks. Sharon gently tugged on her robe, wanting it.

I gripped the robe tightly and drew it away from her. No. She could not have it. It was all I would have left of her.

Sharon granted my doleful request, and I safely let the robe fall across my lap. "Here," Sharon spoke, as she handed me a message from *them*. "I have to go, Michael," she cried. "I *have* to. It's not only *me* they'll kill, if I stay. I saw *you*, Michael—*Dead*! You were *DEAD*! *DEAD*! And I don't want to be here and watch it happen! Oh, God, Michael. I'm sorry. I'm so, so sorry." She left.

I browsed Sharon's letter, then threw a Bible across the living room and screamed, "Nooo!" when it crashed against the wall. I beat my fists on the carpet. What Sharon had seen was my final confrontation in the Dark World. And the Beast stood over my fallen body, boasting:

"I BEAT YOU! I BEAT YOU!"

My emotions were depleted, my physical strength sapped. I propped my numbed body between the corner walls of the living room like a crucified scarecrow. My mind drifted this way and that way. Occasionally, I found comfort in caressing Sharon's bathrobe. I was careful not to dislodge the one strand of her blonde hair that clung to the terry cloth as stubbornly as I did. The lonely shred of her locks reminded me of the many sweet times she'd placed her head on my chest, using me as a pillow while she slept contentedly.

Stroking her robe and thinking Good Things nearly calmed me, until I'd catch a horrifying glimpse of her ominous letter that lay crumpled in the corner. My thoughts fluttered between heartfelt love and terror. Beauty and the Beast. I had lost Sharon as a casualty of war. An unearthly war. A war of the angels.

A bizarre war I learned of while writing about World War Two, a human war that opened up a spiritual window I apparently fell through.

TOP SECRET
From: USS Helm
To: Commander-in-Chief, Pacific
Subject: Search for (Indianapolis) Survivors
August 6, 1945

"All bodies were in extremely bad condition and had been dead for an estimated 4 or 5 days. Some had life jackets and life belts, most had nothing. Most of the bodies were completely naked ... horribly bloated and decomposed. Recognition of faces would have been impossible. About half of the bodies were shark-bitten, some to such a degree that they more nearly resembled skeletons. Sharks were in the immediate area of the ship at all times and continued attacking bodies until driven off by rifle fire."

CHAPTER 2
Top Secret

5 Years Earlier — 1975
Jacksonville, Florida

I was writing a book entitled *Bad Things In The Dark*. It was a true story about the *U.S.S. Indianapolis* based upon Top Secret papers released to me by the President of the United States. It was my first book. I had previously written for a sports magazine and for a couple of newspapers, but never anything of this magnitude. And it seemed that every senior editor in America was contacting me about book rights. A major publishing house even called me at work and told me not to sign with anyone else until they had an opportunity to make a final bid. They also spoke about "movie rights."

The point being, there will be those who say I fabricated *War of the Angels* just to sell a book and to make a lot of money. Fact is, I already had a blockbuster in the works. I was already promised fame and fortune. I had no reason to contrive this story. I had nothing to gain and everything to lose. It just so happened that one evening, angels came to visit me and commanded that I stop writing *Bad Things In The Dark* and to write *War Of The Angels,* instead. I told the angels, no. I'd worked too hard on the *U.S.S. Indianapolis* project to simply walk away and leave it for someone else to write in the future. Angels did not understand how difficult it was to find such a good topic.

I truly enjoyed writing, but until *Bad Things In the Dark*, I had written only as a labor of love. Freelance articles could not pay the bills. I was twenty-four-years-old in July of 1975, when I first went on the prowl for a book topic meaty enough to launch my career as a middle-class author. I never sought wealth. I simply wanted to earn a decent living doing something I enjoyed. Then I stumbled across an article in the *Jacksonville Sun-Times.*

The story told how a series of high-ranking blunders caused the sinking of U.S.S. *Indianapolis* during World War Two, resulting in the largest loss of life ever at sea. But because the tragedy implicated the highest-ranking admirals—even to the Secretary of the Navy, himself—the resulting coverup was quite extensive. The newspaper articles lacked in-depth details because all official documents pertaining to the incident had been classified *Top Secret*. Since I was a native Hoosier born and bred in Indianapolis, I investigated with great intrigue, thinking I may have found a good story if I could get my hands on more detailed information.

My research was in vain, however. I found only general information. Official war historian, Samuel E. Morison, wrote in *Volume XIV* of *History of World War II*:

"None of the findings of the secret court of inquiry were made available to the public."

Further, in Richard Newcomb's *Abandon Ship*, I read:
"The testimony has never been made public and probably never will be."

I was mystified. Something so bizarre had happened to the *U.S.S. Indianapolis* in 1945, that the United States Navy decided that the public could never, ever know. If I could obtain those documents, then I had material for a good book. I began a personal campaign to convince the President of the United States to release Top Secret papers to me. Fat chance, but I had to try.

The political arena at that time was advantageous to me. President Nixon was impeached for dirty tricks and cover-ups. His replacement, Gerald Ford, was sworn into the Presidency with promises of being candid and forthright with the public. Also, *Elections* were approaching and I hoped that President Ford would honor his promises. After three decades of secrecy, History was ripe to release those U.S.S. *Indianapolis* papers to me.

My first inquiry produced only a form letter in return. Something about how happy they were to hear from me. I wrote a second letter, and once again after a lengthy wait, I received another form letter. They were still happy to hear from me. Praise God. I wrote a third letter.

This time when I went to the mail box I found a large manila envelope that I knew contained more than a form letter. I carefully pried loose the seal, so that I did not rip the return address that simply read, "THE WHITE HOUSE." The grandest of all understatements.

I nervously removed the contents from the envelope. Inside was a cover letter from the Navy, saying, "*The President asked that we forward these to you.*" Attached were about twenty photocopies of some very old documents. The heading of each page read, "~~TOP SECRET~~," with the words crossed out. The first page had my name personally scribbled on it. I was ecstatic for a moment, until I read and digested the content of what the President had sent me. I was once again disappointed. The documents were real. They were declassified by executive order of the President of the United States. They were personally addressed to me. But they were all *old* news. It was common, history-book stuff that had been printed over and over for thirty years.

The information concerned minor details about the American Flagship that had been sunk after transporting the Atomic Bomb across the Pacific. The data had been public knowledge for decades. Nothing new. Nothing special. I fired off a fourth letter, then a fifth and sixth. I cannot remember how many more.

I never heard from the President again. Not even to say how happy he was to hear from me. I gave up on my *U.S.S. Indianapolis* project. Then one day I read in the *Sun Times* that President Ford and a large entourage was coming to Jacksonville for a rare, international summit. One way or another, I intended to get the President's undivided attention.

On November 2, 1975, I joined thousands of local residents who lined Beach Boulevard hoping to catch an

Top Secret

historical glimpse of President Gerald Ford and his honored guest, Egyptian President Anwar Sadat, when their Caravan traveled along the scheduled route.

Although it was late autumn, the Floridian sun was strong enough to ripple the air as it bounced hard off the highway pavement. I covered my unshaded glasses with cupped hands and peered far away, to where the road and horizon collided in distortion. I strained for a better view.

I glanced at my watch many times. He was overdue. I slipped behind the crowd and paced haphazardly. I twisted the hair on my mustache and lowered my head in thought. I was planning to charge through the crowd, evade armed security, and stuff my letter into the limo for a personal delivery to the President. I was very nervous, wondering if it was a foolish thing to do.

I picked a location where the Presidential Limousine would slow to a creep in order to make a sharp turn. The President would enter the gated community of a wealthy resident who was hosting the meeting. At that point of vulnerability, I would have the opportunity to rush forward and hand-deliver my request through the window to the President.

As I awaited the Caravan, I paced the highway shoulder, debating with myself about whether or not my plan would work. I clutched my handful of ~~TOP SECRET~~ papers, knowing they were not really valuable. I wondered how much weight they would carry while looking down a Secret Service gun barrel.

The crowd stirred and sirens blared, alerting me that the White House Caravan had arrived. I edged to the front and watched the pompous parade of automobiles, as political hopefuls—from the governor to dog catchers—rode the President's coattails into town.

There was also an impressive display of security either driving in the Caravan with flashing red or blue lights atop their cars, or else on foot engaging in crowd control: the Federal Secret Service, Florida State Troopers, Highway Patrolmen, the Jacksonville Police Department, Duval County Sheriffs, and an assortment of suburban authorities. Besides the usual security concerns for the President of the United States, there was the added fear of assassins gunning down Anwar Sadat (which they eventually would). Hence, a wall of armed guards separated the crowds from the Caravan. I was about to cancel my plans to rush the President.

Suddenly a gaping hole opened in the security line directly across from me, when the limousine slowed for a sharp turn at the entrance gate, just as I had hoped. Fate dealt me a clear approach, completely unobstructed, straight to the President who had his window down while waving to the bystanders. Instinctively I darted through the opening like a running-back who saw daylight to the end zone.

I never saw what hit me. At ten feet from the President, the Secret Service slammed me to the concrete and encircled me. They displayed no mercy as they pounced on their would-be assassin. They frisked me for weapons, but instead discovered the classified documents in my possession.

"Hey, look at these," said one to another in amazement.

"Those are *Top Secret* papers!" I yelled, squirming horizontally in their grasps. They perused my confiscated belongings. They were disarrayed by their unexpected find, and I seized the opportunity created by their confusion. I exaggerated my importance and name-dropped the biggest name in America:

"The *President of The United States* released those to me! They're CLASSIFIED! And don't open that letter—it's the President's!"

The authorities examined my credentials and ...

"Hey, I think these documents are *real*," said one agent into a microphone. They passed them around. Each shrugged his shoulders. They released me.

I stood and brushed myself. I had nothing to lose by exploiting their astonishment. "It's urgent I get that letter to the President. It's Top Secret business."

The head of security seized the documents and returned them to me. "We're sorry, Mr. Mullen. We had no way of knowing. We'll see to it the President gets your letter right away."

"That's okay," I said. "I'll take it to him."

The agent put a quick hand in my chest. "I said we'll deliver it for you." They escorted me to the outskirts, warning: "Don't ever do that again. It's a good way to get shot."

In January, 1976, the President of the United States declassified all secret documents pertaining to the U.S.S.

Indianapolis, several thousand papers, and ordered them delivered to my house.

> *"I can't wait to pay my five dollars and see the movie." (Ted Kreiter, Executive Editor, Saturday Evening Post)*
>
> *"Your project on the U.S.S. Indianapolis sounds better and better." (Harold Kuebler, Senior Editor Special Projects, Doubleday)*
>
> *"Fascinating material. Beautifully presented." (Victoria Darwin, Darwin Publications, Burbank, California)*

CHAPTER 3
Beyond Human Help

I persevered throughout the winter months with *Bad Things in the Dark*. I wrote with mental blinders and did not see the burden I placed upon my wife of two-years to bring in the only income. Still, with good reviews following each new sample I had forwarded to publishers, my wife and in-laws remained supportive.

But by spring, family patience wore thin over the slow, methodical process that a book endures while being pieced together. And adding fuel to an already volatile marriage, I regretfully concluded that my story had reached an impasse. It could not be told by secret papers alone. I needed to interview survivors, few as there were, to breathe life into my characters. I located one, but he lived five hundred miles away and I didn't have expense money to travel. Despondent, I slouched at the kitchen table. I subconsciously opened to the middle pages of the *Jacksonville Sun-Times* and read the community bulletins: "Survivor of U.S.S *Indianapolis* To Give Testimony." It was a *miracle*.

Mr. Hafford Sharp had just relocated to Jacksonville, Florida, where he was employed by Victory Baptist Academy to teach Bible classes. He was giving his testimony that next week at the Bible school and it was open to the public. Not wanting to wait for an impersonal, public event, I hurriedly grabbed the phone book and called the school.

Beyond Human Help

Being late in the afternoon, classes were out and Mr. Sharp was available to talk when the office paged him. "This is Mr. Sharp," he said, answering.

"Hello," I said, introducing myself. "The reason I'm calling is I'm writing a book on the U.S.S. *Indianapolis*, based upon secret documents given to me by President Ford and ..."

"What secret documents are those? From the President you say?"

"Yes. The court of inquiry, you know, with Captain McVay? In Guam?"

"Yes, I'm aware of that. It was all classified secret. You say you've got those papers?"

"Yes. And they're pretty interesting."

"I bet they are. I wouldn't mind taking a look at them, if you wouldn't object."

"Not at all. That's the reason I called. I wanted to get together with you before your testimonial, so I could ask you some questions and let you look over the papers."

"That sounds wonderful. What day did you have in mind?"

"How about tomorrow? Is that convenient for you?"

"Well, I have classes tomorrow. I teach, you know. This is a church, but it's also a twelve-grade school. Now I *do* have a free period at eleven o'clock each day, if that's agreeable with *your* schedule."

"How about tomorrow at eleven, then?"

The entire conversation lasted only a couple of minutes, and scheduling an interview had gone smoother than my best expectations. I penciled in the appointment for March 15, 1976, at 11:00 a.m. "Hey, that's on my birthday," I said aloud to myself. It was a nice present.

When my birthday rolled around after a dreadfully long night, I got an early start. This was my one and only shot at an interview for my book, and I couldn't afford for anything to go wrong. I arrived at Victory Baptist Academy with ample time to kill. I sat in the parking lot drumming my fingers on the steering wheel of my Nissan Datsun, glancing at my watch every couple of minutes until it was eleven o'clock.

I wiped my sweaty right palm, anticipating our introductory handshake. I marched inside quickly to get the ordeal over with. The door to the room was open, and I instinctively knocked on the frame. "Mr. Sharp?"

"Good morning," pleasantly responded the lanky, gray-headed gentleman. "You can just call me *Hafford*, if you like."

I was too nervous to engage in small talk, so I hurriedly launched the interview. "Where can I plug in my tape recorder?"

Hafford was the perfect interview for a fledgling writer, as he commenced right into his story. "There is no way to imagine any of it," began Hafford, in a relaxed Southern drawl that clashed dramatically with the ferocity of his tale.

"It's kind of like a dream. I still find myself asking if it really happened. Not a man would be able to repeat it. For a long time afterwards, for years, I'd wake up in the middle of the night, screaming.

"Some men, even to this day, refuse to talk about it. They *can't* talk about it; it frightens them. All of us needed *psychiatric* treatment, you understand, along with *physical* help, because we'd seen so much.

"At the time it was happening, we couldn't think about it, because the fear was enough to kill us. I don't know how we ever made it, those of us who *did* make it, which wasn't many."

He paused and looked deeply at me. "It was the LORD. It had to be, because we were beyond *human* help. We were physically and mentally shot. We had the minds of cattle. We'd surpassed the human element." Hafford yawned in the middle of a sentence. "Oh, goodness. I'm sleepy."

Continuing his story, Hafford told how Marine Captain Parke caught him sleeping on guard duty, the night before they sank. With a distant glow in his eyes, Hafford mentally slipped away from the tranquil room, back to 1945, and re-boarded the U.S.S. *Indianapolis*.

***

At only nineteen years of age, young Hafford doubted he would ever match the serenity of cruising the South Pacific, unescorted, on a late tropical eve. He savored the experience, storing the exotic sensation as a fine treasure in his mind's vault of most cherished memories.

The water strummed a rhythmic tune—a symphony of the sea—raising the ship in the palm of its swell like a conductor bringing up the softness of his strings, then gently backing off; sswiiIIISSHHH-SSWOOooosshhh went the ship, accompanied by whispering breezes and musical winds.

Indianapolis, America's Flagship, waltzed with the frolicsome waves. As the anxious whitecaps courted her favors, the Queen of the Fifth Fleet granted all a spin, before twirling apart when she lowered her bow as if taking a royal curtsy. The luminous CA-35's ("CA" indicating heavy cruiser; "35" indicating Indianapolis) adorning each cheek of her moonlit face dipped flirtatiously, like a pair of made-up eyes on a romantically dim, tropical eve.

A most relaxing moment. Too relaxing, in fact. Hafford stood Night Watch that July 28, a tortuous deed for a young man who loved his sleep. His odds on staying awake would not have equaled those posted by a wooden horse in the Kentucky Derby. He fell wonderfully asleep.

But Marine Captain Parke caught Hafford in the middle of his lullaby, and planted an angry combat boot firmly in his chest and reeled him backwards.

Startled awake, Hafford's bugging eyes dimly focused on the muscular Marine shaking a wild fist at him. "Do you want to get Killed!?" threatened Captain Parke, heavily emphasizing the last word, as if he would be the one to do it.

"No, Sir," said Hafford meekly.

The Marine slammed Hafford's shoulder with an open palm. "Then stay awake!"

"Yes, Sir."

So the next night, on July 29, Hafford retired early, hoping the extra rest would prevent him from sleeping again on Night Watch.

He said good night to his best friend, fellow-Alabamian Huie H. Phillips, and grabbed a blanket and pillow. His regular sleeping berth sweltered beyond use in the torrid tropics, and he combed the ship for a comfortable place to bed down.

Normally, everyone slept naked on Main Deck. However, Hafford thought it might rain, so he descended one deck, to Number Two Mess Hall, near the fantail. He knew others *would join him later, so he stacked the tables, then set up a cot beneath the fresh air blower, the prime spot. Being first to sleep had its advantages. He slept peacefully.*

At 12:12 a.m. two Japanese submarine torpedoes slammed into Indianapolis and completely snapped off the bow. The explosions launched Hafford from his cot and onto the hard deck. He rubbed his head; it hurt. He groped in the dark for his clothes, finding them between the stacked tables.

A man scurried through the mess hall, lighting battery lanterns on the bulkhead. By that yellowish light, Hafford inched his way to the ladder and climbed topside to investigate.

The moon shone brightly and Hafford saw clearly. He sat on a closed hatch and observed the chaos. Everyone paced back and forth. Nobody knew what to do, nor where to go.

The ship's silence disturbed them: the boilers shut down; the engines quit buzzing. Only boisterous men seeking information broke the stillness. Hafford grabbed someone by the arm, as he ran by. "What's wrong?"

"I don't know. Somebody told me the forward boiler room blew up. I guess everything will be okay, after a while."

Another shipmate ran by. "Do you know what's happened?" *yelled Hafford.*

"Somebody said we hit a floating mine. There's not much damage, though."

All the damage from the torpedoes loomed in the forward area. Hafford sat aft of midship, near the fantail, lacking details. He stopped another, and another.

"What's wrong?"

"I haven't been up forward, so I don't know what it is."

"I don't have any idea. Somebody said we've been hit by torpedoes, but I don't know."

Hafford, afraid to move, timidly watched others run this way and that. Some of the men sustained injuries from flying debris; others suffered burns from a fire.

Hafford suddenly wondered if perhaps Huie was hurt and needed his help. Hafford leaped to his feet to find his friend, when Indianapolis listed sharply. Hafford fell.

Explanations spilled forth from a panicky crew.

"The plane fuel exploded!"

"The kitchen blew up!"

"The paint locker caught fire!"

"The engine room exploded!"

Suddenly the ship capsized and washed most of the sailors overboard. A few men balanced perilously on the overturned hull, but voluntarily jumped into the sea when it grew apparent their ship was going under. Only Hafford remained. Scared, he sat alone on a tiny portion of the stern, too dumbfounded to leave her.

"Jump!" yelled someone from the water. "She's going down!" Others begged young Hafford to abandon ship.

Hafford ignored them. The water looked cold and dark. He felt he was safest right there.

"Jump! She'll blow up and kill you!"

Hafford stared at the group in the water. If the ship blows up, they'll all be killed, too, he reasoned. They were no better off in the water, than he was on the ship, he thought.

"Huie!" called Hafford. Huie would know what to do. He wondered if Huie had jumped. Hafford scanned the water, searching for his confidant.

Hafford sat on the ship and clutched a life jacket tightly against his breast like a scared child grasping a security blanket. "Huie!"

"Jump! Jump!"

Hafford thought that if he jumped, the ship might sail away and leave him. Confused and frightened, he cried. "Shutup! Leave me alone!" Water gushed over the bottom and crept toward him. He removed his shoes, socks, and pants, and wearing only underwear and a blue denim shirt, he walked into the sea and swam away.

A whirlpool sucked him under! He held his breath. His lungs burned from carbon dioxide trying to burst free. He couldn't reach the top. His life jacket proved powerless against the swirling sea. He kicked. He stroked. Painful air escaped his lungs.

Finally his head pierced the surface. He hoarded oxygen, but in the process of siphoning air, he gulped a mouthful of diesel oil, as well. He choked and spat. He vomited profusely.

Likewise, the sea regurgitated the ship that it had so greedily swallowed. Elevated by the water's dense pressure, Indianapolis rose eerily, pointing straight up. Her stern *reached to cling hold of the moon and the clouds, to keep it from plunging to her death. And then down she came, straight toward Hafford like Moby Dick after Captain Ahab.*

Fearful of being crushed, Hafford swam for his life. He thrashed wildly, and the inefficiency of his flailing tired him in thirty yards. He stopped and looked back.

Indianapolis slipped into the sea without havoc: she didn't explode; no further suction drew anyone down with her. Doused flames hissed lightly, emitting a fine steam. The American Flag snapped a parting salute from the fantail.

Hafford swam off to find his friend. "Huie!"

***

While deep into his story, the tape ran to the end of its reel, and the recorder clicked off loudly. "Goodness, I thought I'd been shot," jumped Hafford.

He laughed and eased out of his chair to stretch, while I inserted a new tape.

"Were sharks a problem that first night in the water?" I asked, continuing.

"I'm getting kind of hungry," said Hafford, looking at the clock, ignoring the question. "I'll just get a candy bar or something, before class starts.

"No," he continued, "the thing we feared until daylight the first day, was this:

"If we *were* torpedoed by a Japanese sub, we had no escort and we were helpless. Just as helpless as we could be. I think some of the officers had .45 automatics on their sides, but how can you fight a submarine with a .45? And that's *all* they had.

"This is what happened with other sailors in the war: the Japanese surfaced and killed all the survivors on the water. And we knew this could happen to *us*, if we *had* been hit by a Japanese submarine. But we didn't fear the sub coming to the surface anymore, after dawn the first day.

"Many terrible things happened, even during the first few hours in the water. Those of us who weren't wounded in the blast aboard ship—and there were quite a number of us; not many men were hurt, except the ones who never got off and went down with the ship—began to kid each other about having a thirty-day survivor's leave. Anytime you have to abandon ship, you get a thirty-day survivor's leave. We looked forward to that—even *joked* about it.

"We knew—at least we *thought* we knew—that rescue was only a short time away. But only the Lord knew what was in store for the next five days and nights.

"We had a crew of 1,198: 887 lost their lives in various ways; 311 of us survived. No one knows how many men went down with the ship. My guess is as good as anyone's. I'd say most everyone made it to the water alive, because most everyone slept on Main Deck. It was the time spent in the water, you see, that killed nearly everyone.

"Each of the three hundred eleven survivors has his own story to tell. Not any two of us will tell the same thing, because no two of us had the same things happen to us.

"The whole thing was a nightmare.

"Occasionally now, when I meditate upon it, I find myself asking, '*Did that really happen?*' One hundred twenty-three hours, more than five days and nights with no water to drink and no food to eat. I finally forgot about food, but I never got over thirst.

"Men died almost immediately. They gave up shortly after we abandoned ship. I guess some of them were scared to death. Some of them were wounded. Some of them were in terrible pain.

"We tried to encourage ourselves by saying things like, '*Our Navy's too big, not to spot us. We have too many ships. Surely going from one island to another, we'll be sighted, either by planes, or by ships.*' Or, '*Indianapolis is the Flagship; it's too important to lose track of. We'll be spotted right away.*'

"We grasped at anything, imaginary or real, and encouraged ourselves. We'd think of *anything* to encourage us. And *nothing* to *dis*courage us, because the situation as it was, was discouraging enough.

"Everybody has *closer* friends than they have *other* friends—of course, we were *all* friends aboard ship—but I had one friend especially: Huie H. Phillips. Where you saw one of us, you always saw the other. He was the leader aboard ship. Huie knew everybody and everything. Why, there wasn't anything Huie didn't know. He was a year older, and I guess maybe because he was married he seemed so much brighter and wiser to me. I just really thought he was something. I'd grown to depend on him. But I never saw him the whole one hundred twenty-three hours in the water. That's what scared me, you see. I had to depend on myself.

"We were *every man for himself.* No one was the leader. I did, though, toward the end, find myself giving some orders, even though I was the youngest, simply because I was one of the few who still had sense enough to think. I couldn't think *all* the time, but I could think *some* of the time.

"Almost hourly, I either turned my head, or I'd see somebody die. It wasn't polite to watch a man die. I'd see one of my shipmates take his own life. He'd pull his life jacket off, wave goodbye to us, and go under the water.

"Some of the men went berserk, after a few days. I remember one young boy on his first cruise—it was only my second cruise—but one boy even younger than myself, pulled off his life jacket and put a knife between his teeth and said he was 'Shark huntin.' He kept saying, '*I'm gonna get that shark. I'm gonna get that shark.*'

"We begged him not to do it. He was out of his head. He would dive down, and we'd say, '*Well, he's gone.*' Then after a while, way out there someplace, he'd pop back up. But he kept doing it, until eventually he *didn't* pop up. He finally drowned himself, or a shark got him, or something.

"Sharks wouldn't bother us, as long as we stayed in a group; but sharks got *Loners*. In the middle of the night, we'd hear somebody scream, somebody holler, '*Shark*!' It was the scariest thing I ever heard. He'd drifted off by himself. A *Loner.* Of course that was the end of him.

"By the third day, men died so fast we had to constantly form new groups, to keep the sharks off of us. As far as I know, no one attacked by a shark, lived.

"I heard—I didn't see it, I heard it—one man got his leg bitten by a shark, and he *did* survive. And one survivor showed me later, where something had eaten out the palm of his hand. But he didn't know if it was a shark, or what.

"Many terrible things happened at night. One night, the third or the fourth, all the salt water drinkers went crazy. Drinking salt water and diesel oil affected their minds. Not a man who drank salt water, to my knowledge, survived. They'd go out of their heads and talk crazy, weird things.

"Some of them said they'd swum back to the ship; the ship had come back to the surface, just enough for them to get some water, or to go into the galley for something to eat. And they'd swum back to get us. That's what they said.

"I still had enough mind to know if they did all that, they wouldn't be back out there; they'd still be aboard the ship.

"Some of them said they'd swum to one of the most beautiful islands they'd ever seen; the natives on the island had given them a picnic, with ice cream and Coca-Colas and ice water. Anything we craved, they'd already gotten, on one of the islands populated by friendly natives.

"One day, three of my good friends—not Huie, cause I didn't know what happened to Huie, whether he'd been eaten by a shark or what—but still they were good friends, and they came swimming up to me and said, *'Do you want to go with us? We're going back to the island.'*

"I said, *'What do you mean, you're going back to the island?'*

"*'Well, we've been on ...'* They even gave it a name; it was some far out thing. They'd gotten ice cream and ice water and Coca-Colas, and they'd been fed, and they'd had a good time. They'd come back to tell me about it.

"Now I still had enough mind to think this thing through: *If they've been to an island, and gotten food and water, what are they doing back out here?* I still had that much mind left.

"Some of them popped out of the water and patted their stomachs. They said, *'Look! We have full stomachs.'* And their stomachs were swollen. They swore up and down they'd been to the island. And they wanted me to go with them.

"My mind slipped up for a minute, and I started to swim away from the group, going toward an island, they said. But the thought came to me again.

"My mind came to me enough to figure the thing out. We were four hundred fifty miles from *any* island, *anywhere*. They hadn't been *anyplace*. They were just rattling out of their minds from drinking salt water and diesel oil. I turned back; they went on. That's the last I ever saw of them."

Hafford paused in solemn remembrance. He looked as if he might cry.

The class bell rang.

"You can come back tomorrow, if you like," volunteered Hafford.

***

The interviews for *Bad Things in the Dark* continued throughout the week. Hafford recounted terrifying ordeals that intensified with each new session. But it was on that last day when Hafford truly scared me. And it had nothing to do with sharks. At the conclusion of our final interview, Hafford leaned forward from his relaxed position and told me of some very Bad Things.

Oh, sure, sharks were bad. Drowning was bad. Friends dying ... very bad. The ordeals aboard *Indianapolis* had *all* been bad. But not as bad as these new Bad Things Hafford surprisingly warned me about. He suddenly spoke of other worlds, and demons, and devils, and some very Bad Things that were going to happen to people who did not believe him.

"I was kept alive for a reason," Hafford said ominously. He spoke with a chill in his voice that set a new, hypnotic tone, and his eyes penetrated deeply into me with an uncanny sense of urgency to convince me. He had a frightening determination to explain.

"Something supernatural kept me alive. Some living being from another world brought me out of a desperate situation. I know a lot of people believe otherwise, but to me, they're downright foolish to *not* believe in life elsewhere. We are not the only life there is."

With each word, I wanted more and more to exit the door. But for some reason, I had to keep listening. Those words would haunt me for years and would prepare me for my own terrifying ordeals that were about to commence.

***

Shortly after my interviews with Hafford Sharp my wife came to my bedside and said softly: "Michael, I want a divorce."

I said, "Okay."

"I want you out by Saturday."

"Okay." And that was that. Nothing else was spoken, as she left for work, then spent the rest of the week with her mother until I moved out.

It was not a gruesome departure; there were no children to fight over custody, nor material goods to divvy up. In fact, from the day our wedding announcement was so vehemently objected to by her family—up until that final day—ours had been one of those marriages doomed from the words, "I do."

So the phrase, "Michael, I want a divorce," was like an extinguisher to a grease fire. It was nice to be out. But I suddenly had no where to live, no job, no money, no food, and I was uncertain about my life's detoured path. And I was in no mood to write, so *Bad Things In The Dark* was placed in a holding pattern.

After several fruitless months of sharing a cockroach-infested old house with several teenagers, I migrated back to Indianapolis, Indiana, on August 6, 1976.

I wasted more than a year at my parents' house, being content to live in a friendly environment for a change, and in reuniting with old high school friends I had not seen in years. I played away my precious time and didn't do any work at all, except for a few temporary, meaningless jobs that gave me just enough spending money.

Finally, in January of 1978, I moved from my parents' comfortable house in the suburbs, into a cheap downtown apartment next door to the neighborhood tavern. The low rent allowed me to work only part time, and to focus on my book, should I ever again get motivated enough to sit and write for hours at a time. The publishers were still interested. In fact, they would phone me at work to check my progress and to remind me that their publishing house wanted the final bid before I signed with anyone else. My co-workers teased me about it and called me, "Hollywood."

I worked at the Indianapolis *Gorman* Boys' Club. I wasn't there to motivate underprivileged children, nor was I there to help kids conquer problems and to straighten out their lives. I was there to play and make a few bucks.

I befriended youngsters who—unlike my own shallow obstacles in life—suffered true adversity. Their parents would regularly beat them for superfluous misdeeds, such as using the telephone for too long. I watched police handcuff a twelve-year-old boy who'd raped an eighty-year-old widow. There were teenage boys who got busted for supporting their drug habits with armed robbery; and there were little girls who supported their drug addictions by selling their bodies to every boy in the neighborhood for a buck or two.

I had grown up in a sheltered environment, and guilt slowly crept in for having thrown away opportunities that these kids would never know. I cannot pinpoint exactly when I started to care about the kids, instead of looking at them like a part time paycheck, but I found myself working longer hours and for free. I like to think I played a part in the school truancy rate dropping, as well as the neighborhood crime rate.

As a result of working with the kids, 1978 was also the year I grew up. By summer of 1978, I dusted off my U.S.S. *Indianapolis* papers and renewed my project, working steadily until fall, when an *Alien Being* first visited me.

In politics *nothing* happens by "accident."
If it happens, you can bet it was *planned* that way.
Franklin D. Roosevelt

CHAPTER 4
Holy Murder

Indianapolis, Indiana

The afternoon of October 22, 1978, was a relaxing, sunny Sunday. It was an ideal time for establishing a friendship with my downstairs neighbor. Although I had lived in my building for nearly a year, I had generally used the back entrance and had seen my neighbor only on occasion, in passing.

Now I anxiously proceeded downstairs, to the front apartment overlooking the botanical gardens in Garfield Park. I had often observed pleasant people my own age visiting *Apartment One,* and judging by the constant laughter from within, I envied the popularity of the man who resided there. The time had come to join the party. I knocked on the door.

"Hi," I said, when my neighbor answered.

"Oh, hello," said my neighbor. He looked surprised and flinched his thick, black eyebrows and mustache in unison.

"I'm your upstairs neighbor."

"I know. I was wondering if we'd ever meet. David, come see who's here. I'm Patrick. Come on in and meet David." Patrick was astonished that his aloof neighbor had finally come down to meet him, and he hardly knew what to say to me. He was thankful David took charge of the hospitality.

"God, we meet at last. Hi, I'm David." He smiled as brightly as his blondish hair shone. And the warmth in his soft voice assured me a welcome visit. He broke the ice of a newborn friendship, and offered freshly brewed tea.

The stained-glass front windows allowed little sunshine to penetrate, and Patrick lit a small, antique lamp with a yellowish shade, to supplement the light next to the rocking chair where I sat.

Patrick sighed deeply and said, "Well, I'm so glad. Do you mind if I'm blunt?"

"I guess not."

"David and I are gay; I hope that doesn't bother you. I just want to be open with you because you seem so nice."

Later, I would understand how necessary it had been for Patrick and David to explain their homosexuality up front, with someone they wanted to know. The shock of an accidental discovery had, in the past, destroyed many friendships. Family, too.

Patrick's only brother abandoned him. David's father, likewise, disowned David. Macho men taunted them, and worse, hit them. They'd even been chased by Christians, who'd demanded the "queers" get out of their church. Gays were favorite targets of every prejudiced group. Patrick and David had both been admitted to mental wards for intensive counseling, to become *normal*. Neither had intended, early in life, to *become* gay. In fact, they struggled to be straight and to avoid the ridicule, the hatred, the beatings, and the abandonment. But they *were* gay.

I was taken aback at their "outing" on the first day we met, but I understood their explanation. If I wanted to hit them, or verbally abuse them, or create an excuse not to become friends with them, it was best to do it now.

"Thank you for the compliment in sharing that with me," I said. "Let's make a deal: you don't try and change me, and I won't try and change you. Is that okay?"

"Fair enough." And the darkened apartment grew bright with cheerfulness.

I told them I worked at the Boys' Club. I also discussed my book about the *U.S.S. Indianapolis*. And when afternoon faded into evening, I was telling about my personal life. Patrick and David had a genuine openness that allowed me to share of myself. It was a wonderful gift they had, I thought. Patrick would later confide in me, "You're the brother I never

Holy Murder

had, and always wanted." Our friendship bonded that first day.

As we conversed, the television played in the background. We paid no attention, until the networks ran yet another news bulletin about Pope John Paul II's coronation to the papal throne. David complained, "God, not again? This is a little sickening, don't you think?"

"That's all we've seen for a week," said Patrick. "This guy's getting so much coverage he ought to have his own show."

"Have you been reading about the death of Pope John Paul I?" I asked.

"Ooooooh," said Patrick with a bit of mystical music in his voice. "That was strange, wasn't it?"

"I can't believe he died after just thirty-three days," said David. David always managed to crack a joke even during the most serious of conversations. "It's the Pope-of-the-Month Club," he laughed. "Join now and you'll receive a new Pope about every thirty days. And if you don't like him, just send him home in a box."

"I read something about the Vatican a couple of weeks ago that really freaked me out," I commented. "It was about Pope John Paul I, right before he died."

"What about him?"

"Are either of you Catholic?" I asked.

"We're Lutheran," said Patrick. "That's sort of diet-Catholic."

I explained that I wasn't Catholic and that I didn't understand much about the papal elections or procedures. However, I had noticed something in the newspaper about Pope John Paul I prior to his death that struck me as being odd. On September 26, the newly elected Pope John Paul I claimed that he'd uncovered an organized crime syndicate in the church.

I cut out the article from the *Indianapolis Star*. It was only a short news brief, buried way back on page twenty-six. The Pope issued a statement to the press, saying a '*Holy Mafia*' had embezzled millions of dollars from the Vatican Bank, for what he called 'immoral purposes.'"

On September 28, Pope John Paul I elaborated that *two* crime syndicates had conspired together to steal the Vatican's vast wealth. A secret society of Catholic laymen who worked from *within* the church; and another secret society of non-Catholics who worked from *outside* the church. John Paul personally organized a committee to purge the church of the "Holy Mafia." The Pope said he'd compiled a list of names, and planned to make formal accusations at noon the following day.

The next day, I checked the paper to read about the list of names in the Vatican Mafia. However, when I read the day's headlines I knew there'd be no published list.

"POPE DIES IN HIS SLEEP"

"God! Are you kidding me?" said Patrick. "He was *informing* on the Mafia right before he died? Is that why all this happened?"

"I don't know. Kind of interesting, though."

"Hey, I remember something about that on television," said David. "There were *thousands* of Italians marching in the streets, claiming the Pope was *murdered*! I couldn't believe what I was seeing. I haven't heard anymore about it, though."

"I think it's been censored off the airways," I said. I lifted my cup off the glass-covered, wicker table and sipped my tea. "You know what else? Everybody was *screaming* for an autopsy on John Paul. There must have been a hundred thousand Italians marching through the middle of town waving banners and signs and *demanding* an autopsy."

"What did the autopsy show?"

"Nothing. They didn't *do* one."

Prior to the Pope's death, a church lawyer named Miguel Alvarez was instrumental in creating a new Vatican law stating that it was illegal to perform an autopsy on any Pope. They were "too Holy" for such barbaric human practices. The death of Pope John Paul I was the first opportunity to enforce such a law. No matter how many people demanded an autopsy, it simply could not be performed. It was illegal.

"One other coincidence," I said. "The church lawyer who instigated the new autopsy rule was a prominent member of *Opus Dei*. That's the very same group that John Paul I called the Holy Mafia right before he died."

"Why doesn't anyone else know about this?" asked David.

"They do! Why do you think they're screaming their heads off in Italy?"

"What'd the Vatican say about it?" asked Patrick.

"They just scoffed at the idea. They said it was, 'Pure fantasy.' They don't think anyone would ever conspire to murder a pope. And that's the last anything was ever said about it.

"All the other stuff I got piecemeal from news articles or else from the library. I started searching out of curiosity, but it kept developing into more than what I'd expected."

"What's the new Pope going to do about it?"

"Nothing. The 'Holy Mafia' *elected* the Pope!"

"What? How do you know all this, Michael?"

"It's in the news, but people don't pay attention. Just like today on TV. After his coronation, Pope John Paul II marched across the street and prayed at the graveside of *José Escriva*, instead of to Jesus Christ?"

"Who's he?" asked Patrick.

"Didn't he sing, '*Come on Baby Light My Fire*?'" laughed David.

"That's José *Feliciano*," said Patrick. "Go on, Michael. You'll have to forgive David. Sometimes he just flies off the wall with these things."

"José Escriva," I repeated. "He was the *founder* of Opus Dei—the *Holy Mafia*—the group accused of embezzling money and murdering the Pope. The new Pope is a member of the group that supposedly killed the first Pope. Interesting, huh?"

***

At that moment a Spiritual Being tugged hard on my brain. I did not know who, what, or why, but it was a living creature trying to separate my soul and body. I fell out of the rocking chair and onto the floor.

I grabbed hold of the chair and helped myself back up. I spurted, "Gotta go." That was all I could say. I was confused about what was happening. I did not want it to occur again in front of company.

The Alien Being returned and tugged on my mind again. It was not simple dizziness or a fainting spell. A living, spiritual creature shanghaied my brain and spun it in rapid circles, trying to pull me from my body like a cork from a bottle.

Scared, I resisted. I was like a stubborn hypnotic subject who refused to enter the hypnotist's dreamy world. I engaged the Being in a frightful tug-of-war, over control of my mind.

My soul exited my body. Taken away by the ... whatever it was. My body was an empty shell, and it dropped to the floor.

The Alien Being pulled me toward a gyrating black tunnel, wanting me to enter. It spun my brain like a child's game of merry-go-round, trying to make me dizzy enough to surrender.

It looked scary inside the tunnel. I refused to go. But the tunnel whirled rapidly, hypnotically coaxing me closer, closer. I was now at the fringe of the cone-shaped funnel, at its widest opening. I stared inside, toward the deep exit, where it narrowed, leading mysteriously down to ... somewhere. Somewhere dark.

I determined not to enter the dark cone. The Alien Being pulled from the other side of the funnel. I pulled from Patrick's living room. But the spinning made me too dizzy, too nauseated to continue my meager resistance. I slumped further to the floor. Then once again, I floated above my empty body.

"NO!" I screamed in defiance.

I gained control, stood up, and dashed for the door. I wanted more than anything to run upstairs to the privacy of my own place, where I could at least retain my dignity, if not my willpower and my soul. But when I reached the door, the spiritual force grabbed hold of my brain like an authoritative parent twisting a bad child's earlobe. I dropped to the floor, where I wallowed in the corner to the horrid shock of Patrick and David. They helplessly watched me grope at their door, trying to escape from their place as if I'd seen a ghost.

I struggled to my knees and grabbed hold of the doorknob to pull myself up. I opened the door and stumbled out of Patrick's apartment and into the hallway. I barely was conscious that Patrick and David spoke to me. I shrugged off their efforts to assist me as I tried to methodically scale the two flights of stairs leading up to my apartment.

I gripped the stair railing with both hands and pulled myself up one step at a time. Eventually at the top stair, I paused to lean on the wall. I fought for control of my mind and body. I wobbled a few steps down the corridor, before the Being tugged again and crashed me into the partition.

At ten steps from my own front door, I conceded defeat. I felt Patrick's hand take hold of my elbow, and I surrendered to the inevitable. I slumped to the floor, knowing Patrick was there to watch over my body until I came back for it.

No! Not here. Not in the hall. And not in front of anyone. I battled to my feet, using the wall as a crutch. Feeling my way blindly, I made it to my door.

I pulled out my key and stabbed at the lock, as it quickly faded from view. Again I aimed and missed, before allowing Patrick to unlock my door for me. When opened, I darted in and slammed the door in Patrick's face. I latched the chain quickly, ignoring Patrick's inquiries, and immediately sought refuge on the adjacent sofa.

My brain revved in circles until an overwhelming nausea forced me into submission. It was not as if I was going to vomit, but rather the dizziness was used as a seat belt to restrain me in place, as I protested the impending journey. The Alien Being did not want to hurt me. It only insisted that I follow.

I entered the mysterious tunnel. Out of my body. Toward the unknown. Down to its depths, spinning into blackness. Through to the other side, and into a vast, empty place.

A Dark World.

I could not see anything, but I heard a soft voice from the Alien who had yanked me there.

"Be still. Know that I am," said the Voice.

The Alien pumped thoughts of John Paul I into me. I never saw a vision of the deceased Pope, nor did the Voice speak John Paul's name. But nonetheless, it overwhelmed me with thoughts of John Paul I. No margin for misunderstanding. The feelings were nice. Comforting. Friendly. Warm. Then suddenly the feelings were not so nice. Not so comforting. Not so friendly and not so warm.

The Voice responded, "Murder."

Having said what it wanted to say, the Being released its nauseating grip that held me captive.

I slipped back into the tunnel, narrow end first, spinning the opposite way I had come in, heading towards the original opening. When through to the other side, I popped open my eyes. I was home again.

The next day, I learned from a short news brief that Opus Dei maintained a United States' Headquarters in New York. I wanted to ask them something. I dialed information.

"What city puh-lee-aazz?"

"New York, please."

"New York. What listing puh-lee-aazz?"

"I'd like the listing, please, for 'Society of the Holy Cross and Opus Dei.'"

"Looking under 'Society of the Holy Cross and Opus Dei' I find no listing."

I tried again.

"What city, puh-lee-aazz?"

"New York, and I'd like the listing, please, for 'Opus Dei.'"

Got it! I dialed the number. Instead of identifying themselves when they answered the phone, they evasively referred to their 9 96th Street address, as a generic response: "Nine ninety-six."

"Is this Opus Dei?" I asked.

"Who is this?"

"I just want to talk to someone about obtaining a membership list of Opus Dei."

"Who is this?"

"I'll call back."

"Give me your name and number. Someone will call you."

"No. I'll be out and can't be reached. Is the new Pope a member of Opus Dei?"

"Who is this?"

"Never mind."

"What's your name? Just give me your number."

I hung up. The conversation wasn't going as cordially as I had hoped.

I wrote them, instead, disguising my letter as a query for a college thesis, saying I was Catholic and wanted to know about their organization, and if Pope John Paul II was a member. I would appreciate any help, including brochures or other information they could forward.

Holy Murder

It was days later when I received an answer, of sorts, to my inquiry. I entered the common hallway of my apartment. I stopped abruptly, taken aback at what I saw.

My mail box had been twisted apart from its metal hinges. My letter to Opus Dei was inside, standing on end. It was stamped: "Return to Sender. Moved. Not forwardable." And it had been steamed open, read, and put back.

I placed another phone call to Opus Dei, my hand positioned on the button, ready to cut them off when they answered:

"The number you have dialed has been disconnected."

***

SPECIAL NEWS UPDATE — *On January 7, 1991, the family of Pope John Paul I publicly contradicted the Vatican's version of John Paul I's sudden death after only 33 days into the papacy. They said that Pope John Paul I had discovered an organized crime syndicate operating diligently under the guise and protection of the Vatican. They said that a Holy Mafia had launched an aggressive international bank scandal, designed to embezzle money from banks and savings institutions worldwide. For this reason, family members denounced the Church findings that Pope John Paul I died in his sleep from an apparent heart attack. His own family proclaimed that he had been murdered. They astonishingly claimed that the Church was involved in a scandalous coverup.*

CHAPTER 5
The Beast

Nothing more happened until the spring of 1979. The Dark World faded from memory, as had Holy Mafias and murdered Popes. My family and others helped me understand that what I'd *thought* had happened, *hadn't*. And with the passage of time, I realized they were correct. *Something* had occurred, no doubt, on that first night I met Patrick and David, but not anything supernatural. And most assuredly the deceased Pope had not been murdered.

I was thankful for everyone's, "*What probably happened was ...*"

"*What probably happened was ...*"
      you've been working too hard.
      you haven't been eating right.
      one of those dreams that seemed so real.

Everyone rationalized away what I'd thought had happened. And I was inclined to agree, after Time befriended me.

On April 14, 1979, the Boy's Club officially shut down at 9:00 p.m., but the staff wasted another hour rounding up boys who refused to leave. I was exhausted by the time my '64 Falcon chugged home at about eleven o'clock. I planned to write a page or two on *Bad Things In The Dark*, and to hit the sack early, Saturday evening or not.

I shuffled up the two back flights of stairs to my apartment, then cautiously opened my door. I paused before entering,

The Beast

in anticipation of an attack. I quietly set my briefcase down, so that I had both hands free to defend myself against the beast that I knew awaited me. The door was barely cracked enough for me to slip my hand inside, and I retrieved a pair of shredded mittens and a ragged towel from a chair placed strategically just inside the door. The battles had become routine and my arms were scarred and scabbed with dried blood. I donned the gloves and protectively wrapped my forearm with the rag. I was ready for battle.

When nothing happened, I scooted my attaché into the apartment and softly latched the front door. I was most vulnerable in the dark, but the only living room lamp was in the far corner. I waited for my eyes to adjust. I cautiously shuffled through the blackness on my way to the lamp. I turned on the light and scanned the living room. I was alone.

Convinced there would be no attack this evening, I removed the gloves and padding. I tossed my coat onto a chair and exhaled loudly. I was too tired to sit down at my desk and be creative. I would eat, then call it a night.

Bending at the waist, I eyed longingly the leftover pizza and the one can of beer in my otherwise empty refrigerator. In my fit of hunger, I failed to sense the beast of prey peering down from high atop the cabinets.

Cold, piercing eyes from an extremely large head targeted my neck for a kill. The beast drew taught its hind legs in preparation for a midair pounce across the kitchen and onto its unsuspecting victim. It sprung, airborne, with the grasping talons of an eagle.

George the Kat swept onto my shoulders and bit into my neck. I jumped and screamed, trying to shake loose the rider and its impaling claws. But my screaming only startled George the Kat into spurring me more deeply, like a crazed cowboy hanging onto a *Bucking Bronco* until his eight seconds were up.

Hot blood oozed down my neck and shoulders. "Easy. Eeaassyy," I whispered. I dared not cry out again. A sudden reaction would only frighten George the Kat to rip away more of my skin. I gently reached to withdraw its claws from my shoulders. That's when I dropped my beer. I could not let it hit the floor—it was my last can. I lunged to snatch it from midair and George chomped his lethal fangs into my neck.

"Aaahhh!

"Mmmeeeooowww!"

"Oh, God! Oh, God!"

I bounced through the kitchen, trying to shake the enemy loose of its strangle-hold. I slipped on the pizza and fell, landing on George the Kat, who "Rrrreowed" and regrouped to the living room.

As suddenly as it had begun, the battle was over. All was quiet. I wallowed in beer foam and pepperoni, counting the casualties of battle, massaging my punctured neck and bleeding shoulders. I trashed my soggy pizza, then searched for George. "Here, kitty, kitty, kitty."

Last Thanksgiving, Patrick gave me a kitten to keep me company. At first I declined, not wanting the responsibilities, but then rescinded and took him back. I told Patrick it was the ugliest cat I had ever seen and that it would have to be put to sleep because nobody else would want it. The real reason I wanted him, though, was to have someone to come home to. *George the Kat* lived for the moment I walked through the door. But he truly was ugly. George the Kat had an immensely disproportionate head, with a clownish orange-and-white coat. And he seemed to have grown frightfully bigger each time I returned home. Entering the door had become a bloody adventure. George loved to show affection by pouncing on me. He never tried to hurt me, unless I scared him, which I often did when he startled me.

As I tended to my bleeding, George lounged on the sofa with an indigenous expression of victory. And because he still had that playful look, I approached him slowly and cooed. I talked that embarrassing nonsense Masters say to their pets when alone. I hugged George to display affection, and to show I had conceded defeat. Wanting no more escapades, I said good night and prepared for bed.

I draped a thick blanket over the drawn shades to block the intruding light from the parking lot. I turned on the bathroom fan, wanting its background noise to damper the Saturday night disturbances from nearby Shelby Street and Garfield Park. I quickly dozed off.

The inner-perception of someone being present in my room awakened me. But when I opened my eyes, all I saw was the clock's fluorescent green numerals: 3:15 a.m. The light switch was several feet away and unreachable from bed. Shrouded in darkness, I listened intently for an intruder. Then it seized me. The same Alien Being who had abducted my soul last October in Patrick's apartment, returned. Once again, it pounced on my brain in an unearthly kidnapping.

I resisted, but unlike before, the Being swiftly overpowered me. The speed at which he flushed me in and out of the black funnel, circumvented the nauseating side-effects that accompanied my first journey. This time, I was not gradually forced into submission with a pressure-hold on my brain. Rather, the Alien seemed hurried, as if it had no time for my foolish resistance. It spun my mind clockwise, accelerating rapidly as it dragged me into that same long, twisting, black funnel.

For the second time, I whisked through the spinning cone and exited the other side. I reentered the Dark World. For a teasing moment the darkness receded, enabling me to see my discarded body below, still in bed. My spirit lingered above, observing, like a turtle who had been fished out of its shell and who longed to crawl back inside and hide.

I viewed my estranged body as an IT. IT lay on ITS stomach. ITS right arm extended back toward ITS side. ITS left arm bent around the pillow, reaching toward the headboard. ITS right leg protruded straight back; ITS left one had drawn into a semi-fetal position. And IT had kicked the sheet off, except for a small patterned portion of vivid green flowers that still covered ITS bare buttocks.

Then everything darkened and the familiar sights below vanished. I again roamed the Dark World, as a lost little boy.

As a child I was called, "Little Mikey." I remember graphically when Little Mikey played hide-and-seek at Grandma's and Grandpa's house, often spending most of the day shut away in their dark basement closet. But the darkness of that closet could not have matched the darkness of the Dark World.

One time, Little Mikey ran away from home—way across the street to the cornfield, where he dug a foxhole and lived half the afternoon. There, terribly alone, Little Mikey cried. But being alone in the foxhole back then, was nothing like the frightening solitude of the Dark World now.

And there was that day Little Mikey followed Buck Creek too far back into the woods to fish. It was scary, being so lost. But Little Mikey had not been as lost in the woods then, as he was now in the Dark World. A virtual quagmire of Blackness. I was Little Mikey all over again, and I stayed fearfully quiet and awaited my Dark World fate.

Finally, the Alien Being spoke. "Do not worry."

It was a gentle and thoughtful thing to say. Although I had been kidnapped, my abductor meant no harm. I believed it. Its words were kind and sincere, and they dissipated my fears.

Next, a light appeared. It wasn't much of a light (the size of a pinhead and a trillion miles away), but in the Dark World it sparkled more brilliantly than the rarest crown jewel. The ball of light zoomed across the Dark World, and reached me within a blink of an eye. And it was huge. I backed away to better focus my eyes, as if I had suddenly found myself standing too close at the foot of a movie screen.

Like viewing a movie on a large crystal ball, I watched an image of Grandma project itself onto the sphere. But she looked much older and paler, gravely ill, with her cheeks caved in. I stared into Grandma's bleak future, when suddenly she glowed, illuminating a good portion of the Dark World. Then the vision of Grandma faded.

My mother appeared in the sphere, but she did not glow, as had Grandma. The Friendly Alien spoke again, tenderly. "Tell your mother, 'Do not worry.'"

I asked, "Why?"

It repeated with compassion: "Tell your mother, 'Do not worry.'"

I persisted. "Why?"

Without answering, the Friendly Alien abandoned me. A final reminder echoed throughout the Dark World: "Do not worry."

Moments later, I sensed I was not alone. I saw nothing. I heard nothing. I tasted nothing. I smelled nothing. I felt nothing. All five senses registered zero. Yet I knew hostile eyes pierced me from afar. Cold, steely eyes.

Something in the dark snickered at me.

"Hello!" I called to the Friendly Alien. "Are you there?" I turned this way and that, straining in the dark to find the Alien who had brought me there. I did not like this Second Alien, and more, I was afraid.

The Second Alien laughed at my awkwardness. It mocked me. Nothing was funny, but its laughter intensified, heinously.

Finally it stopped taunting me. But like war drums ending their incessant beatings, the eerie silence frightened me equally as much. Something growled at me like a beast. It growled again. Short, raspy bursts from the back of its throat. It crept closer like a carnivore stalking dinner. It paused and snarled with every cautious advancement. It seemed leery of a baited trap. It used the darkness to camouflage its methodical approach.

Convinced I was alone and helpless, the Beast pounced on me.

I never saw its eerie hands (or claws) lunge out from the dark, but most assuredly a vivid image registered in my mind of what it was that snatched me upside down. The Beast wrapped its fingers (or claws) around my left foot. They were long enough to overlap my tiny ankle and extend far up my calf. And they were cold. Cold as a bloodless corpse. Its skin had scales like snakeskin or lizard.

Its fingertips sprouted long nails that painfully dug into me. There was no escaping the powerful grip. Its growl was menacing. The Beast was going to kill me, but it wanted to prolong the terror. It wanted to kill me without mercy, without pity, and with as much rage as possible. It quavered from anger, reaching the very pinnacle of wrath until it was impossible to express more. It hated me.

The Beast raised me high over its head. It shook me, wanting to jar the life out. It shook me, as if to frighten me to death. It shook me exactly six times, each time screaming the word, "NO!".

"No! No! No! No! No! NooorrrrrrGRRRRRR!" The last word trailed into an awesome growl that vibrated the Dark World like a strong earthquake, only it was not a quake and it was *not earth. Its last rumble nearly popped my heart. It drew me to the peak of its backswing, intending to smash the life out of me. But at that pendulum point where the backswing starts its deadly forward arc, someone (something) gently removed me from its grasp. The Beast fled, apparently afraid of whomever rescued me.*

Then, that same someone cradled me like an infant. Caressed my head. Rocked me gently. Calmed me.

"Do not worry." The Friendly Alien had returned.

***

I went home to my body. I lay in bed and opened my eyes. I was scared. The bathroom fan whirred noisily, but not enough to deafen the thundering pulse in my inner ear. My heart revved in fear. Every gland pumped out of control. My naked body sweat through the bed sheet and soaked the mattress padding. Tears flooded my face and drenched my pillow. Mucous flowed like lava from erupting nostrils. I shivered in the cool dampness.

I opened my mouth to scream, but the air from my lungs just skimmed across my vocal cords and exited out my mouth, as if running away in terror. I could not create a sound. I breathed erratically. Heaving. Trembling. Yelling for help was a physical impossibility.

Then a familiar, warm and furry body cuddled against my shoulder. George the Kat returned from his late-night apartment safari, and perched on top of me for a nap. His purring vibrated my back and arms like I had put a quarter into a *Magic Fingers* mattress.

The purring tickled, and I smiled. I stopped crying and rolled over to wipe my face on a dry sheet corner. When I turned and pulled the blanket, I accidentally tossed George to the floor. I scooped him up on the rebound and stroked his groggy head (top heavy, George seldom landed on his feet). I embraced George until he snored in contentment.

I, however, could not sleep. I stared overhead at the chandelier, afraid to close my eyes. I tried to reason away the Dark World and the Beast. *A nightmare. It was only a nightmare. What probably happened was ... (fill in the blank).*

Suddenly, George awoke. He jumped, hissing at the foot of the bed. He retreated across my face. His actions begged for mercy. In his own way, George was begging me for protection.

I sat up. I flexed my eyes, but it was too dark to see anything. It did not matter—visual confirmation was not necessary. George the Kat was a perpetual killing machine, yet now he feared for his life. That was all the proof I needed. Evil stood at the foot of my bed. I was not sure I *wanted* to see.

The blood vessels pulsated hard in my *left* ankle, exactly where the Beast had grabbed me moments ago, while in the Dark World. My foot seemingly wanted to depart from my body and to run away. George arched his back high. His fur bristled on end. He had never done that before. He was afraid. His muscles flexed for a fight to the death. This was the End. Right here. Right now.

I held George tightly to my chest, until he gashed me with a deadly kick and ran for all his nine lives. My own survival instincts surfaced from their primeval dwellings within and screamed at me to flee from the darkness at the foot of my bed!

My body overflowed with a chilling fluid produced specifically for that one rare moment of terror. The icy adrenaline gushed through my heart and veins and caused me to yank my foot from the end of the bed. But even that superhuman effort was not fast enough. The Beast got me.

Like offering final proof of its existence—that it was more than a nightmare—the Beast broke the plane of the Dark World and invaded my bedroom. It attacked me while I stretched open my eyes to their limits, and while my senses were sharp enough to know real from unreal. The Beast came after me so horrendously that no amount of logic, no semblance of reasoning, no *what-probably-happened-was*, would ever convince me otherwise.

The Beast put me on notice in no uncertain terms that when it was good and ready, it was going to kill me. And It would terminate me with a great deal of *FEAR,* *w*ith more horror than defenseless Little Mikey ever imagined.

Hiding in darkness so that I could not see it, the Beast once again clamped its fingers and claws around my left foot. Evil ran through my veins, and I jerked as if a jolt of electricity shocked my heart. It yanked hard on my foot and lifted me from bed. I sailed from its ugly grasp and slammed into the wall, next to the light switch, five feet away on the fly. I spun the dimmer switch to its brightest output.

The Beast fled, its task accomplished. Its warning had been delivered. Little Mikey would soon be dead, as a hummingbird whose heart would burst in fear. In time, my pretty, in time.

I leaned against the wall. I cupped my face in both hands and cried. My lungs pumped out of control. I ran to the living room. Light from the bedroom shined just enough for me to see the telephone on the table in front of me. I wanted to call my neighbor, but couldn't move to lift the receiver and dial the numbers.

I sat paralyzed in the worn armchair, its rough fabric scratching my naked body. I snatched at the telephone, but knocked it to the floor. My muscular coordination malfunctioned.

I could not breathe. I compressed my diaphragm with both arms and manually injected air into my spastic lungs. I retrieved the telephone and hastily dialed Patrick downstairs. But I could not input the right combination. I dialed again and again, until Patrick's phone rang. I leaned forward and shut my eyes, waiting, praying, begging, for Patrick to answer.

David answered, "Hello."

I sobbed into the phone. I could not talk. My teeth chattered.

"Hello?"

I tried to get David's attention, before he would think it was a crank call and hang up.

"Who *is* this?" asked David. David leaned over to Patrick, who hid his head under the pillow, trying to sleep. He told Patrick, "It's somebody crying like a baby." He lifted the pillow off Patrick's head and passed the telephone to him, saying, "See if you can tell who it is."

"H'lo," mumbled Patrick.

With trembling fingers, I shaped my lips to form a word. I exhausted the small amount of air in my lungs to whisper, "Patri ..."

"Michael? Michael, is that you?"
"Uhhh."
"Michael, what's wrong?"
"Uhhhhhh."
"Michael, are you okay?"
I lowered my face and sobbed without shame.
"Would you like to come down here?"
"Uhhhh." I grabbed the robe I had tossed onto the floor the night before, and wearing nothing else, skipped from the second floor and into Patrick's street-level apartment.

Pounding footsteps telegraphed my arrival, and I didn't have to knock. When Patrick opened the door, I bolted inside. Without saying hello, I darted for the antique rocker next to the stained-glass window, and rocked.

Patrick approached and hugged me. David said assuring words to me. I sat in safe company, although I still trembled, hard enough to rock the chair by itself.

David brewed coffee. He and Patrick sipped away, while I set mine on the wicker table. There was no conversation. In silence, they observed me, as I suppressed my crying as long as possible. Inevitably, I exploded in a convulsion of tears.

A couple of hours passed without a word exchanging. Finally, David asked, "Do you want to talk about it?"

I shook my head no. I was physically able to talk now, but no appropriate words came to mind. I only sat in the chair and rocked. Eventually, I calmed down. I suffered only an occasional shiver. The last of the tears dripped off my damp and gleaming face.

The rising sun peeked solemnly through the rainbow-colored windows. David observed with a sigh, then sarcastically broke the silence when he joked, "What a way to spend Easter Sunrise."

I quit rocking. I wiped my face on my sleeve. My first and only words tumbled off my lips:

"Oh, my God—It's *Easter.*" I stood and went home. No explanations. No goodbye.

CHAPTER 6
The Origin of Bad Things

It was several days past Easter before I reluctantly told Patrick and David about my journey to the Dark World. They were not unbelieving. In fact, as I recounted my brush with Evil, they exposed a dark side of their own.

Many of the people who had wandered in and out of their apartment were either practicing witches or Satanists. Patrick and David were neither, but quite knowledgeable of both because their friends were all involved in the crafts. Their Witch-friends and their Satanist-friends worshipped the very same *Bad Things*, although the witches were ignorant of the connection. Those who dabbled in White Witchcraft argued vehemently at accusations linking them to Satan, while their Satanic friends laughed heartily at the foolish witches and spirit channelers.

Witches and New Agers believe they're using *psychic powers*—connecting with their *inner-self,* and with Nature—to achieve their desired, mystical ends. "They don't realize their spirit guides are Satanic angels," said Patrick. They don't even believe in the existence of a devil. Witches are only involved by *default* ... through *ignorance.* They claim they worship *Mankind* and *Harmony* and *Nature, or possibly a goddess,* instead of God as we think of God. And they get all uptight when you challenge them on that fact.

"Michael," said Patrick, "I want to give you some books to study. You're not going to find what you want by reading news articles." He explained that writers generally focus on blood sacrifices and grave robberies because that is what sells copy. But in reality, Satanists actually *worship* Lucifer as their *God*. The ultimate goal of the Satanic purist is to pave the way for Satan's return to Earth.

Many people scoff at the existence of fundamental Satanism. It is easier for the public to understand teenagers who kill babies, than it is to comprehend a spiritual world of demons and angels. Most of the reported atrocities are *not* common to traditional Satanism. Rather, the media misinterprets. Blood sacrifices are generally ordained by people who have delved too far into something they know little about. Almost always, the worst crimes are committed by young people with Christian or Jewish backgrounds. They are slowly sucked in by curiosity, or by spirit guides they have accidentally or playfully contacted.

Some connect through Satanic music. Sometimes an occult game is their key to a wrong door. Many begin with astrology, which is the mainstay for *all* the occults. Same with worshipping Nature. Worshipping the *created object*, rather than glorifying the Creator. There are many ways to connect.

Soon they hear a voice; see a shadow. Maybe they receive an actual message from a spiritual being. Of course it will not identify itself as a Satanic angel or demon. In fact, most channelers argue that their spirit guide offers *good* advice, which it does for a while. But when the demon has earned enough trust from the channeler, it turns destructive. Suicide. Murder. In fact, some of Patrick's friends would soon be killing themselves. In the end, the demon's only purpose is to destroy, especially if its victim is a former Christian.

But that is *not* Satanism.

Satanism is the orderly worship of Satan, and loyal Satanists diligently prepare for his reign on Earth. They believe Satan has a human counterpart known as the Antichrist. They believe the Antichrist will sweep into power as ruler of a One-World Government. Once he is in his proper political position in The New World Order, Satan will come and incarnate the Antichrist's body and claim to be God on Earth.

That, in a nutshell, is what the Satanic *purists* believe. They never engage in the frivolities of *White* Magic to find a *parking place*, or as a *potion* to get lucky in bed or how to pick a winning bingo card or lottery number. However, such recruiting tactics are used by Satan's angels to gain the confidence of novice witches, channelers and New Agers, prior to sucking them in over their heads. Their imminent demise is caused by ignorance.

Patrick also noted that, unlike witches and channelers, Fundamentalists are *not* tricked or coerced into Satanism. An initiate into Satanism knows exactly which path he takes, and he crosses that boundary on his own accord.

His argument was supported by a passage from the Rite of Initiation, as found in *Satan's Bible*, written by the late Anton LeVey, the High Priest of the Church of Satan in San Francisco.

> " ... *thou receiveth the Vigil of Baphomet and embraceth the Black Flame of cherished enlightenment. Thou hast assumed this Infernal commitment of thine own volition, without let or hindrance. This act being done without coercion and of thine own desire and according to thy will.*"

Patrick and David were instrumental to my research. They allowed me to keep their books. "Just be careful, though," he warned me. "It's real. It's *all* real."

A few weeks after Patrick and David began schooling me in the crafts, Patrick awoke in the middle of the night to see a darkened image standing at the foot of his bed. Patrick nudged David awake. They both sat up in bed, cautiously and without conversation. They were not overly frightened of the Being, who made no effort to hide from them. It made no hostile movements toward them. Neither did it speak. It only stared.

Patrick, an artist, rolled slowly toward the night stand where he kept a sketching pad and pen. In the dark, he hurriedly scribbled its likeness.

The Origin of Bad Things

The Beast was aware that Patrick was sketching its portrait and it even seemed to be holding a pose until Patrick finished a rough draft.

And although it never spoke, threats burned from its eyes: *they shouldn't be educating Michael in the black arts. Michael was the enemy. They were to disassociate themselves from Michael or face the consequences.*

The next day Patrick told me of the ordeal and gave me his sketching of the Beast.

***

I quit my job at the Boy's Club and became a high-commissioned salesman, enlisting students for an airline school. *Money* was not my motivation for being in sales, but rather *Time*. I could make a couple of quick sales, then take time off to write until the money was gone and the refrigerator was empty. I wanted to buy enough Time to learn all I could about the Spiritual Beings beseeching me, and I simply could not waste time on a meaningless job.

On July 15, 1979, I drove eighty miles south of Indianapolis to the rural community of Bedford, Indiana. I preferred working the smaller towns. I was in no frame of mind for making hard-nosed sales pitches, and country people were friendlier, more to my liking. However, my sales prospect canceled our appointment. I searched for a shade tree to park under, while awaiting my next scheduled presentation.

I had driven all over Bedford trying to locate a decent spot to park, but I could not find the smallest inkling of a place to pull over. It was a scorching Sunday afternoon, and I eventually lost my temper and slapped the steering wheel with an opened palm. I needed to pull off the road, to utilize the extra time I had between sales appointments. I had books to read; I carried them with me wherever I went. But I could not find a parking spot and I cursed the town for not having a road wide enough for me to pull aside.

I finally spotted a blacktopped parking lot. I did not care who owned the property, as I pulled in and parked. I looked to see where I was: *Trinity Pentecostal Church*.

My car baked under the mid-summer sun, and I left my windows up and the air conditioning on high speed. I loosened my tie, aware I could not keep the cool air blasting for a full two hours, although I would give it another ten minutes.

I tossed my sales kit into the back seat. I grabbed an array of books and notes to study up front. I thought perhaps that a church congregation ought to know about the Dark World. Maybe they should know about the Beast and the Friendly Alien. Maybe I should speak to them as a group.

I opened the Bible I had brought with me, and searched for passages about demons. However, I could not interpret the King's English or the mystical Prophecies. I closed the book with a thud.

I leaned back and daydreamed. I basked in the scenery beyond the church, absorbing the tranquillity of the hills and the rolling green meadows. I wished I could rent an isolated farm house, to have the required solitude to figure things out. *Somewhere near Bedford would be nice. With lots of land. And horses*!

"Hey!"

I jumped when a man pounded on my window and shouted at me. I thought I was being kicked off the lot for trespassing and I had nowhere else to go. I hurriedly sought an excuse, hoping the man would change his mind and allow me to stay for a couple more hours. I guessed him to be in his fifties. Noting the pin-striped, three-piece suit I also guessed he was an important businessman around town. I shut off the engine and rolled down the window.

"Are you a preacher?" asked the man. He brushed back his long, wavy hair, as he stooped to see inside the car.

"Huh?"

"Well, I noticed your out-of-town license plate. A lot of preachers have been visiting lately—for our revival, you know. That's why I thought you might be one. I'm Charlie Scalf. I'm the pastor here."

I introduced myself and explained my presence in the church lot. I asked if my being there was a bother, which of course, it wasn't. And for good measure, I held aloft my Bible, as if hinting that I was there on church business.

"Say, why don't you drop by tonight? It's the last of our revival and it's been a pretty good one?"

"Oh, I don't know if I'll still be around."

"Course, a lot of folks don't like what I'm preaching about. We're talking about fallen angels and demons. What they are, where they come from, how to deal with them. Kind of scares some folks, you know."

I glanced at my Bible, then at the church. *Coincidence*, I thought. "I know." I picked up the notes off my lap and showed them to Charlie (Charlie insisted on a first-name basis and didn't attach Reverend to it). "That's what I'm studying. I got all kinds of books here about that."

Charlie said, "That's wonderful. Why not come by tonight. Then next Sunday I'll schedule you to speak about what you've been studying."

"Huh? I'm not a preacher."

"That ain't no problem. We always save Sunday evenings for testimonials. We generally get a nice crowd, too."

The invitation stunned me. *Another* coincidence, I thought. I had dug myself into a hole and could not unearth a ready excuse. "Umm, sure. What time?"

"It starts at seven-thirty, but people get here about seven."

Startled by the circumstances falling my way, I assured Charlie that I would be in attendance.

"That's wonderful," said Charlie. "I think you'll like our church. It's not too big and kinduva cozy little place." He mentioned that Trinity had about a hundred members; the building was all paid for, that he did not draw an income from the church, but rather worked a good job with the railroad. And, he and his wife (who played the "Pie-Annie" for the church) were originally from "West Virginny," but were moving to "Flory-da" when he retired next year. "How do you like Bedford?" he asked.

"Fine. I was thinking about renting a house around here someday."

"You know, I've got a house I'm looking to rent."

Coincidence, I thought. "Actually, I'm looking for a farm house—something with acreage."

"It *IS* a farm house. Me and the wife lived there for fifteen years. But we built this new home in town, you see, and the old one's just sitting vacant. Sure would like to rent it to you. Got thirty acres."

By then I was so overcome with the numbers of coincidences that I made up my mind to take it. "Would you mind if I put a horse out there?"

"Land sakes, the horses are already there. You're welcome to ride them, if you want."

Oh, God. The place practically had my name on the mailbox. But I did not have the resources to pay for it. I figured I could handle three hundred dollars, no more. "What are you asking for it?"

"Well, that's a problem. I hate to have to charge so much, but since it's a three-bedroom with a refurbished basement—and with the land and all—I've got to have two hundred a month."

"Uh, okay. I'll rent it. First of the month."

Charlie lifted his hands off my car and stood up, looking surprised. "Well land sakes—don't you want to drive out and see it, aforehand?"

"No."

I attended church that evening, and listened intently to Charlie's spiel about Bad Things.

History of Bad Things: The Story

In the beginning ...
God said let there be Good Things, and there was good. Bad Things simply did not exist. No hunger, no disease. All wealth, no poverty. No Republicans, no Democrats. No brussel sprouts. No television reruns.

Good Things. Nobody worked, everyone played. Teachers taught only recess. Edy's Grand ice cream had no calories. And mothers said, "If you don't eat all your candy, you'll have no spinach," while children argued, "It's my turn to do the dishes ... is not ... is too, you got to do them last night, Mom, tell Billy it's my turn or else I get to do laundry." Hockey games took forever because players kept stopping to shake hands, and Monday Night Football was broadcast without announcers.

In the Land of Good Things, two excelled. Elohim, the League Commissioner, and Shining One, the star athlete—both honored positions in a world where only games existed.

The Commissioner organized the perfect league. If a blemish existed at all, it was perhaps his rule that every angel in town had to participate, including Little Michael. The problem was in finding a role that Little Michael could play. He could not punt or pass. He could not catch. He could not run or hit with power. Fact was, Little Michael could not do much of anything. He could not be water-boy in a world where no one thirst, nor a towel-boy when no one sweat. So Michael roamed the sidelines, leading cheers for Elohim.

At the extreme was Shining One. He won every game. Hit a home run every time at bat. Pitched all no-hitters. Scored a touchdown every play. Made a basket every shot, full length of the court, never missed. So victorious was Shining One, he changed his name to Shining Won and asked to renegotiate his contract.

Elohim, recognizing talent, paid him everything he asked, and more. In fact, he paid him so much more than Shining Won expected, his sports agent asked Elohim to take some back, because nobody deserved that kind of salary for merely playing games.

(The sports agent's request to return money was known far and wide as the first recorded miracle).

The awesome contract offered by Elohim to Shining Won called for rubies and gold and gems of every nature. No-Interest loans, paid-up credit cards. Controlling interest in capital-free business ventures. Company chariot and driver. Designer silk robes. Everything.

"No," declined Shining Won to the offer.

"But why?" asked Elohim. "Is it because you want a long-term contract? I'll make it eternal."

"No," he refused again.

"Is there a problem with your pay? I'll give you as much as a COLLEGE athlete, if that's what it takes."

"What I want—what I demand, or I'll walk—is all of what you've said. PLUS, I want Michael to be leading the cheers for ME. *Shining Won then boasted what became known as "The Fabulous Five I AM's."*

I AM the one scoring all the points.

I AM winning all the games.

I AM the star.

I AM the Top Vote Getter on the All-Star Ballot.

I AM the one making all the plays."

"I can't understand why the crowd cheers for you. I want the recognition. I want election to the Hall of Fame. Why should you get all the glory?"

And Elohim made the greatest "come back" in history. "Because I AM the one making all the plays FOR you," *answered Elohim.*

Shining Won could not have been struck with a more insulting response. Thus he made the first reference to bodily functions and about Bad Things with Mom. In fact, his sideline antics were so infuriating that the crowd hushed in disbelief. And that is when it happened ...

the star athlete in question physically shoved the League Commissioner.

"You're fired," said the Commissioner.

"You can't fire me. Who'll take my place?"

Elohim looked to the bench. Shining Won had a valid point; nobody had a fraction of his skills. And then came an even greater insult; a maneuver that rocked the stadium. Elohim stared Shining Won in the eye and proclaimed for all to hear: "Michael will take your place."

The Origin of Bad Things

"Little Mikey?" Shining Won laughed. And although the crowd was polite, they too, could not help but snicker. "Little Mikey?" Shining Won turned to reenter the game as star quarterback, but Elohim intervened.

"Michael—you're in the game for Shining Won."

Shining Won stormed to the sidelines and threatened Michael. "You're dead meat, wimp."

Elohim called Michael's play from the sideline.

Michael entered the game along with an entire new lineup of scrubs. With the game clock winding down, Michael threw a "Hail Mary" the length of the field. He then sprinted to the end zone in world record time, and caught his own touchdown pass. The announcer cheered, "Holy Cow! Scrubs win! Scrubs win!"

Shining Won ran onto the field in protest, and Little Mikey proceeded to throw him out of the stadium. Humiliated, Shining Won took one-third of the players and one-third of the crowd, vowing to start his own league. He vowed he would be back some day to put Elohim out of business. "And you," he snarled at Michael, "will be dealt with first."

***

And that's the story of Bad Things as I understood it, explained by Charlie Scalf. Except it was not a game. It was serious business. It was war.

Lucifer was God's first Creation. God made Lucifer long before He created humans, long before plants or animals, and even before He created the Earth, or stars, or a universe.

Lucifer was God's masterpiece—the perfect living being. The name Lucifer meant the "Shining One," or the "Light Bearer." He was so wonderfully beautiful that he lit the skies before the sun had been molded into a universal lamp. And God loved him and admired him. "Lucifer, you are full of wisdom and perfect in beauty."

Lucifer had beauty in song, too. He epitomized musical genius. He was a literal music machine, created with flutes and strings for vocal cords. Each and every word proceeding from his mouth was a melodious wonder to behold. All the angels hence created by God would surround Lucifer just to hear the symphonic miracles of his voice.

War of the Angels

God greatly loved Lucifer. They were together, side-by-side in all endeavors, be it in music, in play, in strolls through Paradise, or in Holy solitude on God's highest of the high thrones. God shared everything with Lucifer and withheld nothing from him. There was only one simple *catch*: Lucifer had to give God the Glory and to lead all the angels in Praise and Worship to God the Father.

Lucifer's pride corrupted his thoughts. He hungered for self-adoration. He nurtured a lust for power. He hated performing wondrous signs and miracles to heavenly crowds who continuously gathered around him, only to give all the credit and glory to God. It was embarrassing and it was not fair. He despised everyone's adoration of God. As God's Archangel, Lucifer wanted others to worship him, as well as God. Eventually he thought of himself as God's *equal*.

He rebelled. He corrupted one-third of all the angels into joining him, then launched a horrendous military coup in a wicked attempt at overthrowing God from His throne. But he lost, and was expelled by Michael through the powers granted him by God. God then appointed Michael as his new Archangel, which angered Lucifer even more and made a mortal enemy of Michael.

Lucifer became known as Satan, which means "Adversary." He was banished to his new Kingdom of the Dark World. There he hid in darkness, ashamed to show his face because God had changed him into a beastly dragon. Never did there exist a more repulsive looking monster; not at any time, in any world. He was so hideous to cast eyes upon that he cloaked himself in solitude, unable to cope with his lost pride. To this day, he resides in his dark kingdom, scheming with the rebels he rules about how to get even.

Satan vowed to destroy God's most prized possession: Earth, and every inhabitant. He vowed to destroy all the Good Things. He vowed to destroy Archangel Michael. And he vowed to destroy God, Himself.

Once again, he changed his name: "Apollyon, the Destroyer." Over the mindless millenniums and the countless centuries, he came to have many names: (1) "The Prince of the Power of the Air," who whispered Bad Thoughts to attentive humans; (2) "The Ruler of Darkness," because the Dark World was his kingdom; (3) "Leviathan (the one who dwells in a sea of humanity)," because of his desire to control the human population. He was also called Leviathan for his obsession to exchange his beastly body, for a beautiful human one. And many other names, none kind, all evil.

At the time of his banishment to the Dark World, Satan vowed to return in triumph over God. He, himself, would then become God. Satan issued five ominous threats known as the great I Will's:
- "I will ascend into Heaven!"
- "I will exalt my throne above the stars of God!"
- "I will sit also upon the mount of the congregation, in the sides of the north!"
- "I will ascend above the heights of the clouds!"
- "I will be EL-ELYON!" (meaning, "God of Power!")

Forgive me Father
I have killed a man.
I have loved a woman.
I have stolen for the church.
I Am Opus Dei.
(Anonymous)

CHAPTER 7
Sumpin's Not Right

After my coincidental introduction to Charlie Scalf, I took a leave of absence from my job. I wanted all my time, all my efforts, to be used in preparation for my accidentally scheduled church testimony. Finally, by late Saturday on July 14, 1979, I set aside my notes, convinced I could absorb no more. I climbed into bed for a few hours rest before my upcoming drive to Trinity Pentecostal Church in Bedford, Indiana.

***

Sometime before sunrise, I was rustled from my body for another interworld journey. This time I never entered the black tunnel. I did not travel to the Dark World. Instead, I was exposed to another plane of the same world, as if a curtain of air had been drawn open.
The world behind the wall of air seemed no different than the world I had just left, although I had been asleep in bed back there, and in this duplicate world I was wide awake on a pleasant, sun-shiny day. I stood in the parking lot of the local A&P Supermarket on the southside of Indianapolis. The asphalt parking lot was clean and black. The brick building, a brilliant red. The surroundings were tranquil, until I turned to see the Dark Thing drifting to my left.

It was Death. Although we had never met, I had no difficulty recognizing it. Death was wrapped in a coarse black cloth, a shroud, a dark gauze wound head to toe. It circled in a surreal motion, facing me squarely at all times, as it moved from left-to-left. I was surrounded by Death. Or had Death captured me? Whatever the meaning, Death toyed with me.

I spoke, "You don't bother me."

The shrouded spirit slowly departed, wanting me to behold its flight. I silently watched it retreat toward the "A&P" building. I looked beneath the sign and saw my family huddled as if for a family portrait. They were all present— my mother and father; brothers and sister; aunts and uncles; Grandma and Grandpa. They were unaware that Death hovered above them.

"NO!" Frightened for them, I called out. They never heard me. I jumped up-and-down, waving both arms high over my head to warn them. They did not see me.

I charged forward to attack Death, to save my family. But suddenly a giant military policeman, twenty feet tall, intercepted me and blocked my path. The soldier—dressed in khaki pants, a short-sleeve khaki shirt, and a black helmet with an MP insignia—would not allow me to warn my family about the black-shrouded being that hovered above them, and I was forced to watch helplessly.

I attempted to out-flank the giant, hoping to flee past him and chase Death away from my family. The giant side-stepped and blocked my route. I struck at him, trying to force him away. But how could I fight the mighty soldier? I watched them fade away with Death, into darkness. I cried in defeat.

***

I was still in tears when I awoke, back inside my body. The sun peeked through my window, reminding me it was time to arise and get ready to go expose the Beast to the church in Bedford, Indiana. I thought long and hard about the threats made against my family by the black-shrouded being I had just encountered. I decided to ignore the threats and on July 15, 1979, I drove to Charlie Scalf's church.

The doors to the tiny, cinder-block church remained open between the morning and evening sessions, and I sauntered in alone, six hours early. The lights were shut off, but sunbeams sneaked through the frosted windows and slid across the varnished wood like moonlight on a slick river, enabling me to see my way to the front.

I meandered up three altar steps in slow, ceremonial strides. I was allowing God ample opportunity for a miraculous sign, should He display one, but He never did, not even when I leaned into position behind the gleaming, oaken pulpit. I stared across the darkened chapel and conversed with my soul, while empty pews echoed my thoughts.

In rehearsed gestures, I positioned my chalkboard and strategically arranged my many notes. I had never addressed a congregation before, but I needed to tell someone about the Dark World, and I did not know who else might listen. My own family disbelieved me about Bad Things. My father said, "If you don't quit talking like that you'll go nuts." My older brother said, "I don't want that #^!*&! kind of talk in my house." The nicest thing my younger brother said was to say nothing at all. And my mother said, "I believe you, but what will my friends think if you go around talking like that? Can't you say something funny?" My sister believed me, but she did not count because she would have believed whatever I said. I needed an attentive ear outside my own family.

I ached to inform others about my ventures in the Dark World. But even so, I had not planned on speaking in church—it just happened that way. By coincidence. Nonetheless, when the Sunday Evening worship service began, I was somehow up front on the altar, facing the congregation.

I dreadfully awaited my introduction, while the pastor opened service with prayer, songs, and announcements. I mentally rehashed. Physically perspired. When finally introduced as the featured speaker, I approached slowly, unsure of myself. I acknowledged to the congregation that I was not a Biblical scholar; and I intended to glance toward their pastor occasionally, to seek a nod of approval when interpreting Biblical passages.

"Amens" filled the air, catching me off guard. I paused, scrambling for my notes, trying to reorganize my thoughts.

"I have something to tell you," I began, "and I'm not going to waste my energy trying to convince you that I'm telling the truth. You either believe me, or you don't. I hope you do, but nonetheless, I'm here to tell you there's another world besides the one we now live in."

"Amen."

"I say that, because I've been there on more than one occasion."

Nobody said amen. They seemed a bit stunned at that statement.

"I'm not talking about Heaven. I'm not talking about Hell, either, although maybe it *is* Hell, it's *scary* enough. For lack of a name, I call it the *Dark World*.

"There are *living* creatures in the Dark World. I don't know what *kind* of creatures, even though I've had contacts with them. I haven't *seen* them—it's too *dark* in the Dark World to see them, but I believe they're some kind of spirits. Some are friendly. Some are hateful. One of them in particular is the *Ruler of the Hateful Ones*. One of them in particular is the *Ruler of the Friendly Ones*. And I know—even now as I stand here and talk—that the Friendly Ones and the Hateful Ones are at war in the Dark World.

"I don't know why I'm here tonight," I said with a tone of sadness. "It just kinda happened by coincidence, I guess. I don't even know how to say what I'm trying to tell you.

"Some things happened to me, but from what I've learned about Pentecostals, many of you, yourselves, have experienced ordeals with the supernatural. So I guess I don't have anything special to say, other than to confirm your beliefs that another world does exist, and in it, a struggle between the bad guys and good guys."

"Amen."

"Brother Scalf, am I correct in my interpretation of the Prophecies, that in the final years before the reign of the Antichrist, there shall be a corruption of the church and 'spiritual wickedness in high places?'"

Charlie nodded his head. The congregation saw his approval, and they all nodded, with some "Amens" sprinkled in.

"Well, again I want to reiterate that I don't know very much, but what I *do* know is this: Something's going on in the Vatican that's not quite right. I know many Protestant Christians equate the Catholic Church with the devil. I don't happen to believe that, but that's not what I'm trying to say.

"What I *am* trying to say is this: I think Pope John Paul I was murdered. I think the Roman Catholic Church has been taken over by some very bad people. They've *stolen* the church.

"I can't prove anything. I have nothing but circumstantial evidence, scattered in various print media and history books. But I also have been visited by a Spiritual Being who confirmed to me that John Paul I had been murdered. So therefore, for the sake of argument, let's pretend everything I'm about to tell you is purely, 'Coincidental.' Nonetheless it's all documented, and you can research this on your own, if you have doubts. I think the more you look into this matter, the more convinced you'll be that something doesn't gel.

"Sumpin's not right."

Sumpin's Not Right

José Maria Escriva de Balaguer was a young attorney-at-law in his mid-twenties when political turmoil erupted for the overthrow of King Alfonso XIII, and for an end to the Spanish Monarchy. Never the one to miss an opportunity for personal gain, Escriva took full advantage of the revolutionary atmosphere.

He envisioned himself as replacing the monarchy with his own "perfect society." His Perfect Society would consist of two classes of people: (1) the ruling elite, and; (2) a lesser army of lay people to carry out the elite's desires. A world of "Have's" to govern, and "Have-not's" to labor in servitude. But because opposition to the throne was forbidden as treasonous, Escriva had to repress his aggressions for his own safety. He dared not to publicly declare his aversions.

However, Escriva discovered a loophole that would allow him to legally sew contempt with the Spaniards against their King. He ingeniously abandoned his law career, for the priesthood. As a priest in the Catholic Church, he was legally and morally justified to pursue his ideologies of the "Perfect Society." To carry out his master plan, he established the "Sacerdotal Society of the Holy Cross and Opus Dei," as an exclusive brotherhood within the Catholic Church.

Nevertheless, the Catholic Church refused to recognize Escriva's outlaw organization. The Church claimed that Opus Dei was:

> "(nothing more than) a white masonry, seeking to establish the well-being of it's own members."

Opus Dei was proclaimed a forbidden evil by the Church of Rome. The rejection angered Escriva, who warned the Vatican:

> "Those who will not believe in the ways of Opus Dei, those who will not follow, will be—patiently over the years—convinced through 'Holy Coercion and Holy Forcefulness.'"

The long-term plan for his Perfect Society emphasized:
> "international banking maneuvers (that will) sap economic power from the opposition, and divert

> *their funds (into the holdings of Opus Dei). We will succeed in obtaining our perfect society of the international elite and of the international dollar."*

But he would need cooperation of the upper class who would benefit from his lofty goals, and also of the young intellectuals who would carry on their struggle over time.

Opus Dei recruited important financiers and military help. By the mid-thirties they were powerful enough to back General Francisco Franco, who successfully ousted the King and seized the reigns as Spanish dictator. Franco rewarded Opus Dei with key positions in government. And the General would forever regret that he let Opus Dei in his front door.

Escriva's plans had slowly, but firmly, taken root by 1943. As published by Max Gallo (E.P. Dutton, 1974) in his book, Spain Under Franco: a History, Opus Dei's pattern of growth included heavy enlistments of young intellectuals, recruited by establishing college communities, *"where their lives (were) controlled and supervised by priests and indoctrination."* They would induce student membership with glorious ideals of the Perfect Society, a society in which they would be greatly rewarded for their efforts.

Their undying goal, simply stated in their own words:
> *" ... to gain control over the whole of society, by a judicious placing of men."*

When any of their well-trained members reached a position of power, they were bound by secret oaths to appoint other members, until they had a controlling interest in said establishment, or governmental branch. And to accomplish this magnanimous task of world domination, they'd require *"blind obedience."*

By 1947, Opus Dei spread like a cancerous growth in the Spanish government, controlling nearly every position of power. Other positions, in all walks of life, followed suit. Escriva reiterated that Opus Dei would:
> *"spread throughout all classes of civil society and particularly among intellectuals, in the quest for the (perfect society) within the world."*

War between Opus Dei and the Vatican raged onward. Annually, Opus Dei applied for official admission into the Catholic Church, in order to receive legitimacy. Annually, Rome denied their request.

Rome cited Opus Dei as nothing more than a *"Holy Mafia."* They accused Opus Dei of trying to form a One-World Government, as well as a One-World Religion—which was blasphemous to Christianity and to the Roman Catholic Church.

Opus Dei adhered to their own *"Bible."* Jesus Christ was *not* listed as the way of salvation, as taught by the Catholic Church. Rather, Opus Dei declared their own book, *The Way*, as the true guideline to holiness. Their declared objective on Earth was not to promote salvation into Heaven, but instead, for each initiate to become:

"A Leader of Men, a Leader of Nations, (by adhering to its) 999 Maxims."

The Vatican would repeatedly lambaste Opus Dei for its wretchedness. The Catholic Church consistently accused Opus Dei as being:

"entirely contradictory to the Christian Bible. They are neither Catholic nor Christian of any faith."

By 1952, Opus Dei had grown too mightily to oppress any longer. They had spread their tentacles worldwide. The Vatican dubbed them, *"Octopus Dei."*

They especially targeted the Spanish-speaking Latin American countries. They would find a weak nation to prey upon, win an election or an appointment to power, then bring others onboard. In this manner, they established footholds in international organizations, such as the Vatican's own College of Cardinals.

In 1952, Opus Dei blatantly and defiantly established their own international headquarters in Rome. Using *"Holy Coercion and Holy Forcefulness,"* they applied a ruthless pressure the Church could no longer thwart. Finally, the Vatican granted Opus Dei its official status. *But the Church refused to recognize them as a "Christian religious order."* Rome officially labeled Opus Dei as:

"A humanistic, secular cult of men."

Only about two percent of Opus Dei were priests. The remainder were laymen who carried out the work as instructed by their leaders. The laymen forfeited all their earnings and earthly possessions to Opus Dei, who in return provided all their living necessities. An exception was granted to the wealthy and powerful, who became *"honorary cooperators"* and were not required to make financial sacrifices. In fact, they were often the recipients of financial rewards for having granted generous favors. Such Honorary Cooperators included Nelson Rockefeller, who belonged to the Brazilian Chapter, and several members of the Rothschilds family in the German Chapter.

In 1966, General Juan Ongania was invited to an Opus Dei *"awareness retreat"* in his homeland of Argentina. Afterwards, General Ongania led a revolution to overthrow the government. When he seized power as Dictator of Argentina, General Ongania nationalized all the banks into one central bank, *with the exception of the Banco Ambrossio, owned by Opus Dei.*

A similar pattern preceded the revolution in Chili. General Allende attended *"awareness meetings"* with Opus Dei, after which a revolution ignited, resulting in General Allende's elevation to Dictator. And again, the banks were nationalized, except for Banco Ambrossio.

The method repeated itself, worldwide. Banco Ambrossio, headquartered in Luxembourg, fostered an international group of phony shell banks, most notably in South America and in Panama. And as the norm, in exchange for future political favors, Opus Dei would exalt a cooperator to power. In fact, when a later government of Argentina warred with Great Britain over the Falkland Islands, it was *Opus Dei who purchased the Exocet missiles for their Latin American partners.*

Opus Dei worked diligently with America's CIA. President Nixon sought cooperation for a military coup in Peru, and he needed people with enough savvy to run the operation outside the jurisdiction of the United States. America needed right-wing military support in Latin America, as well as vital military commitments in the strategic Mediterranean gateway controlled by Spain. Those objectives required dealings with Opus Dei.

In 1969, Opus Dei virtually controlled the Spanish Government via their most alluring vehicle of operation—infiltration. They sat on every vital cabinet post. And more importantly, they had persuaded General Franco (with Holy Coercion and Holy Forcefulness) to name Prince Juan Carlos—the most elite member of Opus Dei—as heir to the Spanish Throne upon Franco's death.

> *July 23, 1969: Newsweek*
> "As always, the 76-year old Caudillo ("the Leader," General Franco) remained firmly in control of himself—that is, until he came to the reason for his rare public appearance. Suddenly his voice began to quaver, tears welled up behind his gold-rimmed spectacles and his hands shook violently. 'The relief of the Chief of State is a normal act imposed by man's mortality,' he declared. 'Conscious of my responsibility before God and history, I have decided to recommend Prince Juan Carlos de Borbon y Borbon as my successor.'"

***

While in charge of Spain's national economy, Opus Dei embezzled billions of dollars by granting themselves unsecured loans. Eventually, the national banks declared insolvency and had to be bailed out by the government. The same pattern was carried on throughout the years, even reaching far into the American banking systems where so many banks would be pilfered by Opus Dei that the American government would bail out billions to keep the entire banking system from collapsing.

The Spanish media attacked Opus Dei and sought the arrest of the technocrats in charge of the fraudulent bank loans. But the State's main witness opted to shoot himself in the head with a shotgun. Pursuit of the bank embezzlements ceased.

With their pilfered fortunes, Opus Dei bought a large chunk of the world.

In an October 7, 1968 dispatch by UPI, it was noted:
"*(Opus Dei owns) international newspapers, radio stations, a news magazine, a leading news agency, leading universities, a business school associated with Harvard, an agricultural college and scores of schools and technical education centers, banks, insurance firms, real estate interests and a large industrial empire. The Roman Catholics see them as a threat to the religious tradition ... a Holy Mafia or White Masonry.*"

A 1973 *Los Angeles Times* report on June 24, described:
"*Critics call it 'Octopus Dei,' God's Octopus, or the 'Holy Mafia,' and charge that it exerts immense influence in ... economic, academic and political life*"
"*Further, the critics say, it is an elitist fraternity, the members of which are selected not so much for religious vocation as for their wealth, brains, and even good looks.*"
"*One conservative general described the movement as 'a new white Masonry that is trying to sow discord in the heart of national institutions.'*"

As with the case of the biggest scandal in Spanish history, Opus Dei went about its worldwide mission of embezzling funds to support its Perfect Society. Behind the scenes, they pilfered from banks and savings and loans institutions until the vaults were barren. Often, Opus Dei planted bank officers who would use the guise of unsecured loans, but sometimes they boldly resorted to blatant skimming.

It was Pope John Paul I, himself, who caught them in the act of pilfering the Vatican Bank. The Pope discovered that Paul Marcinkus, head of the Vatican Bank and a member of Opus Dei, was receiving hush money to turn his back on, or perhaps even aid Opus Dei's massive robberies.

Despite denials by Marcinkus, the Pope discovered documentation that Marcinkus had received payments of six million, four hundred thousand dollars from Opus Dei and their outside collaborators, the P-2 Masons. As supporting evidence, the payoffs to Marcinkus were made in fifteen installments to three banks in Switzerland, then transferred to two Opus Dei facades: Riverinvest, and Stanley Brothers & Company. And the Vatican Bank itself, had been depleted.

It was on September 28, 1978, that Pope John Paul I announced his intentions of exposing Opus Dei and the P-2 Masons, at noon the following day.

"POPE DIES IN HIS SLEEP"

Upon the Holy Father's untimely death by *"natural causes,"* the Italian government pursued John Paul's leads. The federal investigators discovered that the international bank frauds ranged all the way to the Franklin Bank in New York, and later to the Continental Bank of Illinois (both owned in large part by Opus Dei).

American banks, and those of other nations, were robbed on a daily basis, depleting the cash and funneling it into Opus Dei and P-2 Mason accounts, while governments borrowed back the stolen funds at high rates to pay their insured depositors. But John Paul I had uncovered key men in the operation, and *the information was confirmed by Italian government investigators!*

An *arrest warrant* was issued for Paul Marcinkus of Opus Dei and for Michele Sindona of the P-2 Masons. Marcinkus took refuge within the Vatican walls and the police could not enter to serve the warrant. However, Michele Sindona was jailed. The headlines read:

"Michele Sindona Dies In Prison"

The coroner's report said that Sindona died of "Natural Causes." Cardiac arrest. He had suffered a heart attack while eating a prison breakfast before his scheduled court-testimony. He simply dropped dead. His last words before his *"heart attack"* were:

"They poisoned me."

In fact, <u>six other witnesses all committed suicide</u> before government investigators could question them. That left only Paul Marcinkus as a link to an international bank embezzlement scheme. And the new Pope refused to cooperate with investigators and offered political asylum to Marcinkus.

Opus Dei and their outside cooperators, the P-2 Masons, had established the nasty habit of granting "bad loans" to themselves, not repaying, and thus putting the banks into insolvency. Thus national governments were forced to cover the losses with taxpayers' money. They didn't stop with individual nations, either, as they also pilfered the World Bank and the International Monetary Fund, chaired by George Rodo Lopez, member and mastermind of Opus Dei.

> According to *CovertAction Information Bulletin #18-W83*:
> *"Opus Dei and the P-2 Masons were robbing dozens of banks daily."*

But because Opus Dei's operations were rooted within the protected confines of the Vatican, the Italian Government could not get at Opus Dei, nor the P-2 Masons, who took refuge in the secrecy of Masonic Lodges. Marcinkus went to the extreme of imprisoning himself within the Church, with the blessing of John Paul II, while authorities waited outside to arrest him should he ever leave the protective confines of the Church.

Nonetheless, Milan magistrate Emilio Alessandrini proceeded to prosecute him, even while Marcinkus hid behind the new Pope. Judge Alessandrini issued an official summons to Pope John Paul II to allow the arrest of Marcinkus, but the Pope refused. When the Italian Government sued for his surrender, the Pope merely extended his protection. The Pope, himself a member of Opus Dei, assured federal authorities that he would never allow the arrest of the Vatican's official banker.

That week's headlines read:

"Communist Red Brigade Assassinates Milan Magistrate"

The case was dismissed.

One member of the secret society decided he'd had enough, and offered testimony to the State. The Italian Government reissued arrest warrants to purge the Vatican of its harbored international crime syndicate. But the day before the court hearing the "Communist Red Brigade" blew up the informant's car. That case, too, was dismissed.

Authorities soon implicated the Chairman of Banco Ambrosiano. An arrest warrant was issued for the syndicate member. But they found him hanging by the neck from a bridge. Quick-thinking police rushed to his office to confiscate damaging papers. Unfortunately, the secretary had destroyed them all, moments before she *"fell out the window"* of the upper floor of the building. Case dismissed.

According to *In God's Name* by author David Yallop, the Italian Government solicited the highly touted services of bank investigator, Giorgio Ambrosoli. An intense, independent review concluded the same as had Pope John Paul I:

> *"Opus Dei and the P-2 Masons have established a direct link to the Vatican Bank and the Church's worldwide holdings."*

Georgio Ambrosoli, himself, issued an arrest order for Marcinkus. But again, Pope John Paul II refused to turn him over to authorities.

But this time, the Vatican was up against a powerful investigator in Ambrosoli. He had discovered John Paul I's secret list of names. At last, the Italian Government had solid proof of an international bank scandal that went right to the Vatican itself. Ambrosoli telephoned the Chief of Police, Boris Giuliano and stated that the list:

> *"Reads like a Who's Who, and it includes top politicians, generals, publishers, industrialists, and financiers."*

Ambrosoli hurriedly went to the home of Chief Biuliano to map a strategy. The next morning:

> *"Communist Red Brigade shoots Giorgio Ambrosoli outside his apartment."*

The case would have been dismissed, but the membership list had been left in protective custody of Police Chief Giuliano. The case was scheduled to go to court.

> *"Communist Red Brigade shoots Chief of Police outside his home.*

The secret list was never found. The case was dismissed for lack of evidence. The Vatican issued a terse, official response toward the accusations:

> *"There was never a list."*

A furious Italian Government hand-carried an arrest warrant straight inside the Vatican, demanding that the Pope extradite Paul Marcinkus. But this time, the rules changed drastically, and mysteriously:

> *"Pope John Paul II promotes Vatican Banker to 'Vice Pope'.*
> *Paul Marcincus ranks second only to the Pope himself."*

> *"John Paul II grants Official Recognition to Opus Dei."*

Furthermore, John Paul II attempted to favor Opus Dei with the highest status in Vatican history. However, Cardinal Giovanni Benelli—the personal advisor to the late Pope Paul IV—protested so vehemently against giving that much power to a secret organization, that Pope John Paul II backed down. Two weeks later, two major news reports came out of the Vatican:

> *(1) "Cardinal Benelli suffers fatal heart attack."*

> (2) *"Pope John Paul II elevates Opus Dei as personal prelature."*

(In 2004, John Paul II elevated Jose Escriva, founder of Opus Dei, to SAINTHOOD!)

Pope John Paul II then rocked the Catholic World when he announced for the first time in history that Masons (of the P-2 variety) could become Catholics and be admitted to the Church.

Soon thereafter, the Italian Government discovered that the multi-lingual Karol Wojtyla (prior to being elected to the papacy by Opus Dei as John Paul II) had traveled around Europe on a speaking tour paid for by Opus Dei, in order to preach their philosophy of a Perfect Society to members and prospective recruits. In exchange for Wojtyla's help, they funneled forty million American dollars to Poland's Solidarity movement.

Now, because John Paul II had elevated Paul Marcinkus to the second highest rank in the Vatican, he could not be touched. He was free to leave the Vatican as he pleased, under complete international diplomatic immunity.

Pope John Paul II then appointed fellow Opus Dei member, Cardinal Franz Koenig to head The Synod of Bishops, in charge of appointing new bishops around the world (of which 68 Opus Dei bishops were immediately appointed; and later, Alvarro del Portillo, the head of Opus Dei, himself). Opus Dei became a majority in the Cardinal of Bishops, and voting rules changed from needing a two-thirds majority, to a simple majority vote. (In February, 2001, John Paul II made the largest appointment in history to the College of Cardinals, nearly all of them members of Opus Dei.)

Pope John Paul II left the confines of the Vatican and became the most traveled Pontiff in history, resounding that all nations should:

> *"... unite not only spiritually, but both politically and economically as well, in a global quest for the Perfect Society."*

Opus Dei had "judiciously placed" their own man into the papacy, and by preaching love and applying a firm fist, had "holy coerced and holy forced" their quest for a One-World Government, and a One-World Religion as the foundation of their Perfect Society.

But dissension arose from within the Vatican. The Catholic hierarchy refused to accept the Pope's guarantees that all was well. Numerous Cardinals *demanded* an outside panel to reinvestigate wrongdoings. And the Italian Government, as persistent as ever, equally insisted that Pope John Paul II reopen the case. The government strongly argued that organized crime ran the church banking system and global economy.

Bowing to pressure from within the College of Cardinals, John Paul II agreed to an inquiry. He personally appointed an outside investigative panel. Further, he commissioned the outside council to *forever remain in charge of the Vatican's vast economic empire.*

> Chairing the *impartial* committee was German banker, Hermann J. Abs, *a Nazi war criminal and high-ranking member of the P-2 Masons. Hermann Abs concluded that nothing was amiss with the Vatican's economic empire and he dismissed the case.*

The Italian government went ballistic and called the findings a hoax. The Vatican replied with an official statement concerning the government's wild accusations:

> *Opus Dei's mission was, "strictly spiritual and has never engaged in business or finance of any nature." Governments should leave the Church alone.*

Finishing my church testimony for the evening, I read an excerpt from the best-selling book about John Paul II's election, *The Making of a Pope*, by Catholic Priest and Author Andrew Greeley. Greeley writes:

> "I've had personal dealings with Opus Dei. They are entirely untrustworthy and totally dishonest."

Greeley also expounded how opponents of Opus Dei were treated to brutal character assassinations and ridicule. And often, if the critics persisted, it was not uncommon for a fatal car bombing from the "Communist Red Brigade" to quiet them.

I wondered aloud to the congregation: "Is this a *holy* organization? Sumpin's not right."

CHAPTER 8
The Burial Shroud Man

The week after my church testimony, I drove to the south side of Indianapolis to visit my parents. I had not seen them or spoken to them in several days. As I leisurely cruised down Madison Avenue, I heard a bleating horn behind me. My eyes shot to the rearview mirror. It was Mom.

She flashed her lights, and overtly pointed for me to pull over. She raced her van to the fast lane beside me and swerved, forcing me into a nearby parking lot. She unrolled her window and I saw that she was crying. She screamed, "Michael, the Devil is after us!"

From inside her van, Mom babbled incohesively about "ghosts" trying to kill the whole family. She cried while she talked, and I sat in stunned silence. Last night she was driving home by herself from a lakeside retreat the family owned in Southern Indiana, when something tried to run her off the road. "It was like a black ghost," she said. She saw it plainly. It was floating right in front of the van as she drove. She swerved left, then swerved right, trying to rid herself of the Dark Thing. She sped faster and faster, daring not to slow down for fear it would get her. It would not go away so Mom tried outdriving it. She was afraid she would crash and die, but she was more afraid of the thing hovering above the hood ornament. She knew it wasn't human. She could see through its transparent shape, her eyes never left it. It was charcoal gray in color. It had two protrusions on the top of its head, sort of like undeveloped horns. It had a full body with no arms or legs, and it tapered down to a funnel shape, looking something like a dark tornado at the bottom. Then it vanished.

Mom pulled off the road and cried. She was so scared that she would block it out of her mind for years, same as Hafford Sharp had done while hiding from the sharks in the Pacific Ocean in the 1945 sinking of *U.S.S. Indianapolis*. It was the human soul's formula for coping with terror—Mom would bury her fear on uncharted isles of memory. She would later say, "Something scared me so badly, I screamed and screamed. But I can't remember what it was."

Now, listening to Mom cry about this and about that, I sat in my car, stunned. Suddenly I recognized a familiar sign on the red brick building in the parking lot. "A&P." I was in the same parking lot where the Alien Being had taken me last week. Mom was describing the shadowy being of Death that I had earlier seen hovering above my family.

While I sat in a spiritual stupor I heard Mom explain more about every member in my family. "And a car swerved off the road Monday and broke Steve's leg while he was sitting at a bus stop. Then Cheri went into a coma Monday and she's still unconscious and nobody knows why, and Grandma went to visit her in the hospital Monday and the escalator broke and Grandma tumbled all the way down, and she's still in the hospital with Cheri, and Jason was attacked by a swarm of bumblebees on Monday and they stung him all over his body and he had to go to the hospital, and so did Dad when he tried to rescue Jason, and I crashed our car Monday when I went to see all of them, cause a bumblebee was in the car with me and it kept stinging me too."

All this had happened the very day after I had spoken in Charlie Scalf's church. I had stood in the pulpit and testified that the Beast had threatened to harm my family. I had told them that Monday, July 23, was the rising of the Dog Star, a holy day for Satan. Then I had forgotten all about it, until now, as I watched Mom cry and shake in fear of things that were suddenly happening to them all. "Why didn't you stop in at the lake Saturday?" she then asked me. I explained that I had been busy in Indianapolis and was not able to drive down. "But we all saw you there, driving around our trailer. We kept waving for you to stop, but you just kept going around the road in circles and then drove away."

"You win," I said aloud to the Beast. "I won't talk in church anymore." And I did not. The attacks against my family stopped, as if their *safety* was my *hush* money.

In August of 1979, I moved into Charlie Scalf's isolated farm house. There, I seldom spoke to *anyone*, about *anything*. Simply stated, there were no human ears within miles. There was only George the Kat and my farm animals, with whom I conversed on a regular basis. But solitude is why I rented Charlie's place. I was schooling myself, to settle a score. And I had never been more studious.

I must acknowledge that I did not live every moment in fear. The peacefulness of the countryside had something to do with that, I believe, as did the companionship of the animals. But another factor, I also believe, was that I kept my part of the bargain, and the Beast kept its. So with all in order, I assumed the Beast went elsewhere. It went about its business; I went about mine.

On the morning of October 20, 1979, I awoke with the first rays of dawn while I lay shivering on the floor beneath a pile of blankets. I had been struggling with sleep all evening, waiting for the weak morning sunshine to come rescue me from the cold night. I was glad when it came at last.

The frost deposit on the window warned that winter was on its way, and reminded me to purchase some heat for the house. I had worked only two days, since having moved into Charlie Scalf's home, and I had no money to fill the propane gas tank. Considering the deteriorating weather conditions, I figured I would need to make a sale or two, in a few days.

For now, long underwear, sweat pants, blue jeans, two pairs of sweat socks, a T-shirt, shirt, sweater, and jacket would make do for sleeping attire, covered by two blankets and a quilt. The only part of me exposed to the cold air was my face, and George the Kat slept on that. The added weight of a giant feline on my head was sometimes uncomfortable, but the extra warmth of fur made up for any inconvenience. Besides, George slept pretty much where he wanted.

Last week, Patrick and David visited from Indianapolis, and while the two of them huddled on the floor in sleeping bags, George bedded down on David's face. David objected,

The Burial Shroud Man

but every time he tried nudging George off him, George growled a fearsome warning. Unbeknownst to me until the next morning, David had spent the night in fear, immobilized like an accident victim in traction, with George threatening to eat his face if he budged in complaint.

Patrick and David never returned.

But George loved *me*. Though he demanded to sleep on my head, not once did he ever threaten me. He simply would not accept "NO!" as an answer to anything.

I would throw him off me at night, but he would simply jump back up before I could roll over. I would throw him down again, and yell, "NO!" He would jump back up. Down. Up.

George knew my limitations on patience. All he needed to do for a comfortable sleeping spot was to jump back up only one more time than he was thrown down. He would manipulate me into believing there existed an endless assembly line of cats, until I was too groggy to argue the case. Some people counted sheep in order to fall asleep—I counted big cats.

one cat ("Get Down!" Jump back up)

two cats ("Down!" Up.)

three cats ("please ga-down-'m-tired." bk-up.)

five hundred eighty-seven cats ("gdn." up.)

two thousand six hundred twenty-three cats, and so forth, until I mumbled, "snfgmblfmmumm," and rolled over with a cat on my head.

When the sun defrosted my room, I eased George off my face, and edged closer to the electric space heater. The tiny heater wasn't much good in a three bedroom house, but now that I had sealed off every room but my office, where I slept on the floor, it helped some. But it was good for only one room at a time, and my bladder and bowels screamed for relief, regardless of the igloo-like temperatures in the bare-tiled bathroom.

The cold air slapped me awake when I opened my office door and slipped into the john, where I relocated the space heater. Having plugged it in and spun its dial to *maximum*, I returned to my office. I pulled the covers back over my head and waited on this feeble effort at warming the toilet seat. I otherwise dared not to venture in and sit down as cold as it was, or else I would have been constipated from shock until spring thaw. And further, I had no hot water to cleanse with in the morning. My whiskers grew. My body stank.

Charlie Scalf came by last week to repair the water heater, but I had gone into town for groceries and was not there to let him in. Since I lived so far out in the country Charlie let himself in to fix the hot water. He was only half-done installing the heating element when, as he explained to me, "I was attacked by a lion!" Charlie ran all the way up the basement stairs and out of the house. The new heating element blew out because he refused to go back in to save it.

Hot water would have been nice, but for now I skipped cleaning. I lived in solitude, except for animals, and neither they nor I objected to offensive odors. I made a note to call Charlie in a day or two to reschedule fixing the water heater.

When out of the bathroom and dressed, I put on my boots and went to the kitchen to prepare breakfast. My refrigerator contained only German potato salad and some baked beans. I could barely afford that. I had a cold bite of each, and washed it down with cheap orange-aide (*"contains no juice, artificial color, artificial flavor, sugar, water"*).

When finished with *my* breakfast, I prepared some *Gravy Train* for George (he preferred dog food to the wimpy feline varieties), and stuffed my pockets with apples for the horses. I grabbed my hiking stick and wandered out to the *back thirty* for my morning jaunt.

As I hiked through the shoulder-high weeds on a narrow trail, a black snake writhed across and gave me the jitters. I gripped my walking stick, which doubled as a weapon: sometimes against snakes; sometimes against giant spiders. I never knew what I would come up against, in the wilds out back.

The Outback split in two: (1) on the left was a wide-open pasture where the horses grazed; (2) to the right was the seldom explored *Badlands*, a heavily wooded area with steep hills and rugged gullies, waterfalls, and a winding creek at the bottom. It was postcard beautiful and an exhilarating walk.

On this particular morning the horses were not in the pasture, which meant they were watering at the creek in the Badlands. I liked when they were far away, because I enjoyed whistling for them to come.

The brown filly, whom I had named "Apples" because she craved them so badly, whinnied in response. She was deep inside the Badlands when she heard my call that an apple awaited her. Her driving hooves beat the hills like drums, vibrating the virgin air and echoing each quarter-note of, *"AP-ple-AP-ple, AP-ple-AP-ple"* She approached me and pushed her nose into my coat pocket, where she always found her treat.

The pinto named "Patches," did not trust me, since she had seldom seen a *Two-Legged Creature* in the uninhabited Badlands. I tossed an apple her way, but she fled, convinced the Creature was trying to pelt her. She lunged to the bottom of the hill and peeked from behind a tree, where like an ostrich with its head in the sand, she thought she was hidden. I gently rolled an apple down her way. She ate it, and I rolled her another.

I turned my back to Apples, pretending to leave. Apples pushed me, as if saying, *"Hey! What's that in your pocket!"* She frisked me with her snout and turned up one more. Finally, I emptied my pockets before Apples believed I was finished.

I sauntered down to the brook, where the pure, spring water swirled its fastest at the bend. I swung across on the vines, back and forth a couple of times over the shallow, rushing water. On the far side, I sat on a tree stump.

On this morning, I talked to God. I spoke to Him like God was a Person, capable of listening. I had not done that before. It was Hafford Sharp's doing. I listened to his taped interviews often. He captivated me when he spoke of other worlds and beings. He made me wonder if God existed as something more than electrical energy, which had always been my guess before ... well, before Stuff happened. So on the morning of October 20, 1979—all by my lonesome in the Badlands, where no one could eavesdrop and think I was crazy—I called God's bluff. *Come out, come out, wherever you are!*

It did not work, but the therapy of self-confession satisfied me to a degree.

An ugly thought entered my mind: I would have to return to the house and schedule some sales appointments over the phone. *What a bummer.* But hunger pangs reminded me how badly I needed a sale. And the morning recollections of the merciless cold motivated me back up the steep, steep hill.

When I reached the carport I knocked the mud and wet leaves off my walking stick. I valued the eight-foot-long branch I had picked up in the Badlands; it was straight, with a sudden crook at the top for a handle, like a cane. Without it, I would have never made it up the incline from the creek, and would have been trapped in the Badlands forever, or so I pretended.

Back to the house, I pounded my stick on the concrete drive under the carport. That is when the Big Hill across the street beckoned me. I had never been there. So like Moses heeding the call of the mountains, I packed my shepherd's staff in hand, and set off to explore lands unknown. To find the edge of the world; to discover America; and to search for God, all on the other side of the street. I leaped my only neighbor's wire fence, half expecting to return with a couple of stone tablets, after first talking to a burning bush.

At the top of the hill, I dropped to my knees and cried. The images of the Beast trying to kill me were vivid. How could I fight it? I begged God to advise me. To say something. Say anything.

Nothing. God was shy.

I did not understand. If God existed, why did He let me fend for myself in the Dark World? Who were those guys I had met there? Did God already know about it? Did He even care? *Hello, anybody home up there? Where are you? Why won't you reveal yourself?*

I stood and dried my eyes. I was astonished I had done such a thing. Fear of the Beast had weakened me. I would not allow it to happen again.

I scouted the terrain. The hillside provided a good vantage point. The heavily wooded areas to the north were not plausible for hiking, but the open pasture at the bottom of the hill looked ideal and picturesque. I did not know

The Burial Shroud Man

where I would end up, but I descended the hill and jumped the pasture fence.

I paused to watch a herd of cows a hundred yards away. I had seldom seen cows, until my move to the country, and I watched them studiously. Cows amused me. They huddled in a circle beneath a shade tree, conducting an oval office meeting. Cows did a lot of that; they were business-oriented and orderly.

I enjoyed watching their meetings come to a close, with all the cows lining up single-file to leave. Each would glance up to see her neighbor going off to God-knows-where, and she would follow. Similar to the way Little Mikey's first-grade class had always marched to the restrooms and to lunch—in orderly fashion, one-by-one, sticking close, not wanting to get lost or to be left behind.

But what entertained me the most about cows, by far, was watching them graze. In order to eat, cows needed a *fence* like people needed a plate and utensils, without which there would be no meal.

They would stretch their necks far through the fence to get a bite of foreign grass. Grass imported from *The Other Side of the Fence* was much tastier. They would take a bite, straighten up, and get lost deeply in thought while eating, like brokers evaluating the stock market in the morning paper at breakfast. Cows focused every thought on how to get a bigger and better bite of foreign grass. How to corner the market.

One morning, I watched them knock down a weak section of fence—their big chance for a hostile takeover. I observed them filing through (*okay, class, one-by-one*), until they were all vacationing on *The Other Side of the Fence*.

And in an orderly manner (*okay, class, one-by-one*), they lined up against the other side of the fence, sticking their heads back across to get a bite of their own grass, which was now on *The OTHER Other Side of the Fence*.

By Fate, one of them *rediscovered* the open section of the fence (their memories being from bite-to-bite), and they all *re-escaped* (*okay, class, one-by-one*), to the land of milk and honey where God had surely led them to *ANOTHER Other Side of the Fence*. A land where Each and Every time

War of the Angels

they crossed there were MORE *Other Other Sides of the Fence*. They had found Cow Heaven!

Now this particular group across the field paid no attention to me, as they busily discussed world events, such as import-export trade balances of grass from *The Other Side of the Fence*, and how to get those darned Japanese cows to stay on their own side. All of them were engaged in heavy discussion. Except for one. A black one.

The black one, I thought, would soon be in big trouble with its peers because it was not attending their cow meeting. In fact, it had completely ignored the other cows and had done nothing but stare at me ever since I jumped the fence.

From a distance, I kept still, watching the cow.

From a distance, the cow kept still, watching me.

I started through the field, on my journey to find God.

Blackie started through the field, on his journey to find hells bells.

I stopped.

Blackie stopped.

Halfway across the pasture, I noticed something odd about Blackie; something different from the other cows. Blackie did not have a briefcase—one of those baggy things underneath. And he had horns, which the other cows did not. I could tell because he lowered his head and pointed them at me.

When Blackie kicked up turfs of grass and came huffing at me, I made sudden reference to a regular body function and hauled butt. Staff in hand, I ran looking for a Red Sea somewhere to part, as the Egyptian Chariots gave chase.

Fifty yards to my right stood an old, vacant house. If I reached that, it was home base. I breathed easier, once I reached the house and dodged inside. Cows did not have sense enough to find a door. Blackie was only thirty yards away, but I no longer worried, as I explored my new surroundings.

The house was in shambles, as if it had not been lived in for quite some time. But at the moment, I did not care. This was my impenetrable fortress. My castle under siege. I would simply wait until Blackie forgot about me. At about the time I was wondering why the house smelled like crap, I saw the pile of manure right in the middle of the living room.

Then I saw another pile in the kitchen. It suddenly dawned on me that the cows *lived* in the old house.

Blackie rooted through the front door like a muscular husband who had come home from work early, only to find the milk man in bed with his bride. The ground quaked in close-quarter combat. I could feel its horrid breath whirling at my feet, in a snorting frenzy. I split out the back, just as Blackie lunged his horns upward at my fleeing butt.

I sprinted for the back fence, now only twenty yards away. Of all the courageous ways possible for a brave man to die, I never dreamed I would be done in by *Elsie Borden's* boyfriend. And way out in the middle of nowhere, my bones would most likely rot before anyone found my remains. I would hate for some archaeologist in a hundred years to excavate my fossilized tailbone, and wonder what tribal custom enticed me to ram that horn up there.

I made it! I scrambled over the fence with the aid of my staff. The barrier was only two strands of rickety wire, and would not have stopped any creature other than a cow. But *all* cows—even Ole Blackie—were instilled at birth with the deepest respect for fences. It was said by those who knew, that cows in India *worshipped* fences, with the hopes of reaching cow-nirvana: to be one with the wire, and to be reincarnated as a mighty chain-link.

Blackie skidded to a halt and bowed his horns in prayer to the holy fence. It eyed me only a few short steps away, but it was not about to violate the sacred shrine of sagging strands.

For the first time, I experienced *The Joys of The Other Side of the Fence.* Yes siree. I would have to detour my mystical journey, of course. And unfortunately, the side of the fence now confronting me led down a steep hill, through thick woods, and no doubt toward the *Castle of the Wicked Witch.* But the alternative was to cross back through the field, where the defiant Ole Blackie reigned supreme.

So with staff in hand, I descended the enchanted side of the hill, half-expecting to run across a tin man, a scarecrow, and a cowardly lion as I searched for God.

Eventually, I found train tracks. The tracks seemed endless, but I knew if I followed them, I would sooner or later locate a recognizable landmark. Being dreadfully lost,

I stepped to the next wooden beam and the next. I never found God, but thousands of wooden train ties later, I found the road home. And that was equally nice.

I slept well that night of October 20, cold or not. Until once again, the Friendly Alien came for me. Before the sun rose on the twenty-first of October in 1979, the Friendly Alien pulled me from my body and led me on another journey.

***

I strolled along the sidewalk of a busy metropolitan area. I was in a hurry to get somewhere, but the old, white-haired lady in front of me was in my way and slowing me down. I decided to pass her. Pedestrian traffic poured by heavily from the opposite way, so I slid around to the right. But she side-stepped and cut me off. I did not particularly get angry with her, because old folks were sometimes confused about where they were going. I reversed to the other side, like a football player cutting back against the grain when the designed hole suddenly closed with a wall of linebackers.

Hey, Lady! She did it again. She deliberately cut me off and blocked my path. Old or not, I was about to angrily confront her, when I heard the elderly person say, "Be patient."

I stopped in my tracks, not because of what was said, but because of how it was said. The elderly person in front was not a woman at all. She was a man, or rather, he was a man. His voice was ...

Hey, you're the Friendly Alien.

I recognized his voice, but had never before seen him. Nonetheless, there he was in front of me. Pedestrians continued to pass by swiftly, unaware the Friendly Alien was amidst them. I was the only one who saw him. But standing behind him, I did not have a good look. I saw only the back of his long, white hair, which I had earlier assumed crowned the head of an elderly woman.

The Friendly Alien turned. I glimpsed his profile in great awe. He was a regular human male, albeit old. His aged skin had weathered to a leathery texture, like that of a salty, timeworn sailor. But his wardrobe simply did not fit the character. The Man draped an elegant, deep-purple cloak

The Burial Shroud Man

around him that was designed for Royalty. Tailored for a King.

I strained for a better look at the Man, who had his majestic collar pulled high to conceal all but a small portion of his face. The Man turned slightly more, offering me a better view. I noticed his hair was not as long as I originally assumed. Earlier I had thought it flowed well beneath his collar, but it was actually about collar length. Then the strangest thing happened, causing me to miss what the old Man said to me. As the old Man spoke, he became YOUNGER; and by the time he finished his sentence he was no older than in his early thirties. AGE meant nothing. AGE had no relative meaning in whatever world I was visiting.

The Man spoke again, and the city—the entire city—changed, or rather disappeared. The Man and I had suddenly traveled to a new place so quickly that I had no time to say goodbye to the city. We were now standing at the intersection of an isolated dirt road in the middle of nowhere.

Suddenly I understood what he was trying to teach me. The big city was still around us, only now it was invisible as if we had simply moved behind a different curtain of air. Furthermore, ALL the cities from Everywhere were around us. In this world, WE WERE EVERYWHERE, ALL AT ONCE. The Friendly Alien was showing me a world that did not recognize TIME or DISTANCE.

The Man briefly raised the cape from his feet, allowing me the quickest of peeks at the flowing, white robe beneath. And I saw that his feet glowed a bright light of some kind. Then he quickly lowered the white garment that covered his feet, and draped the outer cloak back over the white garment. Then he grasped his outer cloak by both corners of its neck collar, and pulled the material high up over the back of his head, as if framing his face like a fine work of art. He turned to face me squarely.

Looking at his face was like he had lassoed the very air at the bottom of my lungs and yanked it out. The Man was not really a Man, although he had the shape of a Man. His dark complexion was uniquely Middle-Eastern. So were his high, solid cheekbones, as was his large aquiline nose. His thick, heavy eyebrows matched his snow white mustache.

A thought suddenly raced through my mind for no apparent reason: "He doesn't have a beard."

Then his eyes disappeared, leaving me to stare deeply into his empty eye sockets. It was as if a switch had been turned on, and an enormous flow of energy emitted from the bottomless wells of his eyes. Looking into them was like seeing everything that ever happened, in every place, to every person, ever born or who would ever be born—all at the same time.

As a simple human being, I could not take such a sight nor could I withstand so much energy. The split-second I saw such a thing I was knocked off my feet and onto my knees on the ground. His vacuous eyes housed the answers to every question ever asked. Every solution to every problem. I'd seen them for only as long as the blink of an eye, yet it was too great an experience for me. My tear ducts ruptured as a broken dam, my lungs quaked in crying heaves, and any sense of self-worth I had ever harbored had abandoned me. I had been reduced to absolute zero. I fell flat at his feet and hoped he would have mercy on me for whatever tortures he had in store for me.

The Kingly Man reached down and picked me up. He hugged me tightly like Daddy used to lovingly squeeze Little Mikey, only I was too weak to hug him in return. He placed his soft hands directly on either side of my face, looked right at me—this time without the tremendous weaponry of energy flowing from his eyes—and gently said, "Well done." His lips never moved when he spoke, but the words came out just the same.

> (And I turned to see the voice that spake with me ... like the Son of Man, clothed with a garment down to the foot ... His head and his hairs were white like wool, as white as snow; and his eyes were as a flame of fire; And his feet like unto fine brass, as if they burned in a furnace; and his voice as the sound of many waters ...
> And when I saw him, I fell at his feet as dead. And he laid his right hand upon me, saying unto me, "Fear not ... Write the things which thou hast seen.") Revelations 1: 12-15

The Burial Shroud Man

The Man backed away—drifted away, rather; his feet never touched the ground. He said, "I will be back shortly. Occupy yourself." He smiled, then vanished.

I was alone in the dirt road, until the scenery changed again. I was trapped inside a walled city; a large one, completely enclosed. I searched in vain for the Friendly Alien to come take me away. Something awful was about to happen. Something terribly bad, and I knew it.

The city was on the verge of destruction. An unparalleled disaster approached. Fear spread rampant. People tried scaling the walls to flee, but their attempts over the towering barricades were futile. There was no escape as they begged to get out of harm's way.

Death sped toward them. Like swimmers drowning in panic, people lashed out at one another, trying to gain a foothold: men; women; children. All hysterical. Everyone for himself.

I looked beyond the walled city at the source of the terror. A deadly tidal wave rolled toward us. It smashed every building, every tree, every person in its path. It consumed all. Nothing escaped its wrath. It was the end. The ultimate end.

When the tidal wave came closer I saw that the source of destruction was NOT water at all—it was OIL. It was a tidal wave of fiendish petroleum sweeping over everyone in its path. Debris and bodies swirled and tumbled within the churning black surf. Oil was the enemy. Oil was Death. Oil was Evil. Oil was the ultimate end of everything. Bad Thing, that Oil.

The Black Wave burst through the walls and smothered the city, gobbling it up, people and all. It hovered above, about to crash down on me as it crested. But before it tumbled down to kill me, I suddenly vanished.

My entire body changed into a transparent substance. Nothing else was changed about me, other than how my spirit was packaged. The part of my soul that was a living creature was no longer housed inside a vehicle of flesh and bone. I still had a body, but it was not made of earthly material.

I was not the only thing that changed, either. The whole earth seemed to have vanished, as well. The oil was gone. Trouble was gone. Fear was gone. Happiness came to stay. I held my breath in awe of my new surroundings. It was so very peaceful, so very opposite of the chaotic destruction going on in the world down below.

It wasn't really a permanent world. I knew, somehow, that it was a temporary shelter to protect me from the Bad Things happening on Earth. It was an in-between world, a barrier separating me from the Dark World above, and the Earth below. The scenery above me was all lined in black, with zero visibility because there was simply nothing to see. It was a solid black curtain. Below me it was a soft, solid white. I was hovering above a Cloud World. These were not ordinary clouds, for they were much too thick for earthly clouds. Their only purpose was to shelter me from the Bad Things that went on down below because of the Oil. I was so thankful to have been yanked from the worldly destruction and chaos of the Bad Oil, and into the friendly confines of the Cloud World. It had happened so fast it had taken me completely by surprise. The only thing I said when I saw the beautiful clouds was, "Wow." And I was not alone. Although I did not see anyone else due to the thickness of the clouds and their resulting low visibility, a new sense of knowledge told me that the Cloud World had a large transient population.

The Friendly Alien, hiding within the cloud puffs, spoke three words: "Do not worry."

***

I returned to my body crying. Sometimes I cried happily. Sometimes fearfully. Good tears and bad tears. Good Things. Bad Things. But I did not understand. The Friendly Alien had established a pattern of speaking to me in riddles and mysteries, never offering reasons or logical answers to my many questions. But when I came home to my own world, I did know that somewhere, somehow, Bad People were doing Bad Things with Bad Oil. And the powerful rulers of nations wanting the oil did not care what happened to the screaming people. Whatever Oil wanted, Oil was going to get at any cost, even to the ultimate end. Wars were going to be fought over oil. The final destruction would be caused by oil. We would all be dead over oil, except for those who would be yanked to safety into an extraordinary Cloud World.

The End.

Although I did not attend church often, I waited until service was over the next day, then drove into town to see Charlie Scalf. I told him about my experience and he handed me a Bible and showed me some related verses that astounded me:

> "All flesh is not the same flesh: but there is one kind of flesh for men ... There are also celestial bodies, and bodies terrestrial ... There is a natural body, and there is a spiritual body. Flesh and blood cannot inherit the Kingdom of God.
> "Behold, I show you a mystery; We shall not all (die), but we shall all be changed (into a new type of body). In a moment, in the twinkling of an eye." (I COR 15: 39-52)
>
> " ... with the voice of the archangel (Michael) ... the dead in Christ shall rise first. Then we which are alive and remain (at the time of the end) shall be caught up together with them in the clouds, to meet the Lord in the air ... (to escape the wrath of the Beast, who's been cast down to earth.)" (I Thess 17)

On Charlie's dining room table, a newspaper lay opened to the *Weekend Entertainment* section. I nonchalantly glanced at the movie listings and saw a display advertisement for a movie: *In Search of Historic Jesus.* "Oh, my God! Charlie, it's him! It's him! It's his photograph! It's the Man I saw! What is this? What is this picture?"

The Shroud of Turin

In the year 1350 A.D. a Knight in Armor rode into the local Church of Lirey, France, and presented to the priest a mysterious object that he had uncovered on a recent quest. He claimed it to be the burial shroud that had been wrapped around Jesus Christ, after he was taken from the cross and entombed. The sheet—14 feet, 3 inches long and 3 feet, 7 inches wide—could not be authenticated by the church to be the actual burial cloth of Jesus, but nonetheless it quickly became one of the most worshipped Christian icons in history. In 1578 the mysterious shroud was brought to a new home in Turin, Italy, where it has remained under rigid security measures ever since.

In fact, security was so tight that seldom was the general public allowed to even see it. Then at the turn of the twentieth century, the Church of Turin put the shroud on exhibit to the public. It had been a long, long time since the mysterious cloth had been opened to the public, and since the last time, an intriguing invention known as a "camera" had made its way into the mainstream of humanity.

In 1898 Secundo Pia snapped a photograph of the Shroud for the first time. When the pictures were developed, an uncanny negative image appeared on the film, invisible to the naked eye but plainly visible to the photographic lens. The negative image displayed a crucified man, in perfect reproduction from head to toe, including thorn markings on his head and an apparent tear in his side from a sharp object, possibly a spear. Christians claimed the photographic image as proof that the cloth was the burial shroud of Jesus. Scientists quickly and emphatically scoffed that the film negative was a clever hoax. The Church of Turin safely stored the shroud back into seclusion and the debate raged for decades.

In 1978, the Catholic Church permitted another photograph to be taken, and allowed a small piece of the garment to be researched. In 1981, the research team from the United States completed its study, after three years of rigorous chemical, computer, and photographic analysis. The 1981 conclusions said:

> "(The sheet) bears a faint, yellowish negative image of the front and back of a man with a thorn mark on the head, lacerations from a flogging on the back, and bruises on the shoulders. (The image is) a real human form of a whipped and crucified man, and not the product of an artist."

The findings not only failed to end the disputes, but caused debates to grow even more heated. Atheistic Scientists were as determined to portray the shroud as a fake, and Christians were equally set on giving due diligence to their Lord.

Christians said radiation from Christ's resurrection created the photograph. Scientists declared the picture to be a clever forgery by an artist. Christians said they could determine that a coin was placed on the crucified image's right eye, which was the Jewish custom during the time of Christ. Scientists said they did not see any such coin. The Shroud was put back into seclusion by the Church of Turin and no further tests were allowed.

However, in 1983, a group of computer analysts at Virginia Polytechnic Institute and State University conducted a series of tests on the remaining piece of the shroud and the previously taken photograph. The research was led by Robert M. Haralick.

Scoffing at the tests was Dr. Walter C. McCrone, a respected microscopist who said that the resolution of the cloth was not sharp enough to determine if a coin was there or not. "I don't care what kind of computer they use," he said.

Professor Haralick and his team of computer wizards were able to break up the film negative into more than 250 various shades of lightness and darkness. They concluded:

> "Shroud imprints fit six Greek letters of a Pontius Pilate coin from 29 A.D., shortly before Jesus Christ was crucified. In addition, the analysis found the face of the shroud image to be similar to the face of an icon of Jesus dating from the sixth century."

Furthermore, the cloth was found to contain fibers that were indigenous to the Middle East.

Dr. McCrone was not impressed. He said he found traces of iron-ore pigment of the type used by artists to make a paint called red ochre. He was more convinced than ever that an artist drew the image hundreds of years ago. He was asked by Christian skeptics:

How could an ancient artist paint a three-dimensional image in a negative form that was completely invisible to the naked eye?

The scoffing scientists went silent. There was no answer. And to this day, no scientist has an answer. No such technology existed centuries ago, and artists were simply incapable of drawing an "invisible" painting that was an exact negative of a modern-day photograph. The artist would not even have known what a "negative" was. Or a camera. So tell us, Mr. Atheist Scientist, how was the hoax created? There was no answer then, and there is no answer now.

***

In 1987, church officials hesitantly permitted scientists to conduct tests on one more small piece of the Shroud. Three separate laboratories, one each from the United States, Great Britain and Switzerland conducted sophisticated carbon-14 dating tests. After a year of testing and re-testing, all three labs concluded with ninety-five percent accuracy that the cloth dated back to the years 1260 A.D. to 1390 A.D., and therefore could *not* be the burial shroud of Jesus Christ.

Cardinal Anastasio Ballestrero, the archbishop of Turin, still claimed that the image on the cloth was not a forgery, and that it was miraculously created, regardless of its age. But he did acknowledge that science could not be argued with about the authenticity of the shroud. "I see no reason for the church to put these (test) results in doubt." The Church of Turin accepted the results from all three labs that the cloth could be no older than about 750 years and was not the celebrated shroud of Jesus.

The Carbon-14 tests used a time calendar known as the Radiocarbon Method to determine the age of organic fibers used in weaving the mysterious Shroud of Turin.

Scientists based their findings on a theory that cosmic radiation from the atmosphere united with oxygen as it approached Earth, and formed carbon dioxide that was absorbed by the living plants from which the Shroud was woven. When the plants were picked, they died and ceased to absorb Carbon-14; they began a decay back into nitrogen at a steady rate. Based on the amount of Carbon-14 scientists found in the Shroud, all three universities agreed that the Shroud was created more than a thousand years after the death of Christ, and therefore, was a clever forgery.

Christians disagreed.

The fallacy, they argued, is that Carbon-14 testing is unreliable. Testing the amount of vegetation and the amount of natural carbon present on Earth at any given moment, would depend upon environmental factors being constant, with little fluctuation throughout history, in order for the steady decline of Carbon-14 to be used as a valid dating method for *anything*. Therefore, whenever science claims Earth to be in the millions of years old, or that the Shroud is seven hundred years old, they are ignoring such events as the ice age and numerous other catastrophic episodes that would throw their relatively crude dating procedures out of whack.

Nonetheless, scientists celebrated their absolute proof that the Shroud of Turin was a forgery. That is, until February of 1989, when one of their own scientists stepped forward and denounced the validity of the Carbon-14 testing on the Shroud, thereby angering his cohorts.

Thomas Phillips, a researcher from Harvard University's High Energy Physics Laboratory, defiantly asked of his peers:

If the Shroud was an artist's forgery, then how was it created?

They, themselves, with all their modern technology, were still incapable of creating a similar forgery. How, then, could a crude artist have done such a thing during the Middle Ages? Furthermore, scientists admitted that the pollen found on the cloth came from *"around Jerusalem."*

Then Phillips offered an astounding theory about the Shroud of Turin that made headlines throughout the world. He believed the image could have been formed by A RESURRECTED BODY.

If the Shroud was the actual burial cloth of Jesus Christ, *"it would have been present at a very unique physical event: the resurrection of a dead body."* Such a resurrection would have radiated light, heat, neutrons or atomic particles. He said in that scenario, the chemistry would have been altered so dramatically that:

"No test would ever be scientifically valid."

IF YOU BELIEVED IN GOD, and in the resurrection of his Son, then you simply could NOT believe in the Carbon-14 testing because it would have been rendered invalid due to "supernatural interference."

Robert Hedges from Oxford University argued in a written response on February 16, 1989:

"If a SUPERNATURAL explanation is to be proposed, it seems pointless to make any scientific measurement on the shroud at all."

Of all the research I did on the Shroud of Turin, it was that one definitive statement by Robert Hedges that impacted me most about science versus religion. From the scientist's own mouth:

If a "SUPERNATURAL" GOD exists, then SCIENTIFIC RESEARCH is pointless.

If God existed and went about His business of working miracles, then being a scientist was meaningless. It was a scientist's *duty* to strike down religion and the supernatural. At all costs. The supernatural was the born enemy of science. Science was duty-bound to manipulate public disbelief. Science owed it to the human population to promote the brilliance of Mankind. Nobody could argue with science. If science said something *was*, then it *was*!

They were not happy campers when one of their own stepped forward with a belief in the supernatural. Science is the systematic observation of the physical world. The Shroud is from the spiritual world. The two collide like oil and water. They do not mix. One side of the fence or the other. As Thomas Phillips of Harvard's High Energy Lab concluded, science is out of its realm when it comes to God and His supernatural powers, if there was such a God.

Science is only capable of studying the physical realm. For example, if an "artist" created the "photographic negative image of a crucified man" on the Shroud of Turin as a great hoax, science would be able to determine within reason via scientific research, who, what, when, where, and how the hoax was created. But it is downright foolish and arrogant of science to think it can research God.

In the physical realm science has accomplished some wonderful things. Many scientists, themselves, are spiritual. God, Himself, has opened up great avenues for Mankind by granting wisdom to scientists. But when a scientist of the physical realm tries to invade God's realm on a fact-finding mission, he is in grave territory. Scientists of Babylon tried to penetrate the supernatural realm thousands of years ago...it backfired.

Science (a mainstay of "humanism") and God are at war with one another, and science is bent on blinding its faithful with long-winded explanations and a whirlwind of fraudulent logic based upon testing of the "physical" world, as if God did not exist.

They are wrong. The Man on the Shroud of Turin commanded that I halt the writing of a best seller about the *U.S.S. Indianapolis*, and to write *War of the Angels,* instead. He is alive, and He is quite the supernatural.

PART TWO

THE RULERS OF DARKNESS

"For they are the spirits of devils ... which go forth unto the kings of the earth and of the whole world, to gather them to the battle of that great day."

Revelations 16:14

"And they had a king over them, which is the angel of the bottomless pit, whose name in the Hebrew tongue is Abaddon, but in the Greek tongue hath his name Apollyon."

Revelations 9:11

CHAPTER 9
Open Wide the Gates of Hell

November 4, 1980

I lost the farm. I had not worked enough to support myself and without rent money I had to vacate the premises in December of 1979. Worse than losing my home was losing my farm family, especially George the Kat. I was moving in with my parents until I made other arrangements, and they forbid me to bring George. He was hardly cute and cuddly, and they were afraid of him.

I could not bring myself to have George euthanized, so I approached the new tenants who took over the farm about keeping George. One look at him and they said, "No way." Their refusal would be George the Kat's death sentence.

I countered with my best sales pitch ever, with George's life riding on the outcome. "He's the finest *mouser* I have ever seen. You'd never have to worry about mice or bugs nesting in your furniture or cabinets. Think of all the money and trouble he'd save you. I'd hate to live way out here without him, with all those dirty rodents lining up outside your house at the first snowfall. It wouldn't even be safe to eat off your plates or drink out of the glasses; not after those things have messed all over them."

"You got a point there," said the man. "Geez, I guess so. Cats ain't that much trouble to care for on a farm. It's better than putting down traps and poison everywhere."

George lived. But George possessed uncanny instincts about changes and he kept jumping into the car with me, even though he hated cars. He knew I was leaving. It was strange how he understood. The new tenants locked him inside so I could leave. George the Kat sat in the picture window and meowed like a kitten when I drove away crying, saying over and again: "Stupid, ugly cat!"

After four months of using my parent's house as a homebase while I drifted town-to-town selling, I randomly settled in Chicago on March 15, on my twenty-ninth birthday. Well, technically it wasn't Chicago *proper.* I lived across the Indiana border in (*Where the heck*?)

A few blocks west was Scherrerville and Munster—but I was not *in* Scherrerville or Munster. A few blocks east was Merrillville and Hobart—but I was not *in* Merrillville or Hobart. A few blocks behind me was Highland and Crown Point—but I was not *in* Highland or Crown Point. Across the street and to the left was Hammond and East Chicago—but I was not *in* Hammond or East Chicago. Across the street and to the right was Gary—but I was not *in* Gary.

I lived *between* them all, but not *in* any of them. I lived in the middle of *Nowhere*, Indiana, Outside Chicago.

My life remained simple and lonely throughout spring and summer. I still had no furniture other than a bed, except for the desk and chair in my spare room that I used for my office. I had not yet made friends, nor had I sought any. Then I met Sharon at a company party on July 4, 1980.

Sharon was brand new with the airline academy when she attended the party. However, her personality and beauty made her the center of attraction. She caught my attention as I sat quietly in the corner nursing a drink, wishing I was as outgoing as she.

Apparently I eyed her too openly because Sharon scooted my way and seductively introduced herself. Everyone laughed when I spilled the drink on my lap, and when Sharon teasingly wiped my pants dry with her untucked blouse. I was embarrassed when she said I was cute and pulled me onto the floor to be her dance partner for the remainder of the evening.

When I left the district headquarters in Indianapolis for my home back in Nowhere Indiana, Outside Chicago, I began writing to Sharon and she wrote back. The relationship developed into daily phone calls. Then in October, I sent her a card—one with a pig on the front, rooting in the garbage. It read: "Do you want to mess around?" Inside the card was a plane ticket, and I asked her to come spend a week with me.

Now, it was approaching midnight on November 4, 1980, as I paced back and forth in the main terminal at O'Hare awaiting Sharon's arrival.

She had boarded the last commuter out of Indianapolis to Chicago because she had taken time to vote in Tuesday's Presidential Election. The lateness was unpleasant for the both of us, but voting was a patriotic duty she would never shirk, even for a more favorable flight schedule.

The flight arrived on time, but commuters landed far from the main terminal. Her shuttle bus would run nearly as long as her flight. I had ample time to prepare a warm greeting for her as I paced the terminal.

I hoped for a good first impression. I had gradually dipped below the poverty level the past couple of years, but meeting Sharon had done something to me. Suddenly I felt like a crystal goblet filled with wine for the first time. I was love drunk. I needed love.

Sharon was an elegant lady accustomed to nice things, and I had worked diligently for enough money to lavish on her. I astounded my company the past month when I wrote a half-year's worth of business in only three weeks. Now a sleek new El Dorado Cadillac slithered in my parking spot at O'Hare, and I paraded around the terminal in my new wardrobe.

Having lived alone in the woods for so long I did not understand fashion, which is why I appreciated the nice black man in the Gary, Indiana, retail outlet who had been kind enough to help me. When I paid him my bill and strut out the door in my new blue velvet jacket and two-toned suede shoes, the clerk yelled a compliment for all to hear: "My man, dig'em threads."

Now I felt slightly embarrassed about being the best dressed man in O'Hare. Everyone glanced in admiration. Passers-by could not keep their eyes off me. I supposed it was not polite to strut and dishearten the less fortunate, but for once I was the cock-of-the-walk and I felt like crowing. *Dig 'em threads.*

The shuttle pulled up and I watched Queen Sharon descend her throne. I also eyed the businessman tugging at her arm. Mr. Executive brazenly asked her out for a drink right in front of me like I was nothing.

"No," snubbed Sharon. "I'm with ... BLUE VELVET?"

It worked, I thought, as I watched her gaze in admiration. *The blue velvet worked.* And when Sharon hugged and kissed me, I watched the executive shake his head in dismay at my slick outfit and scoff away in defeat. (*Dig'em threads*!) The best man won. I sensed it in her eyes, as she loosened her hug to step back and gawk at my hi-fangled, two-toned suede shoes. (*My, man! My, man!*)

Not until Wednesday evening did Sharon and I ease out of bed in time to keep our dinner reservations at a posh restaurant. The dinner proved uneasy for me. I was more comfortable eating a bite of cold salad for myself from a relatively bare refrigerator, while feeding and conversing with a barnyard full of animals. This was my first dinner with *human* companionship in many months.

I learned a lot about her over the course of dinner. She had been a prostitute since age sixteen and had grown accustomed to the niceties earned with long blond hair, full lips, perky breasts, and the eagerness to put them all into motion for men-of-means who could spoil her. She loved the money, the lifestyle, and truth be known, she thrilled to the sex as much as her clients.

Her only drawback was that her breast size limited her earnings to five hundred dollars per evening. Wealthy johns would seldom pay more for a 34-B. She competed with the bigger girls by never wearing a bra and by always managing to give a selected prospect an *accidental* peak. A lot of executives, she learned, preferred a low key approach with a woman of class, in stark contrast to the bustier women who projected themselves as nymphomaniac bimbos. Still, the bimbos made double or triple what Sharon could draw on a given encounter, although Sharon's clients were more apt to return to her on a regular basis because she had style.

Now at age twenty-eight, however, her asking price had dipped to three hundred dollars per night and they did not come back as often. Sex was an occupation for younger women unless she wanted to entertain a lower-class client with more perverse, specialty needs. *That*, she determined, was *not* going to happen.

She wanted out, but going-straight had proven rougher than she had imagined. She did not know how else to earn money. She had no legitimate job skills. She never finished high school and was too embarrassed to attend night classes.

For the first time in her life Sharon was financially strapped with no conceivable hope of bailing herself out. Coping with abusive bill collectors was a new and difficult task. She was no longer willing to pay a mechanic's bill with oral sex, and her car methodically grew in disrepair. She no longer exchanged sex for expensive dinners, nor did she go shopping with a trick's credit card. Sharon had become a regular, cash-paying customer who had run out of cash. Now it was worries, instead of sex, that kept her awake at night. Her ulcers bled, but she was not returning to her old ways as a cure.

Sharon wanted a new direction, and soon. *Time*, she knew, was a woman's worst enemy. Age thirty was in the foreseeable future, and *three-oh* was the end of the line for finding an eligible man, or so she believed. Her self-respect was shattered and she simply could not see the elegant reflections of a beautiful woman in her mirror. The late-twenties horrified her like a ticking time bomb and she anxiously wanted to settle down.

There had been a lot of *"schmucks"* for Sharon. A lot of tears in her large, brown eyes. Men just wanted her for sex. Even her recent job interviews had disgustingly turned into sexual advances and she could not find employment. That is why she was thankful that the district manager for the airline academy was a woman. When she interviewed for the job last July, the two of them had a watery-eyed, heart-to-heart afternoon of true confessions and she had gotten the job as an Admissions Representative (saleswoman) for a proprietary airline and travel academy. In fact, it was that same district manager with whom Sharon had relied upon for advice about coming to visit me for the week.

"Go to him," she'd told Sharon. "You'd be good for each other. I know he's lonely and he seems to care for you very much. He's also the best in the business and he can teach you to be very successful. He enrolls everyone he talks to. His only problem is he doesn't run many appointments. He makes whatever sales he needs, then disappears. Maybe you can get him to work more often. Do you know he set a national sales record last month?"

"That's what I heard."

"And do you know why?"

"No. Why?"

"He did it to impress *you*."

Sharon could have done better—as far as men of means—than with me. She mesmerized me over dinner when she said I was like an answered prayer to her.

I truly wanted to impress her, but I was at a loss in public. I had been such a recluse and hermit that I had no social skills. At the moment I found myself mimicking her dining etiquette.

The table setting confounded me. There were far more eating utensils than I had ever used and I did not know what piece to use with what course. Each item was like a specialty player on a football team that was used merely for one brief situation (*specialty tableware: kick-return forks; punt-return spoons; field-goal knives; third-and-short glasses; second-and-long plates*), until eating had become a game and not a basic necessity.

Sharon peered upwardly at me, the candles flickering in her brown eyes. She stopped eating. Without a word, she resumed, elegantly overplaying her movements for my studious eyes, thereby sparing me further embarrassment.

"Tell me about your book," she said after dinner, over wine. Sharon excelled in directing conversation toward the man, making me feel important. "I hear you have some secret papers from the President. About the U.S.S. *Indianapolis*, I believe. Right?"

"Uh-huh." It made no difference to me that Sharon manipulated the conversation to loosen me up; I liked it. I supposed if I'd have been a plumber, she'd have made me feel important by discussing plastic versus copper pipes.

War of the Angels

I casually mentioned that the sinking of U.S.S. *Indianapolis* was the largest disaster at sea in the history of the United States Navy (the larger loss of life on the *Arizona* was *docked* at Pearl Harbor), and it was so controversial that the findings at the court of inquiry were classified top secret.

I recounted how difficult it had been finding details about the infamous ship. "Everybody said, forget it. You're never, ever going to get those secret papers."

"So how'd you get them?"

I ordered cherries jubilee; I had seen other people having it. I liked the flames. "What makes it burn like that?" Then I explained how I had obtained the papers, and so forth and so on. I told about their contents: about the glorious ship itself, which served as the Allied Headquarters-at-sea; about how it transported the Atomic Bomb across the Pacific to be loaded aboard the bomber Enola Gay; about how high-ranking blunders caused the sinking of the ship, and about a negligent Headquarters that delayed rescue operations. I told about America's most honored admirals and the Secretary of the Navy conspiring to place the blame on the innocent captain of the ship, who later shot himself in the head in disgrace; and about the secret memos I had in my possession, signed by a desperate group of important men trying to hide their guilt from the press. The most disgraceful coverup in the history of the United States Navy.

Those in authority, even years later, determined it would be best if the public never knew the full story. President Gerald Ford honorably declassified the elusive information, after three decades of uncooperative Washington bureaucrats. "This cherries jubilee is good, huh?"

"That's fascinating," said Sharon. "I'd like to see those papers, if you'd allow me."

Of course, I would allow her, I thought. Or if I'd have been a plumber, I would have shown her the plastic and copper tubings. Sharon made me feel important. And she was very good at it. The time and days sailed away when I was with her. We built a good relationship.

***

But on Friday I lied to Sharon.

I said I needed privacy to work on my U.S.S. *Indianapolis* book. Sharon mentioned earlier that she would like a day to see a childhood girlfriend who lived in Chicago, and I suggested this Friday would be ideal for her to go visiting.

Sharon called and made arrangements, then hurriedly packed an overnight bag. I tossed her the car keys, and she left.

But I had no intentions of working on my manuscript. Instead, I planned to summon a spirit from the Dark World. I wanted to confront one. But I did not want Sharon's life endangered, so I lied to her, to get her out of the way in case something went wrong.

I had devoted two hard years for this moment. Patrick and David had given me all the ammunition I needed and I had sacrificed everything to excel at what I was doing. I had disassociated myself from society; I had hungered so badly at times that I'd swung my fists through the air in frustration of the pain in my empty belly; I had lived without heat until my bones and teeth knocked; I had lost everything, including the animals I loved. Tonight was payback time.

I schemed to attack one of the lesser inhabitants of the Dark World, at first, for practice. I planned to trick it: I would act friendly toward one in the name of Satan, to draw it out. And then, I would ambush it in the name of Jesus Christ. I was alone shortly before midnight Friday on November 7, 1980. I trembled, knowing I was not playing games. What I was about to do would cross the bounds of the imaginary, and into the realm of truly Bad Things. It was real and not Hollywood. Determined, I proceeded to a point of no return.

I converted my desk into a Satanic altar. I turned out the lights. I imagined Evil. I relished Hatred. I adored Wickedness. I worshipped the Beast. And in loathsome earnest I initiated the Black Ritual to call forth a demon. "In the name of Satan, as a Brother of Darkness ..."

Hiding my nervousness for my own protection, I lit three ceremonial candles. A white Candle of Destruction burned in the middle. In the Dark World everything seemed topsy-turvy. White was a Good Thing, and Good Things were the Most Hated of the Bad Things. The white candle existed for the absolute depravation of decency. Two black Candles of Compassion flanked both sides. They provided power to execute missions of Evil against the cursed. And I had enclosed all three candles within a chalked circle to concentrate their powers.

The flickering lights danced eerily off the surrounding dark walls. A beautiful place-setting for my expected guests. To rid the air of foul goodness, I rang a purification bell nine times while slowly turning. And to demonstrate my voraciousness for terror, I unwrapped my Dagger of Power (a kitchen knife) from the sacred black cloth I had used to enshroud its forces.

In servitude to the Rulers of Darkness, I faced an imaginary picture of Baphomet, a General in Satan's High-Command. Actual items were not always necessary in rituals, providing that Evil sincerely adorned the heart and soul, and if the mind gave way to imagery of corruptness. The Love of Bad Things. I saluted the dagger toward the goathead. I read from Anton Szandor LaVey's book, *Satan's Rituals*:

> "In the name of Satan, the Ruler of the earth, the King of the World, I command the forces of Darkness to bestow their power upon me.
> Open wide the Gates of Hell and come forth from the abyss to greet me as your brother. I have taken thy name as a part of myself. I live as a beast. I rejoice in sin. I favor the rotten. I curse the just. By all the Gods of the Pit, come to my desires!"

I lifted a silver goblet (wine glass) to my lips. I drank from the Elixir of Life (Sharon's wine). I saluted the dagger to the four corners, saying:

> "Satan from the South. Lucifer from the East. Belial from the North. Leviathan from the West. Shemhamforash! Hail to Satan!"

I concluded.

> "Come forth and answer to your names: Abaddon; Adramelech; Apollyon; Baalberith; Baphomet;

> *Beelzebub; Dagon; Diabolus; Dracula; Ishtar; Kali; Loke; Moloch; Nikasa; Pan; Pluto; Rimmoh; Sekhmet; Set; and, Tammuz.*

I issued my command to them, raising the shadow of my arms on the flickering wall. *Come, manifest my desires!"* I directed the demons toward the sacred circle of chalk:

"Appear! To the Terror of the Earth!"

I consumed the remaining wine as a sign of gluttony. I rang the bell nine more times, while turning, and finished.

"So it is done."

I crouched behind the desk and said nothing else. I breathed softly, watching the candles flicker. Mostly I waited in darkness, hiding. Waiting for a *demon* to appear!

Nothing happened. What a crock of poop. I extinguished the candles, cleaned up, and went to bed.

In Chicago shortly after midnight, Sharon watched television with her girlfriend. They sipped beer and munched snacks. They sometimes watched the movie, they sometimes chatted. Then suddenly Sharon leaped from her chair when the shadowy creature darted past her. Instinctively she screamed, "Michael!"

In a few moments she calmed down and laughed about the incident. Sharon thought she had seen *something*. But she hadn't. It must have been a glare from the television, flashing across the dimly lit room. Silly Sharon.

***

The next morning on November 8, a Saturday, the telephone rang and rang. I disliked answering. Not even my own family called me with idle chatter, knowing my utter contempt for telephones.

My phone conversations seldom varied: "Uh-huh. Huh-uh. Okay. Yup. Nope. Bye." More often than not I simply did not answer, having disciplined myself to ignore the beckoning of *Ma Bell*.

Since having met Sharon, however, I answered more frequently, with expectations of her pleasant voice being on the other end. But she was presently on her way back from Chicago. *It can't be her. Maybe it is. I'd better see.* "Hello."

"Hi, Michael," said Sharon. "It took you long enough to answer. Did you just get in or something?"

"Huh-uh."

"Guess what? Maybe you'd better sit down, first? You're not going to be too happy about what happened."

"What?"

"Your Caddy broke down, about halfway home. It just quit on me."

"Oh, no."

"I'm calling from a service station in Hammond, out on Highway 41. I had it towed in. They said it would be a while before they could get to it. They took your Triple-A for the tow, and I can write a check for the repair if you can cover it for me. Okay?"

"Okay."

"Don't worry about me. It's in a nice part of town and I'm not in any danger or anything like that. I'll be home when I can, but I don't think it's going to be too soon. Okay?"

"Um-hmmm."

"See you later, Sweetheart. Bye-bye."

"Bye."

Sharon called periodically for updates, until afternoon slipped into dusk before the car was repaired. When she finally walked through the front door Sharon expressed disappointment for having missed our dinner and show reservations for the Jazz Festival at the Merrillville Holidome.

Neither one of us said a word about last night. I had nothing to say because nothing actually happened. Sharon had nothing to say, because she *justified* that nothing really happened. The shadowy-gray creature she had seen was in truth, a real shadow. And her abrupt scream had also been for nothing. We ask each other, "Anything exciting happen?" And we each replied, "No, nothing."

Sharon entered my office for no apparent reason. She stood beside the desk I had used for an altar, during last night's bid to beckon a creature from the Dark World.

Open Wide the Gates of Hell

I stopped short of the office doorway, not wanting to go in. "I'm tired. You ready for bed? Sharon? What are you looking at?"

Sharon answered none of my questions. She ignored me, as she slowly traced circles on top of my desk. Around and around, always left. She turned slowly, spookily as if in a trance, and looked at me.

I took a few steps into the room. "Sharon, you look like you're half asleep. Why don't you come to bed?"

She approached me and put her arms around me in a cooing manner. Her touch relaxed me. And when she pressed against me, it made me adamant about hurrying to bed. But instead of succumbing to my suggestions, Sharon lured me further into the room. Like a boxer maneuvering an opponent into the corner while in a clinch, she waltzed and twirled, back-peddled and side-stepped, and used her body to entice me to go where she wanted.

When I encountered the pressure of the desk pushing against my buttocks and Sharon pressing against my pelvis, I believed Sharon was about to make love to me. "Right here on the desk? It's kind of small isn't it? How about the floor?"

She lifted her head from my chest and stared longingly at me. That's when I lost my passion for the moment. Sharon's brown eyes turned green. Not green-green, but not her usual brown-brown, either. Green-brown, mostly green, and like marbles.

I loosened my arms from around her and drew back. I leaned on the desk and edged away from Sharon. But she only came closer, maintaining her tight-hug around the back of my neck. I could not free myself from her. "Sharon, what's the matter? That's enough, okay?"

She spoke in a guttural voice from the pit of her stomach. "Miiichael." It sounded hollow.

"What? Quit acting like that. I don't like it. Let's go to bed."

"Do you know who I am?"

"What do you mean?" I asked.

"Do you know who I am?"

War of the Angels

"No." I saw she was very serious. She was not playing. It *wasn't* Sharon. I was being quizzed, and I responded. "Who are you?"

"I am not who you think?" She did not speak in normal contractions, but rather slowly pronounced every word, full and complete.

"Who are you?"

"You do not know, do you, Michael?" She smiled in jest of my ignorance. She toyed with me.

"Who are you?"

"I cannot tell you. When it is time for you to know, then you will know."

"I don't understand. Tell me."

"When it is time."

"Tell me." I was not playing games either. I put both hands onto her shoulders and shook, pressing my face squarely to her eyes and demanded again, "Tell me!"

Her eyes rolled upwards. No pupils, only whites. "Once, I was a cat. I was inside the tomb."

"What are you talking about? What tomb?"

"Egypt." She glanced toward my desk and said, "Do not do that again."

I had not mentioned about last night's Black Ritual, and wondered how she knew. "Do what?"

"What you did last night. I know what you did."

"How do you know? What did I do?"

"*You* know what you did. Do *not* do it again. It is dangerous, Michael. It is *Evil*." When she said, "Eeee-vill," she drew the word long, scaring me.

Sharon closed her eyes and placed her lips gently on mine, kissing me, dry, mouth closed. She backed away and opened her eyes. They were brown again. "I'm tired," she said in her normal voice. "Let's go to bed."

"What do you mean?" I asked.

She smiled sweetly, unaware of what had taken place. "I mean I'm tired and I want to go to sleep. If you're worked up, we don't have to fall asleep right away, though."

But I wasn't in the mood. I let Sharon traipse to bed alone. I sat up for a few minutes. I was baffled and jittery, wondering who I had just spoken to. Sharon would later confess about the Dark Thing she saw in Chicago at her girlfriend's house at midnight that Friday, and how she had so easily explained it away. But when I eventually described about Saturday night—how her eyes changed colors; how she eerily spoke in mysteries and riddles—her expressed reaction made me realize it *hadn't* been Sharon at all, but someone (*something*) using her as a vehicle to communicate. But it wasn't until next week's visit that I would tell her, so by Sunday morning she returned to Indianapolis with no qualms about planning to come see me again. She looked forward to next week's visit. She did not yet know any better.

CHAPTER 10
There's Something Scary In My Basement

In the interim of Sharon's absence, I proposed to earn a few extra dollars. I did not *need* to work; I had enough money. But I was uncommonly bored without Sharon's companionship. I thought by taking care of business I could pass time, as well as to pad the savings account I would need if our flowering romance blossomed.

I worked only on weekends. I had nearly always done it that way. Saturdays and Sundays were the best days for selling proprietary school enrollments because potentially more students were available for appointments. And I reserved Thursdays for setting those appointments.

I worked myself ragged on weekends, compiling over thirty hours into the two days. My work schedule did not allow much of a social life, but so what? I had no friends to visit on weekends, anyway, and the two-days-on and five-days-off suited me fine.

It was two o'clock Thursday afternoon on November 13, when my part time secretary bounced out to my car. Her name was Brenda, but I called her "Be-Bop." The nickname suited her well. Her giddiness tempered me (*"Can't you ever be serious?"*). Her hyper activity made me nervous (*"Won't you please sit down and work?"*). And her unpredictability infuriated me (*"Oh God, I can't believe you did that."*).

...enty, Be-Bop portrayed the job maturity of ...ear-old, which is why I drove to pick her up for ... It was the only way I could assure myself she would ... there.

I hired her six weeks ago to schedule my sales appointments over the phone. I fired her a week later for tardiness, although I rehired her that same afternoon. I had not *intended* to dismiss her; she had simply driven me nuts by walking in late and yacking and babbling, until I blurted out for my sanity like a whale spouting for air: "You're fired!"

Be-Bop needed the job badly. She stood crying, while I fumed. When I quit screaming she dried her tears and asked, "Am I really fired?"

"No. I want you to be more responsible. Can you get here on *time* from now on?"

"You mean I got my job back?" she asked in amazement.

"Yeah, but don't rub it in."

Her tears evaporated by the warmth of her smile. Bubbles flowed through her veins like good champagne through a straw. She be-bopped to her desk. "I thought you were being a real creep," she confessed to me.

The fact was, I rehired Be-Bop because I could not get along without her. Until I had met Sharon, I worked only four or five days per month. But then needing fast money for the new spark in my life, I suddenly boasted to the company President that I would set a national sales record. And having bragged, I needed secretarial help to reach my goal.

I recognized my weakness with the telephone, and I sought to conquer my shortcomings by hiring a girl to set my appointments. I placed an ad in the paper and interviewed many people. Some over-qualified, some under-qualified. Then I met Be-Bop, while enrolling her into the school. She needed money for tuition payments, and I needed her telephone prowess to help me make money and win Sharon.

Be-Bop was *Ma Bell's* immaculate child. She had bounced out of her mother's womb attached to a phone cord. She had been weaned on a receiver. Talkity-talk-talk. Blabbity-blab-blab. Her enthusiasm for everything carried well over telephone lines. When she scheduled an appointment with one of her peers, they sensed Be-Bop's own excitement about attending the airline school, and they anxiously awaited my

War of the Angels

arrival so they, too, could enroll. Well, *that*, and the fact she teased the boys into believing they would be rooming with her on campus.

The sales record fell. I padded my billfold. A Cadillac materialized outside my door. And Sharon came into my heart. No, siree bob, I could not really fire Be-Bop. I needed her. But I was bewildered about how to get her to work on time. Threats (*"if you're late one more time ..."*) did no good. Motivation (*"if you help break the sales record, you'll ..."*) did no good. Speeches on maturity (*"most people your age ..."*) did no good. Bonus money (*"you'll get an extra ..."*) did no good.

There was only *one* way to assure that she got to the office on time. When she called the very next week after the firing incident to say she could not make it to work on time for some strange reason, I said, "I'll come and get you." A troublesome, but effective, trend was born.

"Of course I don't mind giving you a ride. No problem (*my foot*). No, we can't run by your friend's house first. Be-Bop! No! Would you listen to ... no, just get ready. I'm on my way."

That was then. This was now. And times had not changed. Getting Be-Bop to the office was harder than the work itself. "Hi, Mike," said Be-Bop, smiling big. She came to the driver's window, instead of getting in.

I sensed a delay. There was *always* a delay. "You ready?"

"Come on in, first. I want you to hear the new bass guitar my boyfriend bought for me. They're going to let me play in their band."

"We don't have time for ... okay." It was useless to argue. It would be more efficient to march in and listen to a set or two of Be-Bop on the bass, than it would be to argue for fifteen minutes and then cave into her demands anyway.

Besides, I always allowed an extra hour for surprises, such as: the time I walked into an arm wrestling tournament (she was frail at five-foot-four and ninety pounds, but she won); the time I waited on her to hit baseballs at the arcade; oh, and the spontaneous party I almost never pried her away from, when we had stopped "for just a minute" to see a friend. And not to forget the many times I had called to say I was on my way, only to find myself chasing her down after she'd strayed away to "be-bop around." So I thought listening to an hour of Bmmm ... Bmmm ... Bmmm was not as bad as some Thursdays.

I finally coaxed Be-Bop to my office. Secretly, we were an hour *early*, but I couldn't let her know. She was still an hour away from the time she would sit down at the desk and actually make that first call. I had to always sound desperately late (*we're late, we're late, we have no time to wait*), to have a prayer of getting her started on time. So why did I put up with her nonsense every Thursday? Because she made a thousand dollars per weekend for me, that's why.

Finally, Be-Bop picked up the telephone ... and put it back down. "Is she pretty?"

"Be sure to schedule the appointments in the same area, or at least ... is who pretty?"

"Sharon. I figure she must be pretty, or you wouldn't be working so hard."

"Yes, she is. And don't forget to schedule them ..."

"Does she have big boobs?"

" ... an hour in between, so I can ... huh?"

"You heard me, coz you're blushing. God, I made you blush."

"No, she doesn't. Can we please get down to business, unless you want to know what positions we like, or something?"

"Would you tell me, if I asked?"

"No! Please, please, please ..."

"All right. I just thought you liked big boobs."

"Be-Bop!"

"Okay. Give me the names you want called," she whined, reluctantly.

"God! All these!"

"It's not *that* many."

"You kiddin' me, man? Look at 'em."

She flipped the index cards with the prospects' names on them, then set them aside. She looked at me and toyed with her small breasts. "You like itty bitty ones, huh?"

"Be-Bop, I ..."

"You ought to see the sexy new bra I bought today."

"I ... ummm ... forgot what I wanted to say."

"I'm wearing it. Wanna see?"

"Well, I, uh, oh — I don't really want to work, either," I said, when Be-Bop unzipped her jumpsuit and popped her bra loose in a tease.

"Good," she said, fastening her bra and zipping back up. "Take me home."

Be-Bop jerked open the top metal drawer of the filing cabinet and stuffed the cards back into their proper folder. She grabbed her purse and coat and bounced out of the office before I knew I'd been tricked into a day off. But she abruptly stopped her quick exit, and asked a startling question. "Mike, do you believe in ghosts?"

"Ghosts?" I half-waited for a punch line which never came.

"You know, spirits and junk. You think they're real?"

"Why do you ask?" I did not admit to anything, waiting for her response.

"Because there's something *scary* in my basement."

She broke into tears and her frail body heaved between sobs as she tried to explain. "And nobody boo-hoo-hoo believes me."

"I do," I said. I hugged her and patted her on the back. "I do." But that's *all* I said. Some things were not meant for others to know. "I'll take a look for you, when we get there. C'mon. Let's go."

On the drive home, Be-Bop expounded about the thing in her basement, while I listened intently behind the wheel. She claimed a spirit entered her cellar a few days ago. At first, it performed mischievous pranks: it slammed the washer and dryer lids; it tipped the soap box; it dumped the clothes basket.

"How do you know the machine didn't vibrate the stuff off?"

"Coz it wasn't running! You can think what you want, man. I don't care. I *know* it's a ghost."

"We'll go down there and check it out."

"Huh-Uh, Man! Don't give me that '*we*' stuff. You go by yourself. My *dog* won't even go down there anymore. And that used to be her play area. She grew up down there. She knows, man. Dogs can tell, man."

I thought of George the Kat. George had known — yes indeedy — about the Beast at the foot of the bed.

"My boyfriend *laughs* at me. You can go ahead and laugh, too, if you want. I don't care. You probably think I'm crazy, don't you?"

"No, I don't. Just calm down."

I fidgeted nervously, as I turned into Be-Bop's parking lot. I frantically wondered to myself if her ghost had something to do with my Midnight ritual. She claimed she first noticed something scary in her basement on Saturday morning, only a few hours after my attempt to summon a demon. Maybe it didn't mean a thing. Maybe it did. Was a connection possible? And the desk? I forgot about the desk! Be-Bop used the same desk I had converted to a Satanic altar for my Black Ritual.

And Sharon? Sharon saw a Dark Thing on that same night, way on the other side of town.

Yes, I believed her. Believed the hell out of her.

"Get this, man: yesterday I *saw* it. I had to do laundry, coz my boyfriend was ticked-off at me for letting it go so long. Like I was too scared to go down there and do it, you know, but we didn't have any clean clothes at all, so I asked him to go with me, coz I was scared, you know, and he started screaming bloody murder, you know, coz he was 'tired of hearing about *ghosts!*' God, I had to go by myself.

"Anyway, I went down there and set a basket of laundry on the washer, you know. Like I was too scared you know to be by myself, so I went back up and got my puppy—it's a dachshund and she's really cute and everything; I'll show her to you when we get home; she's only about this big so I named her 'Peanut' coz it's a really neat name, don't you think?—but anyway, she gets so scared she pees all over me, man, so I put her down cause I'm all wet and everything, and as soon as she hits the floor she *flies* back upstairs, man. I mean like, 'va-voom,' man and she's split like a race dog! She's never done that before, man, coz you know, it's like where she plays all the time, down there, you know, in the basement.

"So I went to the stairway to coax her back down—no way I was staying in the basement by myself, huh-uh, man, forget you—so anyway, I was like kneeling at the bottom of the steps, you know, saying, 'Here, Peanut. Come on, Peanut,' and all of a sudden: *Wham!* The soap box flies across the room and hits me in the head; I'm thinking like 'God,' you know, wondering what happened. Then the *laundry basket* flies across the room, too, and hits me smack dab in the back. Then I hear the washing machine lid bang up and down, you know, and when I turn around, I see this shadowy thing coming right at me, man.

"I mean like I'm so scared, I can't even climb the stairs, man. You know what I did? I *crawled* up that sucker and slammed the door shut.

"And my boyfriend stands over me, cussing me out, you know, coz he thinks I threw soap and clothes all over the basement, like I'm sure I'd do that, right? I swear I'm telling the truth, man."

The building where Be-Bop resided was small; it had only four units, and two of them were vacant. It was also very old. Although the bricks had recently undergone a cosmetic sandblasting, the facade of the building screamed its age from tell-tale wrinkles.

I stared at the dirt-caked basement windows. Be-Bop and I reluctantly got out of the Caddy. We ventured inside the building, where we paused at the doorway leading downstairs.

The basement served as common property where tenants did laundry, although Be-Bop's one-and-only neighbor seldom went downstairs because she preferred using a coin-op, instead. Henceforth, the basement was all Be-Bop's. And she wanted no part of it.

"Okay, show me where it happened," I said, starting down the basement steps.

"No way, Jose! I'm not going down there!" She slammed the door on me.

"Thanks a lot," I yelled. "You wanna at least tell me where the lights are?"

The door cracked open. Be-Bop's hand inched inside, and flipped a light switch. The door slammed shut again.

I descended one step at a time, scared of ...

(*memories*).

I walked to the far side of the basement, near the washer and dryer, where Be-Bop told me she'd been attacked. There I noticed another room, which apparently had been sealed off with concrete blocks, long ago. Only now, however, some of the blocks had been dislodged, exposing a dark, empty room.

I poked my head through the obscure hole. *Too dark. Can't see a thing. Is anyone in here?* Suddenly an uncanny feeling rushed through my body.

"In the name of Jesus Christ, demon, I command you to leave." I whispered it without authority, unsure of its potency. I wouldn't have scared away too many demons. But *real* men didn't get scared, and I was embarrassed for having said such a hokey thing. I hoped Be-Bop had not heard me. After all, I still harbored a few doubts.

But mostly, I harbored a sense of *belief.* And I suddenly took command of the situation and did what was necessary: I scurried up the steps, and got the hell out.

I paused at the top of the stairs to catch my breath before opening the door. I could not let Be-Bop see me panting from fright.

She inquired, "Well?"

I stepped into her living room and leaned against the door, resting before I spoke a word. I stared at a row of beastly statues, lining the top of her knick-knack shelf. From Patrick's books, I recognized them as demonic icons and warned, "Get rid of those things. You're inviting trouble."

***

That night while I slept, the Man on the Shroud came to me. He took me out of my body and back to the Dark World. The method of spiritual transport was the same as before, with the spinning mind and the black tunnel. And when I had tumbled all the way through the tunnel, the Man on the Shroud departed, leaving me in the dark by myself.

The darkness mystified me. I kept still while I adapted to the strange environment. I feared moving, as if my first, unguided step would plunge me into a dark and dangerous ravine.

To my advantage, my remaining senses were much sharper in the Dark World, like a blind man who could smell better, or hear better, or who had a more sensitive touch. And I used all my unyielding prowess to assess the eerie situation.

Mostly, my senses were driven by memory, recalling the Beast. I listened for warning sounds of its presence, trying to ascertain the faintest beginnings of that heinous laughter. Listening for the terrifying growl that would follow. Straining to unearth sounds I'd once heard, but had since buried to the deepest confines of my subconscious, in hopes they would never resurface.

The emotion that befriended me most, however, was one of Knowing. The sense of "Knowing" was not an operable function inside my fleshly form, in the world back home. But in the Dark World, Knowing was the most prominent sense.

Knowing was not comparable to "having answers," because I certainly did not have knowledge as to what was happening. Knowing was an awareness of surroundings. And after a few short moments—with my Knowing activated—I knew the Beast was not to be encountered on this journey to the Dark World.

I moved gently. In the Dark World, nothing solid existed to stand upon, so movement was not similar to walking or running, but drifting. Knowing the Beast wasn't nearby, I drifted from one Dark World province to another without fear.

There were many areas to explore. My sense of Knowing told me the Dark World consisted of vast, innumerable planes, with each of the different worlds bearing a distinctness all its own. Distance had no value in the Dark World, for I traveled countless miles in a single movement. Likewise, Direction was immeasurable, for I knew my way around in the dark, no matter which way I turned.

It fascinated me that—as big and as dark as the Dark World was—I was no longer lost, as I had been on my first excursion to the Dark World before I developed Knowing. With Knowing, I was able to navigate any maze, capable of reaching any destination. Maps would have been pointless; all roads led to Everywhere. And then, I discovered Sight.

Although the dark was impenetrable, I could sense shapes and movement, and distinguish various shades of black in an all-black world. That is when I Saw a shadowy creature, the color of Number Two pencil lead, dart away in a blur. It was like a mouse who had been frightfully roused from the safety of its hole.

Instinctively, I gave chase. I was much quicker than the Dark Thing, and I drew within range in a moment. But it suddenly veered off in another direction, trying to lose me. It was afraid.

I paused, baffled. I was not going to hurt it. I continued after the Dark Thing at a leisurely drift. Terror poured from the Dark Thing as I followed. The Dark Thing dipped and darted, this way and that way, entering and exiting one plane after another in a frightful bid to run for its life from me. Its high-pitched squeal echoed in my mind. It was scared. Terrified. It sought refuge in the dark hideaway of ...

Hey, I know this place, I thought. This is Be-Bop's basement. You're the dark angel in Be-Bop's basement.

And while recalling how badly the demon had scared both Be-Bop and myself, I reconsidered my pacifist attitude and thought about revenge. Suddenly the demon scampered out of the hole. This time, I did not give chase. I let it disappear, Knowing it would not be back.

When I saw Be-Bop the next Thursday, she said, "Guess what? That thing in my basement is gone."

(Yes—way, way gone.)

***

It took only a couple of days for me to disbelieve what had happened. Such an outlandish occurrence was simply impossible. *What probably happened was ...*

That is why I was extra glad to hear from Sharon, to put a dose of sanity back into my life. She phoned to let my know how happy she was. "Michael," she said. "I even woke up in the middle of the night because I thought about you so much."

"That's nice to hear," I said in a soft, romantic tone."

"It's just that I thought ... Well, never mind."

"What?" I asked. "Go ahead and say what you thought."

"I heard ... No, I'm sure I *didn't*. But Michael, I thought I heard ..."

"Sharon, you know you can tell me. Now what did you hear?"

"No matter how weird?"

"How weird can it be?"

"Not real weird. I just thought I heard a Voice tell me to call you, that's all."

"Well how bad can that be? I'm glad you did."

"No, I mean like four in the morning. I woke up and heard—or thought I heard: 'Tell Michael, *The blackness of darkness*.'"

On my end of the line, my chin drooped over the mouthpiece. My cheerful smile reserved for one of Sharon's phone calls had vanished.

"That doesn't make any sense, huh?" asked Sharon.

> *"And the (fallen) angels which kept not their first estate, but have left their own habitation ... (are as) wandering stars, to whom is reserved the blackness of darkness for ever."*
>
> *(Jude 6, 13)*

CHAPTER 11
The Drive To Hell

After my journey to the Dark World where I encountered Be-Bop's demon—the one I had unwittingly summoned—I, myself, was thoroughly confounded. I had no sense of *Knowing* back in my own world. The experience was just another piece of the puzzle. This past journey taught me that the Dark World consisted of a structured environment, with greater and lesser inhabitants. I also learned that the black angels had access to *This* world, as if running an underground railway in the cover of night. But for what reason, and to what extent I did not know. So when Sharon gave me her mysterious message, I did not say anything. Exactly what was I to explain?

No matter, I should have said *something*. Anything. But I didn't, and unbeknownst to me, Sharon was driving into a spiritual ambush by coming to see me again. Although we were anxious to see each other when she arrived from Indianapolis on Monday, November 17, smiles were not passed around.

She was already ill by the time she knocked at my Chicagoland door. Not so ill that she needed hospital treatment, but sick enough to keep her from working. That, in itself, was nearly disastrous for Sharon. After four intensive months, she still had not sold her first school enrollment. Her financial predicament teetered near bankruptcy. She grew desperate.

I had assured her over the telephone not to worry, that when she came back, I'd teach her the business. She had started out from home quite well, and was anxious for training. But the farther she drove, the sicker she'd become.

When she reached my apartment, there were no hugs, no kisses exchanged, no greetings. She swiftly walked to the bathroom and vomited profusely. She had me cancel her evening appointments, then confined herself to bed, dashing her hopes of financial recovery.

On Tuesday, I pleaded with her to see a doctor, but she stubbornly argued against it; saying she'd be better soon. She claimed she wasn't really sick. All she needed was a little counter medicine from the corner store. And some chicken soup.

Because my Cadillac quit again, I sprinted to the local convenience store. I loaded up my shopping sack (*doctor's bag*) with buffered aspirin, assorted counter products, and soup. I raced back to the apartment, as if competing for an Olympic Gold medal. But I was a *has-been* athlete, running short-winded on hot and depleted muscles; by the time I returned, I hardly had breath enough to talk. And my legs were too wobbly to stand. I knelt at Sharon's bedside and administered the medicine to her. She eked a smile, asking if I needed medical treatment.

"puff ... puff ... huh-uh ... 'icken soup."

I repeated my sprints on Wednesday. She was slightly better. And by noon Thursday, she groggily swung her feet out of bed for something other than a bathroom trip. "Michael, do we have anything here to eat—besides chicken soup?"

"What would you like? It has to be something within walking distance."

"Isn't there a Chinese place next to the Stop-&-Shop?"

"Are you sure you can eat Chinese?" She was sure, and I was off to the races.

Sharon sat up and ate like she had never been sick. Ate a bunch. Everything on her plate. Mine, too. Stuffed it in. "Ooo gonna ea' dat egg 'oll?" She had never felt better.

Then by mid-afternoon Thursday, the Cadillac was returned in fine order. That's when Sharon asked to use it, reiterating her need to work. She rebuked my arguments against her going out on sales runs. She *did* feel up to it, and besides, she had no *choice.* Bills were due, and she did not want my money to pay them.

I should have told her *something.* Anything. But I didn't.

Sharon was determined that nothing would stop her. On Friday evening, November 21, 1980, she fashionably slithered into my freshly waxed El Dorado and went out and got her first sale At eleven o'clock that evening she was on her way home to tell me the good news, when she passed by the Holidome Piano Bar, made a U-turn and pulled in. She wanted a glass of wine before she traveled the remaining three blocks to my apartment.

Afterward, nearing midnight, she bounced through the parking lot to the car. Her elatedness had not diminished with the brief stopover. She was eager to see my reaction, knowing I'd be proud of her success. With great anticipation, she opened the car door.

Then she eerily stepped away and peered inside the back seat. She had a sudden feeling she was not alone. She looked. And looked again. She did not see anything, but the sensation of being watched didn't go away. She circled around the car, examining. Convinced that imagination was playing tricks on her, Sharon got into the car. Her excitement rejuvenated. *A sale!*

The Caddy responded smoothly at the turn of the key; its engine hummed melodically. Sharon coaxed it gently across the parking lot. At the edge of the lot, where light from the security lamp stretched itself thin, something darted in front of the car. She slammed the brakes. Her speed was slow enough to prevent the car from swerving, but great enough to jerk her forward against the steering wheel. She rubbed her forehead. *What happened? Oh, God, did I hit something? Did I run over somebody?*

She searched the darkness from her car seat, afraid to get out. Hard telling what gruesome scene awaited her. A dog, injured and dangerous? *No, couldn't have been a dog. It was too big for a dog. A man? A black man?* She couldn't tell. It was too dark. She strained and saw nothing. It was late, and was probably just her imagination.

The *Dark Thing* appeared outside her window!

It pressed against the glass next to Sharon's face. Evil peered in at her. A Bad Thing if ever there was one. The shape of a head, but without facial features.

She screamed. She floored the accelerator.

But she did not escape.

The Dark Thing yanked the steering wheel to the left, taking control of the car without entering. Sharon fell to the passenger-side floorboard, at the abrupt change in direction.

The accelerator pressed itself down, driving them hard in left-handed circles, squealing the tires. The Dark Thing remained outside the left window, while Sharon quivered on the floorboard. She bumped to and fro, unable to recover her balance, as if on a very fast amusement park ride with the centrifugal force pinning her against the rightside door.

She screamed for help, but the tight seal on the luxury windows muffled her scream. She tried the electronic switch to lower them, but nothing happened. She flipped the electric door lock, up, down, up, down, up, down. It wouldn't open. She could not escape. Help eluded her.

They circled left, always left. She lowered the center-seat armrest and used it as a prop to drag herself up. She grabbed hold of the steering wheel. It shocked her, and she tumbled backwards to the floor once again.

She screamed. Screamed for her life. But not loudly enough, and no one heard. And they circled left, until it suddenly quit. It went away undramatically, leaving Sharon in shambles, unable to control herself in the frightening silence.

She sped home, then smashed the car up over the curb in my apartment complex, and screamed out the window for help. Screamed a blood-curdling scream that begged for mercy; the type that rarely came in-a-lifetime. The kind *Faye Wray* screamed when she first saw *King Kong*. The type of scream capable of bursting a heart, if prolonged.

I ran to help her, then carried her inside as neighbors peered out their windows to see who died. I set her gently on the bed, where she curled up into a fetal position and quivered. She did not utter a word. She was unable to speak. She only trembled, and when her body allowed, she whimpered a noise. She breathed erratically.

I fixed her a quick cup of instant soup. She sat up and accepted it, but she did not drink. She only sat there in silence, squeezing the Styrofoam, spilling the hot liquid onto her lap without noticing. She squeezed the cup with both hands, gripping for a sense of security, as a child gripping a special blanket in times of concern. She gripped for a hold on reality, needing evidence the *Dark Thing* was gone. She gripped until the cup burst.

I used the blanket to quickly soak up the hot liquid before it scalded her. Her eyes looked up and spoke to me. They shouted! *Look at me, Michael! Read my thoughts. Can't explain. Can't talk. Help me. Help me.*

I saw in her screaming eyes the same fear I suffered two Easters ago — the first time I encountered the Beast. I answered her begging eyes without words, assuring in gestures, "*I know, Sharon. I know. Me, too.*"

When she could talk, all she demanded was answers. "Michael, what's going on? What was that thing? If you know something, *tell* me."

"Okay. Okay. I'll tell you what I can."

I crawled over to Sharon, who sat on the bed's edge. She was physically wrecked, mentally shot. I gently brushed her hair. I wiped her tears. I kissed her on both cheeks. I held her trembling hands.

Delving into her laboring eyes, I said slowly and profoundly, "Listen very carefully."

CHAPTER 12
Demon Priests and Holy Evil

*56 B.C.
Western Europe*

There were demon priests in the ancient days. At least they claimed to be human descendants of Dis Pater, the King of the Underworld—their chief demon. Most historians call them by their more common name, Druids. They are the oldest known religion in the world. They probably originated in Mesopotamia, a gateway between the ancient middle east of Biblical times and barbaric Europe. As a nomadic peoples, they never fully established themselves until they migrated to the black forests of ancient Germain, and more so when they continued on to the isolated isles of what is now Great Britain. Protected by the English Channel from the various conquering empires who traipsed across Europe throughout history, the Druids had the rare opportunity to flourish relatively untouched by civilization once they organized themselves in Britannia.

Hence, not a great deal is known about them today. They shrouded themselves in secrecy. They congregated in deep oak groves, and their grotesque rituals were seldom witnessed. They preserved their primeval mysteries by word of mouth. Seldom did they take a chance to record anything.

What little is known about them is credited to the journals of General Julius Caesar. He and his mighty Legions swept through all of Europe, conquering the barbaric tribes and taking their land in the name of Rome. Caesar was skilled in using FEAR as a weapon. His massive drum corps taunted his opposing forces; their pounding vibrations rocked the very earth his enemies had dug into for a desperate last stand against them. And their colorful pennants and brilliantly red uniforms were hardly meant to camouflage his troops for a sneak attack.

Caesar smashed through Europe with the most proficient military machine ever assembled. When his numerous Legions approached the battle lines, Caesar cockily telegraphed every step he advanced, in order to instill maximum terror into his enemy. Often, the only battles fought were against the backs of men who fled in a panic at the sights and sounds of Rome coming to conquer.

There was no dishonor in retreating from Caesar. In fact, fleeing from his presence was advisable, for Caesar displayed no mercy with those who chose to oppose him. As a warning to future enemies to surrender without a fight, it was Caesar's policy to torture to death those who had chosen to fight.

Such was the case when Caesar chased the ancient Keltic tribes across the European continent. Although fierce by nature, the barbaric Kelts could not withstand the might of modern Rome. Finally, Caesar pressed the Kelts to the sea, and chased after them when they fled to the Isles of Brittany, their last stand.

But it was the Roman Legions who collided with Terror. They, themselves, fled in disarray. Scared. Very scared, when the demon priests of the Kelts made themselves known. The first historical encounter with the Druids was not a pleasant sight.

Wrote Caesar, "Omnis natio Gallorum admodum dedita religionbus. (The whole nation of the Gauls is very much given to religion). Dryades sunt quae quercibus delectantur. Sacrorum Dryades sine templis colebant deos in silvis (The Druids are those who delight in oaks. They attend upon the gods in woods without making use of temples)."

In their holy oak groves, the Fid Nemeds, not even the Druids dared to reside. The oak groves were only for worshipping. They sculptured grotesque gods from oaks, which they revered. They continuously soaked these oak gods in the moist blood of their enemies. Blood was so vital to *their oaken gods, that if a shortage of adversaries existed, the demon priests sacrificed their own people for a fresh supply. So much did they worship the wisdom of oaks, they seldom performed any rite without at least the presence of an oak branch.*

The Druids were those of high class, recruited from the elite. They were exempt from paying taxes to the Tribes, and were also exempt from military duties. Druids were political leaders. The lawmakers. The judges. The executioners. They were physicians, and excelled in the art of poisoning those who conspired against them. Most of all, they had the knowledge of the oaks, the wisdom of The Way.

Druids were highly organized. No tribal decisions were made, without first consulting the head priest, the Archdruid. Archdruids were called upon to foretell the future, and human sacrifice was the core of their soothsaying. Prior to the ritual, the demon priest would cross his heart in a "☦" to acknowledge Tammuz, also known as Dis Pater, their Supreme God.

The Druid would approach the random victim—who had been secured in place by Keltic warriors or else tied to a wooden altar—and slice him open at the midriff. The Druid would reach inside and disembowel the victim, throwing his guts to the ground. All this, while he was alive, because it was the squirming of the victim that determined how the entrails would be read for signs. If the sacrificial hostage also happened to be an enemy, they would drug him, to ease the pain and to keep him conscious long enough to view the horrors of watching his guts being cannibalized, as if slurping a plate of delicious spaghetti. Good Things.

During their rites, the Druids were generally entranced, having given over their bodies to the demons through wild incantations. Their minds, also, were given to their gods in an act of blind obedience. In a deeply sublimable state, they would grip oak branches and flagellate their bodies until their skin wore thin and blood flowed, as a token of love to their God of the Underworld. Then, they would slice open their victim.

First-born males were also important to Druids. They were snatched from their mothers' bosoms and slaughtered in the groves to sanctify them. All subsequently born males were similarly taken from their mothers and given over to Druidic teachers, who raised them in the secret ways until adulthood, at which time they'd return to their parents.

Of course, some of them were needed to burn in the giant wickers they had made as offerings to Dis Pater. Death was honorable. Their severed heads were embalmed and hung with dignity. Others endured the burning sacrifices while still alive, and their bravery was passed on, as the others ate their charred remains.

When Caesar eventually subdued the Kelts and carried their Druids back to Rome, even the most ruthless line of Roman Emperors vomited at their barbarisms. Rome—vicious, merciless Rome—outlawed Druidic practices as being brutally inhumane. Rome forced the Druids underground, to carry on in secrecy throughout the centuries.

However, tell-tale signs of their continued existence prevailed. After performing their gruesome rituals, they would mark a token symbol. They would draw a circle, and enclose three sixes. Each number "6" shared its circular bottom portion, and thereby formed a smaller circle within the circle. Then, they'd extend the top half of each "6" to the outer circle like a spoke on a bike, spaced individually in a triangular pattern. Thus, no matter which way the Druidic wheel rotated, three sixes were identifiable: right-side up; upside-down; sideways. An upside down six was equally holy as a regular six, as long as it comprised part of the group of three: 666, 999, 696. All combinations of three sixes or three nines were holy to Druids.

Further, the demon priests left behind another calling card for historians. Although they seldom wrote, the Druids did inscribe their name upon several altar ruins across Europe. On the rare occasions when they did spell out words for others to read, they used the more common language of their day, a now ancient form of Greek. Druids preferred the title of "Oak Priest," for they alone had the wisdom symbolized by ageless oaks. Oak Priests claimed Supreme knowledge of the origins and workings of the universe. They knew, The Way. Their written name was:

War of the Angels

"Opus Dai"

There were two orders of Druids: (1) the *Opus Dai*, who were carried away to Rome, where they adapted to Roman culture and went underground; and, (2) a more powerful and more dreaded band of demon priests, who remained behind in the Scottish Highlands.

Strange, those Scottish Rite Druids. Even the Opus Dai feared them. Their Kelts built a stone wall, so as not to be foolish enough to venture into their territory. And although Opus Dai was more terrifying and wicked as anyone Rome had encountered, not even they dared to trespass the wall of terror. Evil resided there. Evil too great, even for those priests possessed by the darkest of demons. Julius Caesar stopped at the wall, also, never venturing to conquer beyond, where evil lived.

They had a name for those on the evil side. They did not require oak groves, but rather, they worshipped within circular configurations of stone pillars. They were the wealthiest of the wealthy; the most powerful of the tribal families. The darkest of the dark, and the keepers of the keys to Evil. And they assembled each May 1, in a show of brotherhood.

They became known as the May-Sons, or Maisons. And there existed a slight quirk in their language that easily distinguished them from the Opus Dai Druids. Opus Dai's alphabet included a "Q" sound, but the druids on the evil side of the wall substituted a "PP" for the "Q."

For this reason, they became known as:

"PP Maisons."

I allowed Sharon access to my private journals in those early morning hours. I let her read a final warning from Pope John Paul I, before he mysteriously died. His declaration that the Holy Roman Church had been overrun by:

Opus Dei **and the** *P2 Masons.*

The Catholic Church, itself, had dubbed them as *Anti-Christians who blasphemed the Bible*. And look at this," I told Sharon. "It's Opus Dei's own, separate Bible."

THE WAY:
999 Ways to Holiness
Become A Leader of Men, A Leader of Nations.

Maxim 949:
"Obey your superiors blindly. This is the way to holiness."

"That's not the way to holiness," I told Sharon. "That's Satanic. It's the Druidic philosophy. And look how they utilize the Druidic 666 wheel so often." And I explained how modern Opus Dei was founded.

1926
Madrid, Spain

It was a morning not much different than any other morning for José Escriva, as the ambitious, young attorney prepared for another day's work. He bathed, then stood naked in front of the mirror. He whipped his shaving cream until it foamed up ready to use, then splashed his face from a bowl of fresh water.

Suddenly, he saw something in the mirror behind him. He turned. He set down his shaving tools. An Alien Being had unexpectedly paid him a visit in the bathroom.

The Alien Being assured José that it was a Good Thing, and told him to take a new path in his life. It demanded that José do as it said. He should follow its instructions—obey blindly—and José would be greatly rewarded. He would gain control of the world in the name of "Opus Dei." He'd be recognized as the Father of the Perfect Society, with wealth and power.

José believed what the Good Thing told him. Would a Good Thing tell a lie? Besides, Alien Beings certainly had greater wisdom than simple men. So José obeyed. Blindly.

As a pact, the Alien Being commanded that José perform a ritual of Good Things. Out of love. From the goodness of the Good Thing's extraterrestrial heart.

And because the Good Thing obviously loved and cared for him, José obeyed. He picked up his razor and gouged it across his chest. Then he sliced his arms and legs. Again and again. For love, understand. Escriva's body anguished from the deep cuts in his flesh. His body ran red, and he coated himself in his freshly smeared blood. The Good Thing was pleased. It loved young José, but wanted further proof of Jose's love, in return.

José gripped the razor strop firmly in his hands and beat himself. Leather popped against his bare back. Again. Harder. More love. Deeper love. Skin ripped from his body. Blood splashed the bathroom walls and ceiling. José cried out what a Good Thing it was to suffer for the Alien. He whipped and whipped in a masochistic display of love for the Good Thing.

The bathroom was heavily streaked with blood. The floor ran red. Pieces of torn flesh, ripped ligaments, and battered muscle tissue pelted the room. José collapsed.
Good Things. Very Good Things, indeed.
And every year—and randomly more—Opus Dei members were to beat themselves in a similar display of love for the Good Thing who'd visited their founder that morning in Madrid, Spain. To torture themselves, until they, too, were embroidered in a reddened sheath of love. And to further display their affection on a daily basis, by wearing sharp metal pricks strapped between their groins as a constant reminder of the Good Thing's loving nurtures.

MAXIM 208:
> "Blessed by pain. Loved by pain. Sanctified be pain. Glorified be pain!"

But the Catholic Church chastised Opus Dei. They were not Christian at all, they said.

> "It's best to steer clear of Opus Dei."
> (Father Andrew Greeley)

Neither Sharon nor I slept. We spent the remaining hours of darkness exchanging personal revelations. The most bizarre comment tumbled off Sharon's lips, after my lengthy supposition of Opus Dei and the P2 Masons. I had ask her if she believed me, and if she had ever heard of Opus Dei before tonight.

Sharon's eyes widened. She bit her lip until it turned white and I thought she'd tear the skin. She muttered like a hurt puppy and cried. "I believe you." She nodded her head, yes. She *had* heard of Opus Dei.

She simply and sincerely mumbled, "I believe you because they killed my best girlfriend last year."

Her friend had been dating a member of Opus Dei. She'd approached Sharon one evening with crazy accusations about him, begging for help. But Sharon disregarded her friend's silly pleas. Sharon did not believe in Bad Things back then. She told her friend that she was probably just upset and needed rest. Sharon gave her a *"What probably happened was ..."*

Then her friend was murdered. Sharon became a believer.

"That's who killed my friend. It was Opus Dei. They said she died of a drug overdose. She didn't *do* drugs. Opus Dei killed her."

"Why?"

"I don't know. I didn't believe her. She was trying to tell me something but I didn't pay attention."

***

"Sharon, you know that book I'm writing about the *U.S.S. Indianapolis*?"

"Uh-huh."

"I want you to listen to something." I played my Hafford Sharp interview tapes for Sharon, but this time instead of hearing about the U.S.S. *Indianapolis*, we listened to the end tape—the one about *Bad Things*.

We listened as Hafford suddenly switched subjects, and for no apparent reason—off the wall, out of the clear blue—spoke of the supernatural.

> *"There are demons in the world. Fallen angels. Disembodied spirits. And they're setting a stage. They're running the governments of the world. They're determining the economics of the world. They're invading the highest authorities on Earth, all in preparation of (a time period of the Antichrist known as) 'The Great Tribulation.' Of course, the thing they do best, you understand, is to make people think they don't exist. They operate much more efficiently if everyone leaves them alone, which most people do because they think the whole idea is a joke. We've been brought up to think that the idea of a real devil is untrue; that he's a cartoon character in a red suit, with horns and a pointed tail, carrying a pitchfork. That's how most people see the devil.*

> "But he's real. Satan is real, his Antichrist is real, and his demons are real. Just as real as the two of us sitting here. And he's coming. He's coming for certain, no matter what anyone believes. And he's bringing with him so much fear and evil that people who are still here will be begging to die."

After all the years that had gone by, Hafford's earnest and hypnotic tones still made my bones chill. Hafford made both Sharon and me queasy, listening to ominous warnings about *Bad Things* as if they were ... real?

The tape ran its course and clicked off before Hafford finished. Much of what he had said had gone unrecorded. There were times I would have telephoned Hafford, but I was too embarrassed about four years having vanished without my U.S.S. *Indianapolis* manuscript being written. I had failed, was ashamed of myself, and believed Hafford would have no confidence in me. Besides, I wasn't sure where to locate him, if he had moved on or what. That's what I had told myself, at least. Maybe I just hoped that everything would simply go away. So I never spoke with Hafford again until 1990 at an *Indianapolis* Survivor's reunion. I also would notice at that reunion that he was not the lanky, calm Southerner that I had known from our interviews, but rather someone who was a mental wreck and a bundle of nerves. He relived the fear at the reunion. I was reliving the fear listening to his tapes about evil.

"Is the Pope actually a member of Opus Dei?" asked Sharon.
"If he is, he'd never say."

The Constitution of Opus Dei:
98.1. "After initiation, members may not leave of their own accord."

191. "Members must never reveal the names of other members and must never admit that they themselves are members."

"What's going on, Michael? What's this got to do with us?"

"I don't know."

After conversing the night away, Sharon and I passed out from exhaustion. Our minds and bodies had been overwrought. We did not awaken until the sun had come and gone again, when our eyes slipped open on Sunday, November 23, 1980.

We could not talk anymore about Bad Things. We simply couldn't. We needed to think about Good Things—have some fun. Sharon wanted to go bowling. It was her favorite activity. She bounced out of bed and insisted we go.

"Bowling?" Smoke-filled, beer-laden bowling alleys seemed too unsophisticated for a woman of her stature. Did bowling shirts come made in silk? Were bowling shoes styled in three-inch heels? A sequined glove? Resin bag by Gucci? No, and it seemed queer to watch Sharon squeeze into ragged old jeans, a loose blouse, and sneakers.

"Wouldn't you rather go into Chicago for a play or something?" I hadn't bowled since childhood. I would have rather done something I excelled at, to impress her. "Have you bowled much? What's your average?"

"About two hundred. I grew up bowling. Ma used to bowl professionally."

This won't do, won't do at all, I thought. She intimidated me when she went to the car and got her bowling bag out of the trunk. Our relationship hung in the balance, I believed. If a woman loved dancing, she expected her man to be a good dancer. Or, if she was a movie-buff, she'd expect her man to enjoy movies. Same with the ballet, if she was a ballet-buff; or with gardening, if she was a gardening-buff; or *whatever*, in *any*-buff. Women preferred their men to be *likewise*-buffed. And I was definitely not *bowling*-buffed.

Fortunately it did not matter to Sharon whether I could bowl well or not, as long as she got to bowl all night, as the *"All-Nite Bowling"* sign claimed. Mostly she bowled by herself, as my arm gave way to overexertion.

I sat and watched. On and on, set them up, knock them down. She even strolled back to the table to mark her own score. But she eventually quit out of pity for me.

"Don't stop on my account," I said, changing shoes, happily.

She said, "Okay," and bowled several more games.

When we pulled into the parking lot at home, Sharon put her arms around me before I got out of the car. She kissed me passionately. "Thanks for taking me bowling. I know I put you through a lot."

"Let's go in," I suggested.

"No. You look good in a Cadillac."

"Thank you, but I'd still like to get out of the car."

"*No.*" Play time ended abruptly. She bolted upright and said seriously, "I don't want to go in there."

"Why?"

"I know," she said, changing the subject, "let's make love in the car."

"Can't we go in?"

"No. Right here in the car. We can hop in back if you want."

"I want to go in, if you don't mind. What's the big deal?" I opened the car door and gently coaxed her arm.

Sharon resisted. She had something to say, and she held both sides of my face, glaring at me (*watch my lips*) to avoid any misunderstanding or have any doubt of her seriousness. She exclaimed: "Don't make me go in there!"

I released her, thinking she'd wake the neighbors. "What's the matter?"

"I got bad vibes about going in there." She unbuttoned her blouse to entice me to stay in the car. "Only until daylight. It won't be long."

But I prevailed. With Sharon protesting every step, we went inside.

I hopped onto the bed, much more awake now than I had been at the bowling alley.

Sharon slumped to the floor, in the middle of the room, ten feet from me. She didn't say a word; she just plopped down for no reason.

"Aren't you coming to bed?"

She ignored me. She crossed her legs and assumed a yoga position. Sharon didn't *know* yoga. She faced me as if to converse, but said nothing. She twitched uncomfortably. Perspired heavily.

I scooted to the edge of the bed and observed her strange behavior. I had seen that trance once before, and it frightened me. "Sharon, are you okay?"

"Noooohhh. I do not like this place. It is *eee-vil*."

"Come here. You just need a good back rub."

Suddenly, her eyes rolled upward. No brown, all white. She tilted her head to the side. She spoke harshly to me. The Voice came from the pit of her stomach, in a hard, masculine, grunt. "I do not need *anything*! I do not need *you*! I do not need *anybody*!"

Angry. Hateful. Foul-mouthed.

I retreated across the bed, scared. The Voice inside Sharon laughed at me. Taunted. "Do you know who I am?" The same question as the previous time, only the Voice was not the same. A different *something* spoke *through* Sharon.

"Who are you?" I wanted to know what it was.

Nothing but laughter. Horrid, unfunny laughter.

"Sharon! Sharon!" I reached out to touch her, but her violent reaction backed me off. She swiped at me viciously.

I retreated back on the bed, and Sharon resumed her yoga position, relaxed. She did not say anything else. She just stared at me. An empty look, as if she did not see me.

"Oh Jesus help me," I said.

"I do not like what you are saying," said the Voice coming from Sharon. The Voice cursed me. Spewed hateful, whorehouse-locker room words at me.

"Sharon. Listen to me. Please listen to me. Sharon, please—LISTEN TO ME!" I grieved for her, like a parent helplessly watching a sick child in convulsion.

Then she quit. "Michael, why are you shaking? Are you okay?"

I looked at her. I did not reply immediately. Why the sudden concern? Who was speaking? Sharon, or the other thing inside her?

Blood ran profusely from her nose and across her lips.

"What's happening?" she asked, in her normal voice. She had no recollection. "God, I'm bleeding to death." She jumped up and darted to the bathroom for some tissues.

She came back, still compressing the blood in her nose. With curious eyes peeking from around the red-stained tissues held to her face, she stared at me and mumbled, "Ca we go oo a otel? I on't ike itz p'wace."

I agreed. We left. Sharon never set foot in my apartment again, and I, only long enough to move.

CHAPTER 13
The Pit and the Dark Assassin

I did not like that apartment. Maybe it *was* evil. Maybe it *wasn't*. To me, it did not matter much *where* I lived— Bad Things dogged right along. Sharon insisted a change of scenery was in order. She warned me that if I stayed in my Chicagoland apartment she would never see me again. On December 1, 1980, I got out.

I called Be-Bop and told her that the airline school was transferring me to Kentucky; she would need to find another job, so she could finish paying her tuition. I did not tell her anything else about why I was *really* leaving town. It was best not to scare her needlessly; her basement demon was long gone, and nothing further had bothered her. I owed her one more paycheck and I promised to mail it to her after I settled into my new place in Kentucky.

Then I loaded up to move, something I had done often. I had already packed everything but my lampshade. By tradition, the old, yellow-tainted lampshade—unattached to the base—was always last because of its bulkiness. To me, packing my lampshade symbolized the end of one personal era, and the ushering in of another.

As always, I would take with me only that which I could dubiously squeeze into my car; personal belongings were for *normal* people who had never encountered alien beings. This time I left behind a bed, the first I had slept on in ages, although it was only a ragged foam rubber mattress thrown on top of a simple metal frame. I also abandoned a desk, a homemade one I had purchased for ten dollars in a garage sale. And another cheap set of golf clubs (I had left a set in every city, though I don't recall having ever played golf).

But of all the things I had ever left behind, the most important was another lost dream. My dream of finding a permanent home and settling down. My dream of emulating the laughter from nameless neighbors whom I tearfully envied in every new place I ventured.

I dented the lampshade as I forced it over the front seat of my car and into the back. I had often thought about ditching it, thinking it would not fit, but I had always managed to squeeze it in at the last moment by squashing it along its now permanent crease. I got in the car and slammed the door shut. I sat tall in the seat and breathed in the factory-stained air of Chicagoland for the last time. I pulled out of the parking lot and said goodbye forever to Nowhere Indiana, Outside Chicago.

I was on my way to Lexington, Kentucky, with a brief stopover in Indianapolis to pick up Sharon, who would have to sit in the tiny space I left vacant in the front.

But my dreams were crushed before I even arrived at my destination. Sharon changed her mind. She stayed behind in Indianapolis. She was afraid of making a lasting commitment with someone. She was afraid of leaving her mother and daughter. But more than all else, Sharon said that she was afraid of the Dark Things who battled me and anyone who got near. Worse, she admitted fear of *me*. She kissed me goodbye and said, "I love you. Believe me, I love you. But I can't go with you, and I know you don't understand."

I fought back tears, until I reached the privacy of my car, which I now felt was packed with meaningless nothings. The drive to Lexington was lonely, even with all the cars zipping by.

When I reached my new apartment, I felt sure I was unloading my old lampshade for the last time. I had found a permanent home. I even looked forward to trashing my lampshade, as soon as I purchased all new furniture, as I knew I would.

Afternoon wore into evening, as I piled everything out of the car and into the living room in a bedlam heap. I was too tired to unpack and rearrange. I would sort it all out tomorrow, except for one important box I found a proper place for that very minute.

As the lampshade had always gone into the car last, my secret papers on the U.S.S. *Indianapolis* had always been the first to find its permanent spot, once inside a new home. Tradition bade me to locate an immediate, safe storage area for my papers: this time for certain, I would finish writing my book about the U.S.S. *Indianapolis* (another continuing promise that always came with new territory).

I sweat profusely, lugging a huge carton of five thousand pages up two flights of stairs. I tucked them away, inside the walk-in closet of my spare bedroom, which would soon be my office. Nothing else mattered as much. I would wait until morning for the rest of my belongings. It had been a long, rough day. The nice, hot shower I craved was also placed on tomorrow's busy agenda. I was way too tired to find the shower curtain and towels. It was bed time.

I unrolled the fuzzy green blanket that I used as a mattress. I spread it neatly over the carpeted floor, and threw my only sheet on top. I unfolded a crinkled brown cover to pull over my naked body. I slept soundly.

I had lost at love, but tomorrow promised the birth of a new life, without the Shroud Man, the Beast, or the Dark World. But the road from the Dark World led to everywhere. And I had been followed.

***

Late that night while I slept, the Shroud Man tugged gently on my mind, awakening my spirit, without disturbing my body. It spun my brain faster and faster, until it separated my soul and body. As before, the Shroud Man escorted my soul to the Dark World and left my body behind.

But on this excursion the Shroud Man detoured off the main highway of the Dark World, to a place where no roads went in, no roads came out. Getting there was by special escort only. He led me to a place in the Dark World where not even Bad Things wanted to visit. My sense of Knowing warned me, before we had even reached our destination. Knowing told me that we were approaching a Dark World dungeon. A Keep, where Evil had been taken prisoner of war by the Shroud Man. To a place more secure than Alcatraz, where no Thing had ever left, once inside. Angel prisoners of war.

"Do not worry," was all the Shroud Man said. He lowered me into a large, dark Pit. I squirmed in defiance, grasping at air to avoid going into the dungeon. Once I was inside, the Shroud Man abandoned me.

But I was not alone. My "sight" adjusted rapidly in the darkness. I would have preferred not seeing what I saw. The Pit was somewhere underneath the deepest of the Dark World. The walls were well defined, though not visible. Cubical, not too wide, but very deep as if it had no bottom. I could have dropped a pebble and listened for the rest of my life, without ever having heard the echo of it striking bottom.

The Pit With No Bottom was inhabited by some very strange and scary looking creatures. There were hundreds—THOUSANDS—of them! More than thousands! An entire civilization of creatures. They were all shapes and sizes, and they were quite ugly. They were not like the Dark Angels I had seen before on previous journeys. These creatures were all very different from the generic Shadows of the other Alien Beings. These had definitive features. These beings had faces, noses, and bodies, only their bodies looked painfully distorted.

I noticed one had a long, dog-like snout. Another had abbreviated ears atop its head—reminding me of pig ears—although the creature who wore them was certainly no pig. All of them appeared to be reptilian in nature, with scales, instead of skin. Some were dark green, some dull brown. I hadn't noticed colors before in the Dark World, but now I did, though none were brilliant, and all were dull or drab.

The inhabitants of the Pit With No Bottom were all four-legged creatures, but they stood mostly on their back-quarters, while working their upper two feet as if they were hands. And they were old. Many were wrinkled as if they had grown ancient in the Pit that imprisoned them. Their worn scales overlapped into aging folds. I wondered how long they had been imprisoned there, as I drifted high above them out of harms way, observing.

They wantonly eyed me like I was their key to freedom. They pawed at me with sharp claws, wanting to pull me down to a vengeful death, as if I had been responsible for their dreadful predicament. They uttered various sounds: some gurgled, some squealed in high-pitches, some in low-pitches.

They were all climbing on top of one another trying to reach me. I don't know what they were standing on since the Pit had no bottom, but I wasn't going down there to find out. Then frightfully I sank, slowly, like a helium balloon with a tiny leak. I inched downward to their murderously outstretched limbs. They pawed and gnashed, but still could not touch me. Something held them back, like an invisible buffer. I was terrified amidst them, even though I was shielded by something and they were not hurting me. I searched for an escape, but there was none.

The Shroud Man returned. He was the only Being who could come and go as he pleased. The prison warden with the only set of keys. He lifted me from the Pit, and sent me home to my body.

***

Horrified, I blocked the Pit Creatures out of my mind quicker than Hafford Sharp forgot about sharks. *Poof ... gone. Nobody home, Mr. Fear. Gone Fishin'. Sweep the Bad Things under the carpet. Stuff them into the closet. Hide them under the pillow.* That was the only way I coped with my horrors, same as Hafford Sharp. How often I had thought about Hafford when situations grew beyond human help.

When the days wore on, my fearful ordeals faded into nothings. The Pit With No Bottom? Pit Creatures? I locked those bad memories into a lead safe and sank them to the far depths of my consciousness. I conveniently forgot.

And then Sharon called. She said a "Voice" told her to read something to me from the Bible. Bull! I wanted no reminders and did not want to hear it. But I did anyway:

Sharon read:
> "The Beast that thou sawest ... shall ascend out of the bottomless pit ... and they that dwell

> on Earth shall wonder ... when they behold the Beast." (Revelations 17:8)

I supposed that is why Sharon received mystical messages. I needed a second opinion, and she had been drafted into a spiritual army to provide confirmation. That is why she feared to be around me because unexplainable things happened. Then again, she felt compelled to return.

On December 6, Sharon re-decided to come live with me in Kentucky. I was to pick her up in Indianapolis, next week. Sharon's return was all I could think about. I had no room for Dark World thoughts. My mind was cluttered with Sharon. She was coming back.

She would have preferred Texas, but having been to Lexington once before, she thought it looked cozy—nice, clean. A cute little city that catered to the pleasures of the many wealthy people who resided there. Lexington seemed like an oasis amidst the isolated coal fields of the Appalachians. And its green pastures were enhanced by white picket fences along its perimeters to protect the valuable grazing lands of the town's main industry, race horses.

But of all the beauty in Lexington, the one place that caught my eye was the bowling alley on the loop. Seeking a way to kill the Eternal Week I had to wait before picking up Sharon, I vowed to earn a spot in her heart and get *bowling-buffed*.

I bowled most of the night away, trying to build up my stamina for the game, to keep up with Sharon. My scores vastly improved, and the number of games I could roll, greatly increased. Nonetheless, I sorely toggled home and groaned in pain when my aching shoulder was put to bed on the hard floor.

***

When the Shroud Man visited me for the second time in my new apartment, I fought him. I wanted the ordeals to end. I wanted a new life, free of beasts, and dark things, and shroud men. I resisted strenuously, as much as I had on that first evening at Patrick's place. A flood of bad memories from my last journey awakened me. I opened my eyes. I wasn't going. No way, Man.

The Shroud Man was equally determined. He reapplied the nauseating pressure that had forced me into submission on my first venture. I grimaced from the sickening tension. My eyes rolled to the back of their sockets. At that point, the spinning resumed, and the Shroud Man slid my spirit from my body and into the tunnel. At the other side, the Shroud Man released the pressure and vanished.

I felt resentment, similar to a child who had been wrongly punished by a loving parent. I did not feel hatred for the Shroud Man, but I did exhibit dislike for what he had done to me. Nothing good ever happened in the Dark World. I did not understand the punishment. Why the continued journeys? Once more, Little Mikey was by his lonesome in the Dark World.

Hey, wait a minute! Mikey wasn't Little. Not on this journey. "Knowing" told me. A keen new sense had been added to my repertoire of Dark World attributes. It was exhilarating! It was Power!

I moved, unafraid, exalted by my awesome strength and courage. I no longer drifted, but rather soared through the Dark World, self-assured. I had never done that before. Then I saw it. A Dark Thing, far away.

As with the Bad Thing I had encountered in Be-Bop's basement, this creature also feared me and fled. But its evasive maneuvers only stimulated my newly discovered Powers, and I felt as a lion who spotted game taking flight. I had to chase it. It was my nature. I existed to hunt Dark Things. Before, with the Bad Thing in Be-Bop's basement, I tracked it only out of curiosity. And in the end, I let it go. But this was not the same. I wanted to kill it.

This Dark Thing was very much afraid of me and soared at twice the speed of the first one I had encountered. However, its quickness made no difference to me. I knew I could chase it down and cut it off whenever I wanted. In fact, I prolonged the chase. I pursued at a slight distance, hanging back to study.

The Dark Thing was a semi-formless, gray shadow. It had a bounded shape, yet no clear-cut features. It had a round head, except for two short protrusions on top, something resembling stubs. It had no arms, but it did have curvatures suggesting shoulders. Its body tapered to a single point where it should have had feet, but didn't. It moved in a flowing manner, rapidly, as it emitted a high-pitched squeal.

It seemed to know I wanted to kill it. It zoomed up, down, around, dodging me. Whenever I advanced, it retreated in haste. I savored its recognition of my Power! Then it stopped running. It suddenly whirled around to face me, head-on.

I engaged my brakes. "Knowing" told me I faced a Fallen Angel of a different order, of higher rank. I froze, gazing into the holes in the Fallen Angel's head. Unlike the empty eyes of the Shroud Man, these more resembled hollow slits, than eye sockets.

The Dark Angel locked-into my dumbfounded stare and fired an invisible bolt of energy from its slits that surged through my eyes and lodged deeply into my bowels. It hit with such force, I tumbled across the Dark World. I had tremendous pain in my stomach. I was seriously hurt.

I burned from the inside, out. It was not the same as a fire burn. It was similar to how a steel knife blade could feel "cold" on the outside of the skin, yet be "burning hot" once it penetrated the flesh. What I felt was intensely hot. My insides were melting.

I was too stunned and crippled to flee, as the demonic assassin sped after me. The Dark Angel closed for the kill, making frightful grunts and groans. With superior skills, it swarmed over me, maneuvering for an opening.

I knew better than to confront it head-on again; the eye slits were its weapons, and the Dark Angel needed to penetrate my eyes in order to blast me. I humbly covered my face in fear and pain, turning my back. I twisted and turned. Away, away. That was all I knew how to do, was to turn my back.

Swiftly, it broke my defense and zoomed around to the front. It locked-in for another assault. Its force penetrated my eyes before I had time to react. Again, the burning power surged downward to my midriff, as I tried unsuccessfully to regurgitate it.

I was about to explode from the combustible energy that pressurized inside me, when "Knowing" instructed me. Suddenly, I abandoned my meager defenses. I no longer *sought to cover up: I attacked! My surprising change of tactics startled the Dark Angel. I faced it head-on, in Battle Position.*

I raised my arms overhead and stretched them high. I flattened my hands and turned my palms over, facing upward. I was an antennae, reaching to gather energy beams from the Shroud Man. I was a lightning rod begging to be struck.

External Power from the Shroud Man rushed through my upturned palms, down my outstretched arms, and into my body and to my midriff. There, it engaged the stream of invading energy from the Dark Angel. My borrowed Force expelled the Dark Angel's power by pushing it upward from my intestinal pit, until it exited my bulging eyes.

Our opposing powers, mine and the Dark Angel's, collided outside our bodies, halfway between us. Then I stretched my arms again. The higher I raised them, the more Power I received from the Shroud Man.

My eyes thrust open, and an eerie barrage of energy spilled forth, toward the Dark Angel. It was not laser power, nor light, nor beams of any kind. It was not anything I could see. And it wasn't sound. It wasn't electrical energy, either. It was simply awesome Power!

The Power lanced its target, the eye slits. It raced down its innards, where it glowed an unearthly orange, then red from the heat gnawing at its guts. Its insides grew redder, hotter. The Dark Angel squirmed, suffering. Then it happened. Spontaneous combustion. A gaseous ball of fire erupted. A miniature, white-hot Sun engulfed the Dark Angel, in continually burning flames.

But strangely, the fire did not consume its victim. The Dark Angel did not die, although it wanted to. It suffered horribly, still alive and still burning. It tried to scream, only nothing came out. Its previously rounded face, distorted itself, twisting in agony. Suddenly, another burst of energy struck the Dark Angel. Only I hadn't done it. The Shroud Man returned and fired a bolt, causing the burning Dark Angel to soar far away, to the outer parts of darkness until it was out of sight, cast beyond the boundaries of the Dark World. Imprisoned forever in a ball of fire.

***

The Shroud Man helped me back into my body. In bed, I opened my eyes. I had been thrust into some kind of spiritual battle between the Shroud Man and the Beast. I had been shown how angels fight. My insides pained greatly, and I sorely moved. It would take me many days to recover. A continuous reminder of the reality I could not deny.

I didn't need an ominous call from Sharon to convince me. But I got one, nonetheless. "The Voice", she said, "told me to read this to you.

> *"And they had a king over them, which is the angel of the bottomless pit, whose name in the Hebrew tongue is Abaddon, but in the Greek tongue hath his name Apollyon (the Destroyer)."* (Revelations 9:11)

CHAPTER 14
Christmas Terror

Every time I denied something, Sharon fired a supernatural message at me. I grew to depend on her. Somehow I felt safer with her around. For more than obvious reasons, I was happy when the time came to go get her.

It was Friday evening, December 12, when we reunited in Indianapolis. Her things were packed, and I wanted to load them in the car and head straight back to Lexington. But instead, we went bowling at one of Indy's all-night lanes. Sharon bowled into pre-dawn Saturday, the thirteenth, while I struggled to keep my eyes opened at the scorer's table.

Sharon's eyes were focused intently on a five-seven split. She was on the verge of bowling her high game of the evening—well into the mid-two hundreds—and she needed only to pick up a critical and difficult spare. Suddenly, she broke her icy concentration. She stopped her approach, lowered her ball into a resting position, and walked back to me and said, "I love you."

She had interrupted her bowling to tell me. That is how I knew her words had not been a case of sunrise-insanity, to be undone at noon. "I really, really, love you," she told me. And although I never scored in bed that evening because we had taken up temporary living quarters at the bowl-a-rama, I did score a two hundred, bowled about twelve thousand games before tiring, and won Sharon's heart. I was *officially* bowling-buffed.

(And Sharon picked up the spare.)

"Do you mind if I bowl by myself now?" asked Sharon. "I can go faster." She rolled a few more games, then we went for breakfast—which was actually our dinner, since getting to the lanes in time to beat the waiting list had received a higher priority than had eating. We finally got to her house at nearly eleven o'clock, and it was time for me to go in and meet her family—having bowled a two hundred, and all.

Reba, or simply "Ma," was pretty at forty-nine, but she could have been prettier. Her hair was colored a dull, truck-stop diner black, and not styled. She retained a shapely figure, but her simple, loosely worn slacks and blouse toned down her appeal. Sharon's eleven year old daughter described Grandma as *"Cotton,"* and Mom as *"Silk."* She was correct.

"Where's Jodi?" inquired Sharon about her daughter.

"She's out skating. Where else?"

"I wanted her to meet Michael." Then she turned to me and said, "She got such a thrill helping me open all those greeting cards you sent last week."

KA-BOOM!
KA-BAM!

Jodi hit the front door like Godzilla stepping out from the sea and into downtown Tokyo. "Mom, I need five bucks."

"Well, hello to you, too."

"Hi. Like hurry up, I'm going skating."

"I thought you were already skating."

"That was *street* skating. I came back to get my *rink* skates, okay? Geooodd (God)! Grandma I need five bucks."

"Hey," said Sharon, "how about some manners?"

"Pleeease. Like I'm in a hurry, okay?" She grabbed her skates and changed into her sneakers, while she argued her case.

"Okay," said Sharon, "here's five bucks. And I want you to meet Michael."

"Like, hi. Are you the one who sent all those greeting cards to Mom?"

"Yes, I am, but ..."

"Like, neat. You got five bucks?"

"Jodi!"

"Jodi!" repeated Grandma.

"Geooodd (God)! Like what'd I do?"
"No problem," I said. "Here, you go, Jodi."
"Michael," protested Sharon, "don't give her that."
"It's only five bucks."
"Yeah, Mom, like it's only five bucks. Grandma, I need five bucks."
"Whu ... I can't believe this."
"Come on, Grandma."
"Okay," she said, handing her the five, "but stop calling me, *Grandma*. It makes me feel so old."
"Grandma! Grandma! Grandma! Grandma!"
"Jodi!"
"Grandma! Grandma! Bye everybody."
"Tie your shoes, first," said Sharon, "before you trip and break your neck."
"I can't."
"You can't break your neck?"
"No. I can't tie my shoes. Like it's not *in*."
"Pardon me?"
"It's not *cool*. Like okay?"
"It's not cool to tie your shoes? Tie them."
"Geooodd (God)! Don't you know anything?"
"I know you're going to tie those shoes."
"Geooodd (God)! Like you're so old fashion."
"Old fashioned?" gasped Sharon.
Grandma laughed. "Sounds familiar, huh?"
Sharon stood up. I am *not* old fashion. You come here young lady. You tie those shoes or you're not going, and that's final."
"Geooodd (God)! Everyone'll laugh at me."
"Well, then they'll just have to laugh."
"I'll tell 'em *you* made me, and like, they'll laugh at *you* for being *Old Fashioned*."
"I'm *not* Old Fashion."
"Are too. Are too."
They went into the back room for a lecture. Sharon scolded her about the shoe strings, and also for having asked me for money.
"Geooodd (God)! It was only five bucks, okay? Like he's rich, isn't he?"
"No, he isn't rich. Does everyone have to be rich?"

"Well why do you like him then?"

"If you don't want a *rich* man, you should at least get a *hunk*."

It was true. Sharon could have had a hunk, or she could have had a rich man, or she could have had a rich hunk. Instead, she had me.

Sharon did not answer Jodi because it was impossible to explain to a kid the wonderfulness of two people being *likewise-buffed*. She could have expressed, perhaps, that Jodi might someday meet a man who was neither rich nor a hunk, yet she would be willing to sacrifice her *Prince Charming* for someone who was *skating*-buffed. *Buffs* were important. She could have explained it that way, but to an eleven-year-old, five dollar bills were more easily understood than buffs.

Jodi took the money and ran through the living room yelling, "Grandma! Grandma! Grandma!"

"Stop that!"

"Grandma! Grandma!" Jodi blasted out the front door.

KA-BOOM!
KA-BAM!

"That was my daughter," Sharon informed me, grinning.

"I noticed."

"Michael, I need some sleep and I know you do to. You want to take a nap with me?"

"No, you go ahead and sleep. I'm going to visit my parents, before we go to Lexington in the morning."

"We can see them tonight, can't we?"

"I was hoping you'd go somewhere with me tonight, if you don't mind. It's kind of important."

"Where's that?"

"You remember me telling you about Patrick and David?"

"Your neighbors where you used to live? Yes."

"Well, Patrick's father died."

In spite of his father's long-expected death from cancer, Patrick hosted a Christmas Tree Decorating Party. He desired the company of his many friends to ease his depression. He had been told by friends that his father's eventual death had been a blessing since his cancer had lingered for so long.

War of the Angels

But such endings were never true forms of relief. It was painstaking to hang wreaths and homemade decorations throughout the apartments, but Patrick was bent on having his party, as planned.

Only the landlady—a *Jehovah's Witness* who deplored Christmas as an instrument of the Devil—refused Patrick's invitation. She removed the wreath from her door, and warned her tenants they would all go to hell for celebrating the holidays. Patrick hugged her and gave her a kiss on the cheek. "Merry Christmas, anyway."

The evening was doubly sad because this was also a farewell party for Patrick. He was leaving Apartment One at the end of the month, to move back home and take care of his recently widowed mother.

His mother lived only a few blocks down the street, but Apartment One was the only place he had ever lived away from home. And he shared countless, rich memories with the many friends who gathered to bid farewell to "Patrick's Place."

When Sharon and I arrived, Patrick walked across the crowded room, past the tree decorators and gave me a hug at the door. "Oh, Michael, I'm so glad you made it." I introduced Sharon for the first time. Then I inquired about David's whereabouts. Patrick nearly cried. He tightened his lips and said, "Michael, David moved to California."

"When?"

"Last week. He just needed to get away. Everything's been coming down hard, lately. Oh, Michael, you haven't heard, have you?"

"Heard what?"

"His father went berserk and shot himself."

"He what?"

"And you know what else? David was robbed his second day in San Francisco. His left arm was broken so badly they don't think he'll ever be able to use it again. Oh, and the week before he left Indianapolis, his car was totaled. He wasn't even scratched, but they said it was a miracle he wasn't *killed*. And the license plate of the guy who hit him was, "DAVE 666."

"Oh, God."

Christmas Terror

"David freaked, Michael. He said he can't be around us anymore." It would be years before I learned that David hadn't stayed in California, but had returned to Indianapolis, unbeknownst to Patrick. He'd found another partner and was very much in love with him and did not see Patrick anymore. As far as Patrick and I were concerned David was gone forever, and Patrick would die a few years later without ever knowing his whereabouts. The party was lonely without David.

Guests interrupted our conversation. They mischievously hung ornaments from Patrick's shirt pockets and belt loops, and strung silver icicles on his head and shoulders. "I think they're trying to tell me something. You and Sharon help yourself to refreshments, and join in the decorations." Patrick left us to mingle.

Parting the crowd, I escorted Sharon toward the food and drink in the kitchen. "Hello," I said to the elderly woman standing at the counter. "I bet you're Patrick's mother. I'm Michael—the one who used to live upstairs." I waited for a response, but didn't receive one.

"Hi. Patrick's in the front room." She looked coldly at me with abrupt rudeness. She carried the conversation no further.

Sharon and I shuffled across the room with filled plates and a drink, past the tree decorators and to a seat near Patrick, who paused to take a break from hosting. Sharon took the remaining spot on the sofa, squeezing next to Patrick, while I claimed dibs on my favorite rocker, next to the sofa and Sharon.

I greeted Patrick's three cats—George the Kat's sisters—all of whom balled up safely in the far corner. "Hello, Kitty Pat," I said to my favorite of the litter. Kitty Pat was named for the black mustache on her white face, which looked identical to Patrick's.

"She's the climber," I said to Sharon. "She'll perch on the highest object she can find. She even climbs up to that curtain rod."

"That curtain up there?"

"Yeah. I don't see how she balances on it, but she'll stay up there all day. She even takes naps up there. Don't you, Kitty Pat?" I stood, stepping toward her when I spoke. I extended a loving hand to slick back her fur, just the way she liked. Suddenly, Kitty Pat jumped and hissed at me. She had never done *that* before.

Patrick scolded her. "Kitty Pat, shame on you. That's your Uncle Michael." She ruefully meowed in pain.

"Oh, baby, what's the matter," cooed Patrick.

I reached over again to touch Kitty Pat. Then it happened. A shadowy creature—a charcoal-gray ghost—ripped painfully out of Kitty Pat's body to escape my reaching hand, and scrambled toward the door. It ran toward the exit, but a girl standing in its way screamed, startling everyone in the room, including the ghost cat. The phantom feline changed routes. It ran for its life toward the sofa, veered away from Sharon, jumped onto Patrick's lap, leaped to the floor again, scooted under the coffee table, and disappeared into the kitchen.

A guest said, "God, we just saw a ghost cat!"

"That wasn't a ghost," said Patrick, correcting his friend. Patrick wiped blood from his arm where the demon had cut him, when it scampered across in its frantic bid to escape.

"Oh, yeah? Well, what the hell *was* it then?"

"Something else—in the shape of a cat." He saw how upset his guests were, and added, "Never mind. It's gone."

Sharon's glassy eyes shouted at me in stunned terror. She did not need to speak. Before she could open her trembling lips, I said, "Come on, let's go—we really can't stay. I just wanted you to meet Patrick."

Patrick escorted us to the door, in a show of understanding. He smoothly said, "Let's get together soon." But Patrick and I would *not* get together, soon or otherwise. Circumstance always intervened. That was the last time I ever saw Patrick, and he would die a few years later.

When Patrick closed the door behind us, he turned and bumped into his mother, who had followed him. She startled her son with an ominous warning about me: "Satan is one step behind that boy."

Sharon did not come with me to Lexington directly from Patrick's that night. Rather, she said if she was going to live with me, she would need her own car, which was in for repairs. I had my doubts. She was still upset about the demon cat, although we had seen worse. I only hoped it

Christmas Terror

did not trigger her most dreaded memories. Surprisingly, as of late, she had come to realize that she was a part of whatever it was that was happening, and she knew I needed her. She did, indeed, get her car right out of the shop and head down.

But she moved-in only *some* of her things, far from *all* of her things. I thought long and hard about her implications. I did not bother telling her of my further adventures, since she seemed to have moved in on a trial basis, to see if more ghost cats or shadowy beings would materialize. It was selfish of me to withhold information. Nonetheless, there she was, next to me in my bed-on-the-floor.

In fact, she was in my bed-on-the-floor nearly all week, sick again. She had gotten up only for bathroom duty, except for the one night we went bowling. She was still ailing that night, but she would have made Death wait for a game of bowling. When at long last we made it to the car, she moaned sweetly, "Michael, do you think you could give me a massage when we get home—and use some oil?" She sat there a moment in silence, feeling sickly again. Then she smiled and said, "You bowled pretty well tonight. God, you beat me (one out of infinity). I'm so proud of you, Michael. You practiced just for me, didn't you?" She kissed me.

And for once, the Bad Things left us alone our entire time together in Lexington. Other than for Sharon's illness, which spoiled every night but one. But even her illness suddenly went away by the time Christmas Eve rolled around, when we drove north to celebrate the holidays with our families in Indianapolis. Our troubles were behind, and the mood, bright. Times were nice. Good Things.

Although it was not something I could physically see, I sensed that a Christmas Spirit truly existed. It was in the air. The most joyous season of the year, Christian or not. Good will toward men. Charity. Giving, instead of taking. People forgetting their petty differences and uniting to end worldly oppressions for a day. Bad Things took a leave of absence.

My brothers, sister, and their families all congregated in the living room of my parent's house on Christmas Eve. And although it was late, the Big People and the Little People mingled. By tradition, we exchanged presents on Christmas

Eve (technically it *was* Christmas, we justified, because it was midnight). None of the children objected, and it allowed the adults to sleep-in somewhat later on Christmas Morning. Of course, the children's best toys were held back in reserve (as gifts from Santa). So when the radio newscaster interrupted the music with periodic reports of an unidentified flying object around the North Pole, the excitement mounted.

As with any family, we engaged in happy, frivolous conversation, to the background of our favorite holiday carols and other sounds unique to Christmas.

Here's what the Big People said:
> *"Well after all, Christmas is for the kids; Oh, isn't that lovely; I had to work half a day today; I've always wanted one of these; I can't eat another bite; I don't need to return it, it's exactly what I wanted; I can't believe he ran that kickoff all the way back; it's just the right size; I'll start my diet after the holidays; and, save the bows."*

Here's what the Little People said:
> *I already have two of these; Hey, I got gypped; Billy already knows what he got coz he peeked in the closet; I want what Sissy has; Daddy, it's my turn to play with it and tell Bobby to give it to me; is this all I got?; Ummm I'm telling; I get some more from Santa tomorrow; huh-uh, man, it was your fault; and, Mommy, Stevie broked it ... did not ... did too."*

When everyone finally called it a night—after all the family hoopla was through for what remained of the dark hours—Sharon and I retired for what was left of the evening, in the privacy of my childhood bedroom. I felt like it was my best Christmas ever. A wonderful end to a wonderful Christmas Eve (Christmas Day, past midnight). Now it was time to sleep.

Sharon snoozed, her head on my chest, but I couldn't sleep because excitement encompassed me and kept me awake. And it was dangerously past the time when Santa might see my opened eyes and bypass our chimney (*"but we don't have a chimbley, Daddy"*; *"He comes in through the*

Christmas Terror

wunk hole, now get to sleep, Mikey, before all you get's a lump of coal").

Finally, I slipped away to the land of sweet dreams—until the Beast attacked Sharon, and her screams woke everyone in the house.

***

Before Christmas daylight shone its blessings on the world, the Shroud Man visited Sharon. He gently tapped her soul awake, without disturbing her body. He rapidly spun her mind around and around. He eased her down a black tunnel, while leaving her empty flesh and bones next to me. She would not need them on this journey.

Once on the other side of the black tunnel the Shroud Man left Sharon alone. She was in a tomb. It was an ancient tomb, dank, carved into a cliff. It was centuries old. Thin beams of light filtered in, and they spotlighted the many dust particles suspended in air, in no hurry to settle, and with no place to accumulate if they did.

She heard the Voice utter a single word, "Empty."

That one word hung heavily in Sharon's mind. "Empty." She wondered what it meant. She snooped around, wondering whose tomb she was in. The chamber was small, but being petite, she had ample room.

She paused at the musty slab of stone. At one time, a body was put to rest there, long, long ago. But now the body was gone, and a discarded burial shroud was left behind as the only evidence the crypt had ever been occupied. She touched the cloth and immediately felt the presence of the Voice. She said aloud, "You're not dead."

Then came laughter, from outside. She had not said anything funny. She was serious, dead serious, in a tomb. So who laughed?

(One laugh; two laughs; three laughs; four ...)
"Who are you?"
(five laughs, six, and a whole lot more ...)
(taunting, teasing, outside the door ...)
"Who's out there?"
(nothing was funny, not in the least ...)
(it wasn't a joke, so stop it, you—BEAST!)

"Stop it! Stop it! Stop it!" She ran for the exit.

Somebody threw something, and it hit her in the face. Suddenly a barrage of things were thrown at Sharon. Her face and body ached from the pelting. She turned her back and covered her head. Sharon recognized the smell of oranges.

The Beast tried beaning her to death with oranges. It threw with such velocity, she could hear the grunting of each pitch. Then she heard oranges splattering the walls of the tomb, and realized she was no longer the target. Sharon opened her eyes. Facing the stone slab, she watched hundreds of oranges smash into the shroud, drowning it in juice and pulp.

The barrage stopped.

"Sharon," called a voice from outside the tomb. She waited for more oranges but no more were thrown. "Sharon."

She uncovered her bruised head and straightened up. She stepped toward the exit, wanting to forsake her defenses and charge out the door. But was the Beast out there? Waiting? Setting a trap?

"Sharon."

Wait a minute. That sounds like ... "Grandpa! Grandpa!" Yes, it was he. She knew Grandpa anywhere, in this world or in the other one. She had rocked horsey on his knee too many hours not to recognize his voice.

"Oh, Grandpa," she cried, when she rushed outside to greet him. She missed him greatly. He had been long, long dead. In her troubled childhood, Grandpa had been father, big brother, friend, and Grandpa. She scoured the area to find him. She wanted to lose herself in that warm and secure hug. She craved for his wavy gray hair to spill onto hers, as he snuggled against his little "Punkin' Head."

"Grandpa. Where are you Grandpa?"

The grass, green and tall, cushioned her bare feet like it had when she had been a child. And the cool meadow breeze rushed between her toes. There he was! Down by the river. "Grandpa!" Her feet peddled fast, running after one of those scrumptious hugs.

"Stay where you are, Sharon. Stop!"

The harshness in his voice shocked her. He had never said an unkind word. "I love you, Grandpa."

"I love you, Punkin'."

She raced to him again.

"Stay where you are! You can't come here."
"I don't understand, Grandpa."
"Listen, Punkin'. Do not come to the river."

She looked at the peaceful riverside, where Grandpa rested with his back to her. "Why, Grandpa?" All she wanted was a hug. She took a step forward, quietly. And another, another. Until she was close enough to steal her hug. She touched the back of his black cape.

Grandpa turned around. Sharon opened her arms for the hug. But Grandpa did not hug her. Instead, he pulled a black veil from his face. The skeleton underneath said in a raspy voice, "Do not come to the river."

(Scream-Punkin'-scream. But don't come to the river, because Grandpa loves you.)

***

Now we all sat at the breakfast table trying to calm Sharon. "No, I don't know what it means." The others in my family gathered to find out who had been murdered in the dark, to have screamed such a terrifying scream. "Can you remember anything more?" I asked.

"I ... I ... uh ... sniff (*fear, fear*)."

"We'll talk about it later." I hugged her, and it felt good to her. Not as good as Grandpa's hugs, but I understood more than anyone and ...

"Wait," said Sharon. The Voice had given her a message for me. The Voice always gave her messages. She never understood them, but she always repeated them as instructed.

The Voice told her: "Tell Michael, 'The Evil House is Spanish.'"

"What?" I asked. "I don't understand."

"*The Evil House is Spanish.*"

The Antichrist
"The Evil House is Spanish"

There are, indeed, powerful organizations in the modern world who are paving the way for Satan's return. The example of Opus Dei bears a striking resemblance to the ancient order, Opus Dai, perhaps too much to be considered a coincidence. If the research arguments hold true, then what exists is a powerful order bent on forming a one-world society, with a one-world economy as a throne for their King of the Underworld.

The most prominent member of this anti-Christian organization is King Juan Carlos of Spain. He was actually born in Rome, where he was given up at birth to Opus Dei priests. Nicknamed, "The Boy," Opus Dei groomed him from birth to be the, "Leader of Men, Leader of Nations."

According to Biblical Prophecy, the Antichrist will arise from the city that destroyed Jerusalem in 70 A.D., which was *Rome*. Therefore, the birthplace of the Antichrist *must* be *Rome*. The following facts apply:

> *King Alfonso III of Spain had to flee the country following his overthrow by General Franciso Franco, who was backed by a powerful group called Opus Dei. While in Rome, his wife Maria, gave birth to a son, Juan Carlos. Juan Carlos was born a Roman citizen and was raised from birth by Opus Dei priests. When he was an adult, he returned to Spain and became King, bypassing his father who was rightfully in line. Thus, the King of Spain is a Roman.*

The "King of the Jews" is a Roman Emperor!

In November of 1975, Opus Dei successfully lobbied the Israeli Parliament to restore an ancient rite for the King of Spain to be the Royal Protector of Jerusalem. In 1987, Juan Carlos became the first Spanish monarch in history to enter a synagogue, and on March 31, 1992, he received a special synagogue blessing with President Chaim Herzog of Israel. So what we now have is a Roman Emperor—dominated by a mysterious demonic order trying to establish a global throne for the God of the Underworld—being proclaimed as, "King of the Jews."

Furthermore, Spain was the eleventh nation admitted to the European Common Market, the so-called revised Roman Empire.

> "There will be ten nations, and another shall arise after them, an eleventh ... the Beast "
> (Paraphrased Book of Daniel)

"The Evil House is Spanish." King Juan Carlos could very well be that person. Regardless, the truth will be known when a representative from a European Coalition signs *a 7-year peace treaty with Israel*, guaranteeing Israel's right to exist as a Jewish nation under the protection of the European Coalition, and that Jerusalem shall be recognized as the Israeli capital. To this end, whoever signs that Treaty of Death is the Antichrist.

WORLD WAR III
"The Treaty of Death"

The Middle-East conflict between Muslims and Jews will continue to escalate, until people and nations fear a global spread of their terrorist activities. No nation on earth will escape militant operations from Middle East martyrs. Not even America. But the problem is twofold: (1) innocent people are killed via terrorism, and (2) the world's OIL supply is disrupted, threatening a heinous economic breakdown. World Leaders are concerned about people dying, but they are more concerned about getting their nation's supply of OIL. God showed me that OIL will dictate policy.

Time and again world leaders will attempt and fail to get the Palestinians and Israelis to agree to a peaceful co-existence. Finally, as the world tires of the warring factors, a union of European Nations will force a treaty upon the Middle East. The European Coalition will instigate the perfect peace treaty (known in the Prophecies as, "The Covenant with Death"). They will stress the need to be fair to all parties: Israel and Palestine both have the right to exist as autonomous nations, and each has the right to live in peace and harmony.

The Peace Treaty will establish national boundaries for both the Jews and the Palestinians. The Jews will get Israel, with Jerusalem as their capital. The Palestinians will get the West Bank and the Gaza Strip. The Treaty will be policed by the mightiest force in the world, a United Europe.

As a prominent member of the European Union, the living Antichrist will sign a Seven-Year Covenant with Israel. He will have already been hailed as the Champion of the Jews, Protector of Israel, and he will seem to be the perfect choice to usher in the Perfect Society with his signature. *The identity of the Antichrist, will be the King who signs this seven-year peace treaty.*

The treaty sounds great to the average person, but to the Muslims and Jews, it is a matter of life and death to have control over their Holy City of Jerusalem. The perfect solution to peace is a well-designed trap. They know that Muslims will never settle for anything less than having Jerusalem as *their* capital. They will have no choice but to declare Holy War, since they can never peaceably regain their sacred Jerusalem.

The Arab Nations will approach Russia with a deal they can't refuse. They will offer the Russians all the Arabian oil in the world, in exchange for the total annihilation of Israel. (On March 13, 2001, the new Russian President signed a "weapons-for-oil" treaty with Iran. This is a prelude to the bigger oil-for-Jerusalem deal about to occur.)

To Russia, it is a no-brainer. They have become one of the poorest nations on earth, and the Arab Coalition offers them the greatest riches in history. Moscow accepts. But America will never allow Russia to attack Israel, so Russia must first eliminate America with an all-out surprise, nuclear strike.

So when European nations begin wondering HOW TO SETTLE THE DISPUTE OVER JERUSALEM, the time is near. They will sign a 7-Year Peace Treaty giving Jerusalem to Israel, and they will protect Israel with a European army to enforce the treaty. When they say "Peace and Safety" over Jerusalem, then World War Three will happen within hours.

***

Christmas Terror

The Man on the Shroud came and took me with him to a place above earth, where I stood beside him on his right side, as he sat. From our vantage point we both watched World War III unfold on earth. My sense of Knowing told me I was watching the United States.

Overlooking a large city, I observed warning sirens blast without ceasing. People scrambled for cover underground. I looked for my own family and was concerned that I did not see them. Others were equally concerned about their families, as they called out for loved ones. Surprisingly, though, most of the people were unaware of the catastrophic conditions and they continued milling about the city as usual. I wanted to shout at them, but did not.

From up above with the Shroud Man, I watched a multitude of red-colored missiles converging on the city. There were too many to count and the manner in which they sped towards America was frightening to watch. I wanted to stop them, but as a mere spectator, there was nothing I could do. Strangely, the red missiles began dropping harmlessly from the sky as if the Shroud Man swatted them down. And then larger white missiles from America launched by the thousands, heading in the direction of the red missiles. The white missiles seemed filled with emotion, with immense anger, as they cruised toward their destination. I felt as if the Shroud Man was orchestrating the events down below.

Suddenly a red missile glided menacingly over the American city. It happened so quickly that all I could do was shout, "Noooo!" The red missile exploded with a brilliant white light.

However, because the speed of light is faster than the speed of sound, I never heard the thundering boom that followed the white light of the nuclear explosion. At that micro-moment between the flashing light and the sonic boom, the Shroud Man yanked me and millions of believers into the Cloud World. We were safely tucked away and kept oblivious of World War III down below.

***

Satan's political powers, whoever they might be, are going to start World War III. It is not as unusual as you might think. International bankers have been fomenting wars ever since the first government borrowed a dollar. The biggest fortunes in history have been made by financing both sides of two feuding armies, and then causing their fuses to be lit. This time, they will spark a nuclear holocaust to create the desired global chaos needed to bring into power the Antichrist and his economic Mark of the Beast. The irony is that they will use a peace treaty to start the most destructive war ever.

> *"And he shall make a firm covenant (treaty) for (seven years) And when they shall say, 'Peace and Safety,' then sudden destruction cometh ..." (Daniel 9:27; 12:1)*

> *"And at that time shall Michael stand up (against the Beast) ... and there shall be a time of trouble, such as never was since the first nation." (I Thessalonians 5:3)*

CHAPTER 15
Ancient Secrets

Nothing ruins a good celebration like an uninvited demon. Once again Sharon lay in bed, strung out, missing another day recuperating from Bad Things; only this time they had been the ruination of her Christmas. She had planned on spending only Christmas Eve and early Christmas Morning with my family. She should have been joyfully celebrating at her own home by now, instead of trembling under the covers at my parents' home. Not until the Christmas sun had come and gone did Sharon get out of bed, wobbly, and ill again. "I'll feel better when I get something in my stomach," she said. "Besides, I have to go see my baby. It's *Christmas*, Michael."

I searched the Yellow Pages for restaurants opened on Christmas Night. I found a diner in a shopping strip on the north side of town. It was a far drive from where we were on the south side, but Sharon said a long trip suited her. She cracked the window and devoured the crisp, meaty air, along the way.

At the restaurant Sharon ordered from the blander, breakfast menu to acclimate her lonesome tummy to food. She ate cautiously, picking at her food and conversing between bites. She avoided the subject most on her mind (Bad Things). Other than that, she behaved like she had never been sick a day in her life.

"Can I drive?" she asked, afterward.

It was dark out, and I did not know the back roads to her house. She wanted to drive because she didn't feel like directing me where to turn all he way home. She hurried me into the passenger side of the car. She took the wheel. Her anxiety increased at the realization of going home for Christmas. "You missed the exit," I said, as Sharon passed the highway entrance and cruised the parking lot's outer perimeter.

"I know."

"You know? And you still missed it?"

"I don't know what I'm doing," she said, confused. "I didn't mean to turn this way." And instead of going back, she turned left again, away from the road.

"What are you doing?"

She started trembling and crying. "Nothing!"

"Stop the car."

"I can't! I'm not doing it!" Her hands weren't gripping the wheel, which turned by itself, left again, toward the rear of the shopping strip. At the back alley, the car stopped.

"God, what's happening?" I asked, not expecting an answer.

Sharon saw something. She left the car and ran away from the alley, screaming, "No. No. No."

I leaped out and chased her. When I finally caught up with her, I huffed in her face, "Wassa matter?"

Sharon did not hear me. She did not see me. I held her by both arms and shook her, trying to get her attention. She hit me. "No! No! No!"

"Sharon! Hey! Calm down. It's okay." I hugged her. She cried into my chest, being too short to reach my shoulder.

Standing in the parking lot, Sharon explained. Several years ago she had eaten at the same restaurant we'd just left. She had even parked in the same spot. On that night, she had come out to her car alone. When she got in, a gun was thrust to her head. She was told to drive around back to the alley. The man scaled the front seat and forced Sharon to perform oral sex with the gun barrel. Then he raped her, over and again.

"It was right here in this alley," she cried. She had not returned to the scene again until this evening. She had blocked it from her memory and had not recognized where she was. And now the fear of it came back to haunt her. She had not steered the car. She would have never returned to that spot. Something eerie had guided her. The same kind of something that drove her in circles at my place in Chicagoland.

"Michael, they're after me again. I can't take anymore. They're killing me. They're after you, but they're using me to get to you. Aren't they? Michael, it's got to stop. I can't take it anymore."

I tried to comfort her, but she pushed me away.

Suddenly, she ran through the parking lot, swinging her fists at the air. "They're killing me! They're killing me!" Exhausted, she slumped to the ground, leaning on a garbage dumpster. She looked at me and turned away in tears. "Michael, I *can't* see you anymore. I don't *want* to see you anymore."

I put my arm gently on her shoulder, but she swiped at me, meaning harm if I touched her again. I backed away. She jogged across the street to the Holiday Inn, where she checked in for the night. I returned home, embarrassed to face my family. I was thankful the guests were gone, except for my grandparents. As midnight snuffed away Christmas, my grandmother sat on the sofa trying to comfort me, her arm around my shoulder.

"She's gone," I said. "Sharon's gone."

I shielded my tears with cupped hands. "They drove her away. They attacked her. That's what happened this morning. And again tonight. They've got to split us apart. She tells me things, to help me fight them. She's like a messenger, of sorts. But they *won*. They finally drove her away. And now I don't know what to do."

"Who drove her away?" asked Mom, who also stayed by me, listening to a woeful tale in bits and pieces. "What's going on? Who did what?"

I lifted my face. "*They* did. They don't want us to be together."

"I wish you'd tell us," said Mom. "We don't understand what you're talking about."

"You know we'll help you," said Grandma.

I never forgot my vision about Grandma; it was the first one shown to me by the Shroud Man. I also noticed that

Grandma was beginning to look a lot like the pale, sickly old lady of the future I'd seen nearly two years ago, inside the sphere that had glowed like a Holy Omen.

As I now sat talking to her, I had no way of knowing this would be the final year that Grandma would possess anything vaguely resembling a mind. Alzheimer's Disease would be eating away at her brain soon. And I would be quitting my job and moving into her remodeled attic to try and take care of her after Grandpa died. She would venture up to the attic at three o'clock in the morning, where I'd be writing the night away, renewing interest in my U.S.S. *Indianapolis* manuscript, when she would say to me: "God told me to come up here and have you quit writing *that* book. He says to do the *other*. And I'm not to call you, 'Mike,' anymore. He says to call you, '*Michael*.' And hurry up. You're wasting time."

But for now, I just sat by her side on the sofa and sighed. My Merry Christmas had been ruined by Bad Things in the Dark. Ruined by Sharon's departure. Since my ordeals had started with a vision of Grandma, I decided it was best to tell her *everything*. Drawing a deep breath, I explained into the deepest part of a dark morning.

When I was all finished I waited for them to tell me I was crazy. But Grandma had a secret of her own. One she had locked away tightly in her rusty memory bank for thirty years. A secret about me.

Not everyone present at my birth was human.

And Grandma—having patiently listened to me throughout the entire explanation—said, while her mind was still a mind: "I've got a secret I've never told anybody. There were *angels* in the room when you were born. No one else saw them. But I did. They were singing and waving their arms."

I dried my tears and turned to see the truthfulness in her eyes.

Suddenly, my mother added, "When they brought you in and placed you on top of me, I heard a Voice. It said plain as day, '*This one is for me.*' I never knew what it meant, but I cried when I heard it."

I stood and loped to the kitchen, speechless. Grandma and Mom followed, staring at me, both of them in tears.

Mom removed a silver cross from her neck and placed it around me. "Now I know."

"Know what?"

Mom put her hand to her lips and backed away. Never answering. Never explaining. Never again repeating those simple and stunning words.

I did not realize it at the time, but Sharon was hearing similar stories about the supernatural when she was a toddler. She'd sought immediate refuge with friends, after she fled from the Bad Things and me. Then, on January 5, 1981, she finally made it home to her mother's. She was hoping for at least a small welcoming committee since it was her birthday. But Christmas break was over and nobody was home. Ma went to work and Jodi returned to school. Alone, Sharon wearily plopped onto the sofa and sighed.

She was depressed. Twenty-nine years old. She needed to put her life in order, quickly. A woman had a limited number of prime years to find a good man. She reevaluated her relationship with me. Last night, she telephoned and said she had decided to move in with me, after all. But even as I drove from Lexington that morning, she was having third thoughts about her second thoughts. Was she doing the right thing?

I *scared* her. Not me, myself, but the Evil following me. She wasn't sure about her continued role. But the choice, she feared, wasn't hers. The Voice used her as some type of spiritual messenger. It was true that I scared her; but she was equally scared to *leave*.

She battled opposing instincts. She was a compass needle pointing *South*. Drawn to me by one force, repelled by another. Now, her compelling urge was to try again with me.

She had actually started down to Lexington for the New Year's Holiday, but never made it. She took ill shortly outside Indianapolis, and returned to her friend's, where she stayed. She regretted getting sick around me so often. It spoiled our togetherness. She wondered if the Dark Things were making her ill. Was there a pattern to her illness?

(*knock knock*)

"Who is it?"

"Michael."

Sharon opened the door. I stood on her front porch, naked, except for a green, terry cloth bathrobe of hers, which she'd left at my place.

She wasn't in the mood for humor. "Oh God, Michael. Get in here before someone sees you. I can't believe you did that." She turned away, tossing her arms in disgust.

"Hey, I'm sorry. I'll go get my clothes out of the car and ..."

"No, you won't. You're not going out to the car like that," she blurted, pushing me away from the door. "The neighbors already think we're weird enough. Where's your clothes? I'll get them for you."

"Sharon, wait a minute. Look at me. I did this because you're depressed as hell, and you need to laugh. She finally did smile. I had not heard her giggle in a long time. I changed clothes before Ma and Jodi came home.

When Ma arrive home from work, we exchanged small talk at the kitchen table, while Sharon prepared lunch.

KA-BAM!

KA-BOOM!

"I'M HOME, GRANDMA!"

"No kidding. I thought maybe Russia dropped the bomb."

"Is Mom here?"

"Yes, Jodi, I'm here, and quit yelling." Jodi went into the kitchen and hugged Sharon.

"Happy Birthday, Mom."

"Thank you, Sweetie. I liked the card you left for me this morning."

"I would have put some money in it, but Grandma didn't have change and said I'd have to wait until after school."

"Grandma?"

"Okay, get my purse." She handed Jodi a ten.

"Here, Mom. You can get something with this."

"Aww, that's sweet. I'll get some makeup with it." Sharon stuffed the money into her jeans. "How was school, baby?"

"Izzallrite (It was alright). Like I need five bucks real bad, okay? I'm going skating."

"Well ..."

"Come on, Mom. I'm in a hurry. Grandma, tell her to give me five bucks."

"You tell her."
"Geoood! (God!) Maahh-aahhmm (Mom)."
"I'll *give* it to you. Just tie your shoes first."
"Geoood! (God!)"
"I don't want to argue about it."
"Like okay, okay? I'm tying them. Now give me my five bucks." Crouched down over her shoes, Jodi looked up and saw me. "Have you got five bucks? Like Mom'll pay you back."
"Jodi! Michael, don't you dare. Here, baby, here's the *ten*. But don't hit me up for any more the rest of the week. I'm broke."
"Like okay, okay? Grandma ..."
Grandma stood and put her hands on her hips, pouting, mimicking Jodi to demonstrate how immature she acted. Then she whined like her pleading granddaughter, "Geoood! (God!) Like okay, okay?"
Jodi stared at Grandma's antics. Her eyes grew in wonderment. She blurted, "Like, NEAT, Grandma. Where'd you learn that?"
"Like *NEAT*? Is that all you got to say for yourself?"
"Can I have five bucks?"
"I give up." Grandma responded with a couple of bills. Jodi snatched them up and hit the door.
Sharon yelled, "Sit down and eat before you ..."
KA-BAM!
KA-BOOM!
"That girl's going to make a lot of money, someday," predicted Sharon.
"Why does it seem so quiet when she leaves?" asked Ma.
Sharon put lunch on the table.
"Why did you miss Christmas?" asked Ma, insisting on an answer
Sharon explained about *Bad Things*.
Ma was not phased by her daughter's tales. Scary tales of the Voice, of tombs in other worlds where beasts pummeled her with oranges, and so forth and so on, about many *Bad Things*. "Sweetheart," said Ma, "now there's something *I* have to tell *you*. It's about your Grandpa and you."

Grandpa's Story
The Beast and Baby Sharon

Once upon a time, when Sharon was a teeny tiny baby ...

Grandpa babysat Sharon, like he often did. As always, Grandpa opened the refrigerator and removed his Little Punkin's orange juice. He cradled her in his arms while she fed.

Suddenly her tiny hands pushed away the bottle. She was choking to death and her face turned blue.

Grandpa pried opened her mouth and inserted his finger, expecting to clear orange pulp, or maybe a seed. But what he found, instead, was an unearthly, slimy green substance filling her toothless mouth.

The orange juice had supernaturally changed into a gummy-gel. And the gel had seemingly come alive. It knew what it wanted done, and it strategically blocked her vital passages: nose; throat; esophagus; windpipe.

Grandpa scooped out the sludge, yelling: "You can't have her! You can't have her!" But the more he scooped, the less good it did. It grew.

While Grandpa panicked over Little Punkin, a dark, frightening shadow materialized in the kitchen. It laughed. Laughed at Grandpa's useless actions. Laughed at the blue baby with the green gel stuck down her throat.

Grandpa screamed again: "You can't have her! You can't have her!" He kept scooping, shoveling.

The Beast laughed and laughed. But when a Friendly Alien entered the kitchen, the Beast vanished.

The Friendly Alien looked at Little Punkin' and smiled. The gel changed back into orange juice. She spit up, and it trickled harmlessly down her chin.

Grandpa stared at the Alien Man. He had tanned skin that contrasted well with his snowy-white hair. He also had a thick, white mustache, but Grandpa strangely noted to himself that the Alien Man had no beard. He wore a long purple garment that covered him up all the way down to his feet. His feet did not touch the ground when he drifted away from Grandpa and Baby Sharon. The Alien Man smiled again and left, as mysteriously as he had appeared.

"Michael's seen him," said Sharon to Ma, speaking of the Alien Man that Grandpa described.

I looked at Reba and said slowly: "He's on the Shroud of Turin."

Ma gasped. *"That's it! That's Daddy's secret!"*

***

"I saw Grandpa," Sharon told Ma. "That man Grandpa saw took me out of my body and I ended up in a tomb." She recounted the story about a beast laughing at her, while pelting her with oranges. "Grandpa helped me get out," she said. She mentioned how strange it was that Grandpa's encounter with Baby Sharon involved orange juice, and now she'd had an ordeal with oranges. "But what's the green gel chocking me to death got to do with anything?"

PART THREE

WAR OF THE ANGELS

And there was war in heaven: Michael and his angels fought against the Dragon: and the Dragon fought and his angels ... And the great Dragon was cast out, that old serpent, called the Devil, and Satan ... he was cast out into the earth, and his angels were cast out with him ...

Woe to the inhabiters of the earth and of the sea! for the Devil is come down unto you, having great wrath for he knows he has only a short time.
(Revelations 12:7,12)

CHAPTER 16
January 10, 1981
Get Out of That House -- NOW!

The Baby Beast lurched at Sharon. It latched onto her face, sealing her mouth and nostrils so she could not breathe. It was killing her! It pumped a thick, green gel down her windpipe. It stuck to her face and she could not free herself. It was suffocating her.

She slithered her long fingernails beneath its belly. She pried as a lever beneath a big rock. It made a slurping sound when it popped loose from Sharon's face. A wet, green slime splashed all over her. Sharon vomited the sickly-green gel. Her windpipe cleared. She gulped air, then blew her nostrils free. She held the Bad Baby at arms length and squeezed it. "YOU SON OF A BITCH! YOU BASTARD!"

The Baby Bad Thing begged with its eyes. Then it talked. "Please, don't Sharon. Please, no."

Its voice startled Sharon. In her amazement, she loosened her grip. She tightened back up, just as it made another leap toward her face. She grabbed hold with both hands. "Squirm, you little bastard!" She squeezed it. She squeezed for her life, and squeezed for its death.

"Noooo!" the Baby Bad Thing changed its meek tone and yelped a loud and final, "Please no, Sharon! Plleeaasssee, NooOO!" Then its head splattered as a green volcano erupting.

Green gel splashed Sharon's face: It oozed down her arms, dripped down her chest. "I crushed you!" yelled Sharon. "I finally crushed you!"

"Noooo!" screamed Sharon, awakening to the black of morning, the tenth of January.

At my touch, Sharon hit me. "You Bitch!" She unknowingly battered me. She thought only of the Creature that had lunged at her seconds ago; she believed she was still in the Oak Forest, clawing and scratching for her life.

Suddenly, Sharon leaped off the piles of blankets that served as our bed. She rushed to the walk-in closet and flipped on the light. In one motion, she yanked her two suitcases off the rack, crashed them to the floor and popped them open. "I gotta go."

"Go where?"

"Outta here." She haphazardly packed her clothes, and paused only long enough to turn to me and say, "No more, Michael. They're KILLING me!"

She fled downstairs, skipping steps and banging her suitcase alternately against the wall and stair railing. She slowed her exit and approached me in the corner.

"Here," Sharon spoke, as she handed me a message from them. "I have to go, Michael," she cried. "I have to. It's not only me they'll kill, if I stay. I saw you, Michael—Dead! You were DEAD! DEAD! And I don't want to be here and watch it happen! Oh, God, Michael. I'm sorry. I'm so, so sorry." She left.

I browsed Sharon's letter, then threw a Bible across the living room and screamed, "Nooo!" when it crashed against the wall. I beat my fists on the carpet. What Sharon had seen was my final confrontation in the Dark World. And the Beast stood over my fallen body, boasting:

"I BEAT YOU! I BEAT YOU!"

Ouch. I had passed out, hard telling in what position on the living room floor, and the pain stirred me awake. I could barely turn my stiff neck, as my eyes scanned the darkness to gather some familiar bearings, while my grogginess slowly faded.

I stood, but not easily. My legs were like cardboard tubing, and my ankles were rigid like a new pair of army combat boots. My chest felt like a massive heart attack had come and gone, and my shoulders felt like I had run the football into the Chicago Bears front line without padding. I was sore.

What time is it? My protesting eyes did not feel up to the shock of a bright light, so I illuminated the kitchen barely long enough to read the clock on the counter: *six o'clock.* I flipped the light off and sat back down on the living room floor.

Six o'clock when? I didn't know if it was *six-in-the-morning* or *six-in-the-evening.* It was dark out, which it would have been for either time on this day of the year. *What day is it?* Was this the day the Beast was coming to kill me? I thought long and hard, when suddenly an idea popped into my head. An invisible urge whispered to me. I felt whisperings that I needed to learn more about the Beast, to defeat it and save myself. *That's what you want, isn't it, Michael?*

I went to my office and gathered my collection of Satanic Rites, along with the many notes and materials Patrick had given me. The mysteries of the Dark World. The thoughts came faster. I opened a manual on the Black Mass. Inside were the answers I needed, whispered my thoughts. Everything I needed to learn the secrets of the Beast. Knowledge of Evil—if I would only concentrate. I needed the proper atmosphere.

I needed an altar, so I hurriedly rearranged my desk. Instead of three candles, I used one oil-burning lamp. It wouldn't matter, if my heart was sincere, which it was. I *had* to know more.

I recited the Lord's Prayer backwards. " ... name thy be Hallowed." *Good, Michael, just obey your thoughts and we'll be fine. Feeling better?*

Yes. Yes, much better.

I removed a ball of string from my top drawer and made a circle on the carpet. "Is this the way?" I spoke aloud, to whom, I didn't know.

That's right, Michael. We'll give you the wisdom. We'll show you the mysteries to save yourself. You'll have your answers. You don't need Sharon for answers. Sharon ran out on you. You'll need her photograph; it's already on the altar.

"She did run out on me, didn't she?"

Put Sharon's picture in the circle and you'll have your answers. You'll have knowledge. You don't need Sharon. You don't need anybody.

I *didn't* need anybody. I felt it. Spiritual wisdom flowed through me. Now I understood. I knew Sharon had done a Bad Thing. Then even more wisdom sped through my enlightened mind. Sharon was guilty of more than simply *doing* a Bad Thing. Sharon WAS a Bad Thing.

That's right, Michael. Got to remove her. Remove her.

I tore Sharon's picture in half and tossed it back inside the circle. I grabbed hold of the string, where it overlapped. I yanked the string up from the floor, unbinding the Bad Things, leaving Sharon's destroyed photo by itself, in the open. "Remove her! Remove her!"

"Do not dwell on these."

What? That wasn't the same voice.

"Do not dwell on these."

That was the Shroud Man. He had come into my room and was talking to me, though I did not see him.

A flame shot high above from the oil lamp on my desk. I jumped. I leaped to my senses, suddenly ashamed at what I had lapsed into. I blew out the lamp and flipped the wall switch. I went to my desk and knocked the Satanic materials off so hard, they scattered.

For the third time, I heard: "Do not dwell on these."

Okay, I would not ever dwell on them again. I gathered the papers haphazardly, wadding and crushing and tearing, until I had two boxloads. I ran to the trash bin outside and heaved them over the open top. I slammed the metal lid down with a crash.

Then I slumped to the ground and rested, feeling instant reprieve. I seemingly weighed less than the air I slowly breathed. The Voice was right. Dwelling on Evil was dangerous. Bad Things and Good Things did not mix. Bad Things trapped even those who knew better.

"Tell Sharon to get out. Get out of that house."

(*What?*) I sat there, not responding.

The Shroud Man repeated his warning, much louder, sternly commanding: "Tell Sharon to get out! Get out of that house!"

Okay! I ran inside and reached for the telephone, then thought better of dialing the number. *No, it's too late to call. Especially as upset as she was with me. I had already called her once at home, and she'd burned me with blistering words. She was adamant about getting away from me. "Leave me alone, damn it!" she'd screamed.* I decided not to call, to ignore the Voice, and placed the receiver back on its hook.

"Tell Sharon to get out! Get out of that house! Get out of that house—NOW!!!"

The inexplicable warning frightened me. Forget the time. Dial the number! The phone rang and rang.

"H'lo."

"*Oh, God,*" I thought. Without a word, I hung up. I went upstairs to bed. But at 4:13 a.m., before I had fallen asleep, my telephone beckoned.

When I placed it to my ear, Sharon screamed at me. "Damn you! What did you do? Damn you! Damn you!"

"I didn't do anything, Sharon! What's the matter?"

"Didn't you just call me a minute ago?"

"Yeah, but ..."

"I told you never to call."

"I had to! Sharon, get out of that house! Now!

"Make them go away! They're after me! They're everywhere!"

"What is?"

"Those things! You conjured them up because I left. Damn you! Damn you!"

She interrupted her conversation to scream and to cry.

"Sharon, what's going on?"

"Michael, get them out of here! They're flying all over my room! I hate you! I hate you!"

"Sharon, I ...."

She slammed the phone down.

That was the last I ever heard from Sharon.

CHAPTER 17
I Beat You! I Beat You!

I stayed inside my apartment for the remainder of the week. A couple of times, I went to the corner store for a bite to eat. But that was all. I ignored *this* world around me, and concentrated solely on that *other* world out there. When I slept, it was mostly in daylight. I did not want to sleep at night. When it got dark, I would simply sit or stand by the window all night until sunrise.

Late on January 23, I stared out the sliding glass door of my upstairs patio, outside my bedroom. I gazed at the blackened skies, waiting, remembering, and cringing. *There's a war up there*, I thought, looking out, looking up. The crisp, wintry sky offered a clear picture: bright, gaseous stars; mysterious planets; untouched galaxies; innumerably unnamed universes. Beyond that, who knew?

***

The Shroud Man finally came for me on the thirteenth night after Sharon's frightful departure. Strangely, I understood it to be my last voyage to the Dark World. Nobody had to tell me; I simply knew. The Shroud Man had shown me something new on each trip, as if he had been educating me about the dark angels, their habitation, and the wars they were fighting. In all the journeys, the Shroud Man had never taken me to see the Good Angels—only the bad, as if he wanted me to explain their existence and to send a warning by writing this when the proper time had come. All of the previous trips had been mere warmups, in preparation of this, the final showdown. I knew what awaited me. I did not want to go, either. Not on this journey. When the Shroud Man tugged at my mind, I tugged back. Nonetheless I went into the black tunnel, twisting my way to the Dark World for the last time.

I had an appointed rendezvous with the Beast, which is why I was so hesitant about making this journey. I moved through the Dark World very cautiously, hoping I was wrong.

And then I heard it—the Growl!

From the depths of its throat it rumbled, like a distant, brewing storm. It was an ultra-low vibration. A ragged, heavy bass that grew into a vibrant thunder. The Dark World reverberated. I slowed my advance, afraid. The Beast lurked out of view, but I had heard that gnarl before, and I'd never forgotten the terror. I knew who it was. It camouflaged itself in the blackest black of the Dark World, taunting me with its growls.

And then there was nothing but silence. It was the scary side of Silence, the calm before the storm. I backed away, keeping my senses glued to where I had last heard the growling. I prepared a meager defense, having been shown by the Shroud Man how angels fight. I was hoping it would not come to a confrontation, but Knowing told me otherwise.

The Beast attacked me from straight ahead. I abandoned all thoughts of fighting back because the difference in power was so overwhelming. I turned in full retreat and fled as quickly as I could. I flew through the darkness looking for safety, hoping the Shroud Man would come rescue me as he always had in the past. But he was no where to be found, as if he had done his job training, and now it was up to me.

The Beast closed in, and with superior speed, and with a good deal of pleasure, it cut me off and diverted my escape.

Although the Shroud Man had personally tutored me in the skills of angelic warfare, fighting the Beast was out of the question. This was a battle that should have been fought by the Shroud Man himself, not by me. All I could hope for was to avoid a deadly look into Its eyes. From past experience, I knew the blast of power would come from his eyes, then into mine; I spun and circled, always keeping my back to the Beast. I simply could not face It. It toyed with me like a cat playing with its catch. Finally, when It was ready and wanting, It zoomed around and faced me, head-on. I froze. It was my very first, full-frontal view of Satan.

He is not the devil who has been portrayed in comics. There is nothing funny about the way he looks. He is the epitome of horror. His body is covered with scales, instead of skin. He is reptilian. His scales are brownish-green, with no highlights in color. He does not have horns, although a protrusion on the top of his head fans out to both sides. The Beast does have a tail, although it is not like the cartoon character whose tail is rope-like and ends in the shape of a spearhead. In reality the Beast has a tail similar to that of a large crocodile.

His face does not have scales like the rest of his body. It looks more like the wet and slimy skin of a catfish. His mouth is oval shaped, toothless, and flabby like that of bigmouth bass. And his mouth opens and closes like a fishy nostril puckering for oxygen.

His face is disfigured by two elongated scars that rise above the rest of his skin. It looks as if the raised marks were caused by a cowboy's branding iron, like a rancher marking his livestock. One line runs from his forehead to his chin, and the other from cheek-to-cheek. Somebody a long, long time ago branded the mark of a cross square in the middle of the Dragon's face.

And like the Shroud Man, the Dragon had no eyes. But instead of projecting wondrous thoughts and beautiful visions from the eye sockets, as had the Shroud Man, I sensed the Dragon's hatred spewing out at me. Everything evil poured from those voids in his eyes. The creature inside those frightening sockets had long ago given birth to Terror. Deep down inside was the womb of Death. The place where all Bad Things originated. And they stared straight into my face.

I had no choice but to fight, so I took advantage of firing the first volley of energy, exactly how the Shroud Man had instructed. I raised both arms high, then turned my palms face up, reaching like a satellite dish to absorb energy beams. A Force oozed into my palms and ran down my arms, to my brain, and Power shot out of my eyes in a mighty surge. The invisible Power made no noise as it burst out. Nonetheless, whatever streamed out was Forceful. Power exploded from my eyes, toward its target. Power hit the Dragon squarely in Its penetrable face.

The Dragon laughed at me. It ridiculed my meager effort. It returned a burst of its own, and knocked me to my knees. It laughed, evermore, wanting to prolong the game.

The measure of hot energy tore through my insides. It roasted me from inside-out. I got back up to run, knowing I could not fight the Dragon. But he blasted me again with a fiery jolt that electrocuted me. I collapsed, face down. I was defeated. I waited for It to kill me, and I wanted to end the pain of burning. I did not fight anymore.

The Dragon delayed killing me. It wanted to gloat, as It squirmed over me. As I lay there, I could not believe that this was happening. The Dragon was grunting and groaning, rapidly shuffling over top of me. It was so excited, that It didn't want the moment of victory to end. Each time It stepped over me, I could feel Its tail dragging over my back, and Its paws and claws poking at me in torment.

It stepped on the backside of my burning belly, and I screamed. The Dragon laughed. My pain was humorous to It. Then It quit laughing. It was time to terminate me. The Dragon planted a foot into my back and pushed me down. It posed over my body as a hunter in triumph, with one foot on my back, and one foot grounded. It belted a shattering proclamation of victory:

"I BEAT YOU! I BEAT YOU!"

Those were Sharon's exact words of prophecy. Suddenly I rolled my eyes upward and saw a glowing ball of light (a mirage? there is no light in the Dark World). It appeared from somewhere at the far boundaries of darkness, like an intruder in a strange land.

And the light was ALIVE! A living creature! A Being so bright I could not look directly at it. The alien was a Bright Being.

Suddenly, the Bright Being zoomed across the Dark World before I could even blink from its brightness. It invaded me! The Bright Being stormed inside of me, uninvited, and took command of my stricken body. It yanked me to my feet. Bright Being extended my arms into battle position. He thrust open

I Beat You! I Beat You!

my eyes in great wrath. Bright Being was very, very mad. He had stood off in the distance and watched the Dragon do Bad Things long enough, and now He was intervening. Bright Being was not just intervening on MY behalf, but on behalf of EVERYONE who ever existed and had suffered from Bad Things, and for every creature ever forced to creep on the ground, and for every tiny bird who ever fell from the sky, and for every tear that ever dropped, and for every instance of Bad Things ever done to anybody, anywhere, at anytime.

All I could do was cry as I was manipulated like a marionette by the Bright Being inside me. I bawled like a baby because of the awesome power brewing inside me. Bright Being could have detonated every volcano all at the same time with the mere breath of a single nostril. And he was so enraged he was going to HIT somebody with all his godly might.

Then I saw the Dragon.

Suddenly, the scene looked to me like a slow-motion replay. I flashed back to the first time I had encountered the Beast. How terrified I had been! I remembered how I had been unable to breathe, unable to talk. That's how fearsome the Beast had looked to me then.

Now when I stared into the Dragon's eyes, I saw the definition of real terror. It was now a RECIPIENT of Terror (Let's see how YOU like it!). A devouring horror screamed from the Dragon's eyeless eyes.

A colossal burst of power spewed from my eyes and into the Dragon. A gaseous ball of fire ignited and engulfed the Dragon, but its flames did not consume him. Rather, the Dragon was imprisoned within the fire, and the flame's purpose was to torture, not terminate. The pain and terror distorted the Dragon's ugly face. He tried to scream, but the fire sapped his breath. The heat dissipated the words inside his beastly throat before they escaped. His cries were silenced by the flaming, miniature sun enveloping him.

I was witnessing Hell. A physical state and place.

Bright Being was showing me the ultimate result of its wrath toward Bad Things. Hell will not be a party with bad angels and bad people all having fun together. It will be mano-y-mano, inside a painful ball of fire that will never burn itself out, and will never consume unto death, and the *prisoner will be caged in his own personal solitary furnace forever and ever.*

The Dragon endured such indescribable torment, such pure pain, that I felt sorry for it, grimacing at the sight. I would have never guessed I'd be pleading mercy for the Beast, but I did.

(Put it out of its misery. Kill it. Please, please, please— KILL IT!)

But Bright Being did NOT kill it. He would not EVER kill it. Instead, Bright Being grew angrier and madder and increased the pain. Still, it was not ENOUGH pain. Bright Being did something that hardly seemed possible—He made the fire hotter. He hurt the Dragon more. He increased the suffering because it was not yet enough to make up for all the misery the Beast had caused in the past. Bright Being added more terror. More hurt.

I cried more for the Beast. (Kill it! Please, Kill it!)

But Bright Being still refused to kill the Dragon. He did just the opposite. He froze Time itself, at the very height of pain, so that the fire and suffering would continue forever, and the Dragon would remain for always at the height of his agony and terror.

I watched the Dragon try to scream away the excess hurt, but he could not. His face and mouth stretched out of shape. Bright Being shot another jolt of energy, and cast the Dragon and his flaming capsule of fire to the farthest edges of the Dark World, so that I no longer had to witness the suffering.

> *The Son of man shall send forth his angels, and they shall gather out of his kingdom all things that offend, and them which do iniquity; And shall cast them into a furnace of fire: there shall be wailing and gnashing of teeth.*
> *(Matthew 13: 41-42)*

CHAPTER 18
Michael and the Living Star

My encounters in the Dark World were finished. For that, I was more than thankful. But I had not worked since Bad Things began their heaviest assault, when Sharon first visited me last November. I was now out of money. It was January 31, and with double-rent past due the landlord was evicting me at daybreak. On Saturday evening I complacently packed my belongings in preparation of being homeless by sunrise, in stark contrast to the joyful neighbors around me who got into their cars and drove away for some weekend fun. I envied them. For me it was simply time to move on again.

I should have been sadder than I was, but what I felt most was relief. My ordeal had played out its hand. At long last, it was over. At the same time, an emptiness gnawed away at me from the inside. Why had this happened? As I packed, I recapped the scenarios again and again.

Exhausted, I went to bed for the last time at my home in Lexington.

***

Early Sunday morning the Shroud Man came to visit me one more time. He took me out of my body and directed me to a beautiful countryside. No more Dark World. In the middle of a plush green meadow, workmen briskly constructed an interstate freeway. The crew worked only on the right side of the highway, a double-lane going up a steep hill. The left side of the road was not being built.

I asked, "What is this?"

The workers stopped. They all pointed to the top of the highway, where the road peaked with the blue horizon over the hill. I looked above the inclining road, high in the clouds, where I saw a large white sign. On the sign was a name printed in bold, black letters for me to see, as if it were an elevated billboard along an interstate system, seen for miles:

MICHAEL

"What does this mean?" I asked the Shroud Man, who stood beside the workers. The Shroud Man never said. But instead, he nodded toward the workers, who in turn, glanced once again at the sign in the clouds, then back toward me. They pointed their fingers directly at me, and all said in unison:

"Michael."

I returned to my body. I opened my eyes. The sun said its first hello of the day, gently, like a merciful snooze alarm awakening me softly: *"pssst pssst."* I did not budge from my bed, but lazily pondered, "Michael?"

The sun reached into my bedroom window and reminded me again: *"Time to get moving, Little Mikey. Places to go. Things to see."*

I rolled up my bedding and carried it to the car. I carefully positioned it in the back seat to pad the breakables. I set my lamp gently in front, on the passenger side of the floor. Routinely, I squeezed the lampshade into the back, piling it on top, blocking the window. I rearranged this, pushed down that, and cleared a path for the rearview mirror. Then I sauntered back to my apartment and locked the front door behind me for the last time.

I drove away in search of Good Things.

Homelessness is not something that is understandable until it happens. It is not a Good Thing to have nowhere to go, especially when it is bedtime. At least I had a car, although they would soon be repossessing it. I wasted away the daylight by mall-walking, resting on benches, and just thinking. But when the sun went down, I learned how foolish I had been complaining about not having had a bed. Now, I longed for my bed-on-the-floor, or for that matter, a plain hardwood floor under a roof.

I drove west on Interstate-64, stopping often at coffee shops along the way. I had no destination, just driving with a full tank of gas and thinking. Out of habit, I headed north when I reached I-65 and crossed the Ohio River. It was late by then, and I was sleepy. I pulled into a rest stop. I parked far enough from the other cars to have my privacy, yet near enough for protection against robbers who preyed on travelers.

I tried to get comfortable in the front seat, but I did not have room to stretch out. And I simply could not sleep sitting up. I threw my lampshade in the dumpster. When it disappeared over the trash lid and out of sight, I felt as if I'd lost part of my family. But the car wasn't big enough for both of us.

Finally, after I had stuffed everything from the front seat into the back, I eased myself down and pulled a blanket over me. But I still could not sleep. It was too cold. Occasionally, I would blast the car heater, but for the most part I left it off to conserve gas. I was jostling under my bedroll when someone startled me with a sharp bang on my side window.

Alarmed, I unburied myself and sat up. A man in a short sleeve, red-plaid shirt and dark dress slacks stood beside my car. He was not wearing a coat, and his attire looked cold and out of place for a wintry night. I rolled down the window. "Yes?"

"Michael, I'm supposed to tell you: *'Do not worry.'*"

"Huh? Thanks." I turned to throw the blankets off, to get out of the car. But when I turned around, the man was *gone.* Vanished.

I jumped out of my car to find him. I stared one way, then another. There was no place he could have gone in such a hurry, yet he was no where to be found. Not a trace of the man. *Where'd he go? He couldn't just disappear? How'd he know my name?*

And when I was standing in the middle of the lot, finally convinced that—well, maybe he *had* just disappeared—something else happened.

A star fell.

Not your average falling star, but one that divinely "floated" only a few hundred feet above the parking lot, over me.

(*A star with a brain?*)

It had four points, cross-shaped. I watched to see if it would move again, but it didn't. It stayed put, overhead, very, very low. It was not an aircraft, nor a helicopter, nor or a flying saucer. It was a *Living Star* that knew exactly what it was doing.

And its light shone like a *spotlight*, illuminating the interstate entrance ramp in front of me. I could not move, in awe of the Living Star. It seemed to be pointing the way for me, a sign indicating I would be spending some time on the highway. I had already known *that*, but what I *hadn't* known up until now, was *not to worry* about it.

Having seen the Living Star, I understood it would be futile to search for the mysterious messenger I had just encountered. He had come from "up there."

Finally, a man in the parking lot got out of his car and walked up to me, as I continued to gaze at the ominous Living Star. The man had a scraggly beard, biker clothes, and was definitely from the same world as I. He, too, was in awe of the Living Star. I was glad to know someone else was seeing what I saw. Together, we two strangers watched the Living Star for several moments. All he said was, "Far out."

After a short silence, the man next to me said, "That's a sign from God!" At that, the Living Star whisked away. Vanished, in mid-sentence, as if it had been waiting for that acknowledgment. "And I'm not even religious," the man continued his previous train of thought.

"You know what I think?" I asked.

"What?"

"That's the Star of Bethlehem."

"We can't ever tell anyone," he said. "They'll think we're crazy."

CHAPTER 19
It Ain't Over, 'Til It's Over

I lived out of my car for months, although sometimes I worked enough to rent a cheap motel. Finally, by July of 1981, I moved into a slum house near the Ohio River, on the Kentucky side of Cincinnati.

I shared a one-room apartment with thousands of roaches, hundreds of mice, and with a childhood friend of mine who'd gotten divorced and had nowhere to go. We laughed that our $40-per-week dump was just a rung above homelessness. But it was ours and it wasn't on wheels. I had a small bed with a mattress and he had a sofa to sleep on. We had the bare essentials, paid for by selling blood plasma each week (although I always fainted). Before long we each had a plate and a fork and spoon, until one of our neighbors broke into our abode and stole one of the forks and a dish rag (wasn't much else worth taking).

The nicest part about our place was its proximity to the water. I could stand on Main Street Bridge overlooking the Ohio River and dream about better things to come, on my long road back to being normal again.

The fun part about dreaming at the river was making believe I had some *"spending"* money. Maybe I could save enough for the movies (or even to buy a television—a used one; small; black-and-white). And get some money for dating. Maybe I could find a steady girlfriend (*one who knew nothing of Beasts and Bad Things, since they were now gone*). Spending money could be used for a lot of things, I thought. It would be great to have enough food to *snack* on; eating just for the *fun* of it. But other than the thought of having ample food, my fantasies centered upon having enough money to watch a *Reds* baseball game. I truly loved sports; and the stadium was right over there, at the end of the bridge. I would watch crowds enter the gates, listen to them cheer, then watch them stream out. I would pretend I was among them. That is why I liked the river. It brought my little fantasies to life. Then one day I was inclined to realize my fantasies by working hard again to achieve them. I was ready and determined to make some airline school enrollments once more.

I hired a secretary to schedule my appointments, the same concept as before with Be-Bop, when I had established a company sales record. I had actually talked to Be-Bop once from Lexington, to see how she was doing. She was doing fine with the home study portion of her airline school training, and was anxious to get down to Florida for the resident training. I also called to let her know I mailed the two hundred dollars I owed her. My departure from Chicagoland, Indiana, had been rather hectic, and I'd forgotten all about Be-Bop.

"You mailed my money? Wow, my boyfriend bet me you just skipped town and like I'd never see my money coz you didn't really have to, you know, since you weren't in town anymore, if you know what I mean and everything but like I knew you'd pay me, though."

"You'll do really well," I said. "I've never met anyone who loves to talk as much as you. That's half the job in the travel industry; the other half is showing up to work on time."

The secretary I hired in Cincinnati was not as loquacious as Be-Bop, but instead, was much more mature. For one, she lived in the same apartment building. I never had to chase her down and haul her in to the office. I let her telephone from her own apartment (she was the only one in the building who had a telephone).

Gladys and three of her five children lived in the building's remodeled attic. At forty-two and divorced, she was determined to better herself. She and her children had grown up in various rough neighborhoods, where they often had to fight for their lives just to get to work or school. It was a life I never understood, but I knew she was determined to make changes. She attended a local college, intending to be an accountant. She was the top student. I admired her grit, and I gave her rides to class (I no longer drove a Cadillac, but I did have a hundred dollar monstrosity that ran).

As always, Thursdays were reserved for scheduling appointments by telephone, and July 23 was her first day on the job. I did not worry at all about Gladys. She was well prepared and needed no supervision. She had memorized her telephone spiel, and she possessed a professional phone voice. I had no qualms about leaving her alone to work, while I made my appointed rounds. It was nice to be attacking my job again, instead of attacking beasts.

I knew today marked the rising of the *Dog Star*, a Holy Day for the Beast, but my extra-worldly battles had ended, and I now had enough time under my belt to shrug off the past and to move forward on my job. And my enthusiasm quickly paid off. I enrolled the first two students I interviewed. I earned a pretty good commission for a night's work. I thought they would both do well in travel careers, too, so I felt good about making the sales. Everything about my life was shaping up, at last.

I returned in a joyful mood to see how Gladys was doing, on her first day of setting appointments for the upcoming weekend. I opened the door and walked in.

Gladys screamed at me. "Michael! It's after me." She curled up in the corner of the room, sobbing and trembling. She was terrified. "Something's after me!" She ran toward me, seeking protection. She babbled, and it was hard for me to understand her frantic exasperation.

"I tried to make your calls, and every time I picked up the phone, there was so much static I couldn't talk. And one time the phone shocked me and I dropped it."

"Calm down, Gladys. I know what it was. You don't need to explain."

"No, you don't understand. Something laughed at me, and said, 'You won't make those calls for Michael.' I said, 'Yes, I will.' And then it *growled* at me!

"Gladys, I under ..."

"It said I can't help you, but I did anyway, and that's when the phone shocked me."

I held Gladys and patted her back, trying to calm her down. She trembled so hard, she had difficulty breathing and talking at the same time.

"I said, 'I'm making these calls!' and then it said 'You'll be sorry,' and laughed. I'm scared. Michael, it said it's going to *KILL* you!"

Then she quietly asked, "Michael, what was that thing? What's happening?"

"Let me fix some coffee. I have something to tell you."

Bad Things returned.

I thought IT was over. The reappearance of Bad Things hit me like a truck and I quit my job and ran away. But I could not run away from the war of the angels.

IT was back. I was taken by surprise since so much time had passed. I had mistakenly thought it *was* over. But TIME is an *earthly* element. *Humans* are unique about mapping everything into bits and pieces of TIME. We pay billions of dollars *annually* (another unit of TIME) to make comparisons of TIME, or to get somewhere on TIME, or to see if we have enough TIME.

There are *someTIMES*, and *all-the-TIMES*, and *past TIMES*, and *last TIMES*, and *next TIMES*. When we're young, TIME flies. If we sit still TIME passes us by. To the business man, TIME is money. To the incarcerated, TIME is something to kill while doing TIME. Athletes seek to increase playing TIME, while coaches call TIME in order to preserve playing TIME. And when the game of life winds down, we sit in rockers and mentally capture lost TIME to reminisce—the best of TIMES and the worst of TIMES. To us, TIME is everything.

Elsewhere, TIME is simply a highway to get from one dimension to another. A spiritual interstate system. I thought I had put enough Time and Distance between me and the Bad Things, prior to this latest visit. I had allowed TIME to cushion the horrifying memories. TIME can be a wonderful friend in such cases. TIME heals all wounds.

Unfortunately, the Beast is no respecter of TIME. ITS sudden reappearance carried that frightful reminder. IT is TIMEless. Although the celestial battles have already been fought and the outcome determined, it's as if the wars were fought in a different TIME ZONE, and they have not yet happened here on Earth. It is like when New Year's strikes midnight in Paris, it is still on its way to Los Angeles, where it has not yet happened.

The Beast has not yet come to Earth, but nonetheless it will come, and it is bent on terror and total destruction of everything created by the Shroud Man, including me, you, and your little dog, too. Yes, Virginia, there *is* a Kingdom of Darkness. And in it, a Beast. It commands an army of Fallen Angels. Every one of them evil. All of them, coming: "To the Terror of the Earth!" And IT ain't gonna be over, 'til it's over.

A Bad, Bad Baby

I was visited in my sleep by two newborn, male babies, placed in front of me in strollers.

One baby was sweet. He was the type of baby that made a parent wish for another baby and another and another. Although I did not recall any recognizable scent, he seemed to be the kind of baby that would have smelled like Johnson & Johnson™ baby powder. All fresh and clean. He was always smiling. His eyes were soft and easy.

The other baby was not so nice. He did not smile. He did not gyrate with joy. In fact, he stayed unusually motionless, his eyes keyed upon me so intently that I felt violated.

Then the sweet baby went away, strangely, on his own accord. Nobody came and carried him off; nobody wheeled him out. He did not crawl away. He simply faded.

The quiet baby stayed, laid out before me as I stood watching curiously. Now that the sweet baby was no longer in my presence, the quiet baby began to stir uneasily. Its steely eyes held me prisoner. I could not move. Its eyes were old. They looked older than Time. It was a stark contrast that a brand new baby would have such very old eyes.

I had seen that evil look before, only it had not come from a tiny, newborn baby. It was the Beast, only this time it was incarnated inside a baby. A human baby; at least to the average onlooker it was human.

The scenery changed to that of a busy sidewalk in a large downtown area. The Bad Baby was inside a carriage, with the top down, so a throng of passersby could stop and admire it. The Bad Baby was now a smiling, laughing, beautiful baby. In reality, it was a mere imitation of a beautiful baby. I tried to warn those around me as to its evil nature, but they did not believe me. How could a little baby be bad? The Bad Baby won public admiration.

The crowd dispersed, laughing at me for saying silly Bad Things about a Good Baby. Then once again, the Bad Baby and I were alone together inside a building. It quit smiling.

Then it tried to kill me. It tried to muscle its way through my eyes with its evil power.

I squeezed its head. It fought me. I yelled, "I'm going to poke those eyes out!" I screamed at the evil in them.

As I gripped the Bad Baby, its body changed. The body of the Bad Baby was now cold and lifeless. It was a plastic imitation, an impostor, born to deceive people that it was a good baby. It vanished into the crowd.

***

That baby is all grown up now. Waiting. Quietly. And his armies of dark angels have pulled back the curtain that separates the celestial world from the terrestrial, and demon encounters will dramatically escalate as the TIME gets closer. There may be times that you sense someone, or something, in your presence. Something that you cannot see, yet you have this feeling that IT is there. Maybe you will hear a Voice. Maybe it will actually materialize in front of you, and introduce itself. Remember, Good Angels are servents who serve their Master and never emphasize their own importance, while Bad Angels are prideful and want to glorify themselves. They want to be your "spiritual guide." They will slowly gain your confidence until they control you. And someday if you rebel against them, bad things will happen.

But wait. The Shroud Man has a secret weapon for you.

***

I visited my widowed mother in the sleepy, pioneer town of Nashville, Indiana (population 814), near the scenic country hills of Brown County State Park, the most visited State Park in America. By December, however, the visitors were long gone, and the only people there during winter months were those wanting to escape the world and do absolutely nothing, in a place where there was absolutely nothing to do. Time stands still in Nashville, Indiana, where everything has pretty much stayed the same since the first log cabin was built a couple hundred years ago. That is the charm of the town. The place civilization has bypassed. The relaxation was pure therapy for my soul. But I could not hide from the Beast, and once again, he did not really care if Time stood still or not—he came back in another attempt to kill me.

I was asleep at 4:13 a.m. when my subconscience (spirit) warned me that I had stopped breathing. My spirit went into action, while my body remained asleep. The Beast was weaving a black shroud over my face, causing me to suffocate to death. It was not a finished cloth that was pushed into my face, but rather it was being woven around my head as I lay on my back. I watched the thin threads increasingly dim my view, as if I was being buried alive within this black shroud.

I knew I would be dead if I allowed the Beast to finish weaving my burial shroud, so I reached up with one arm and pulled a handful of the black web off of my face until I could breathe. As soon as I dropped my hand back to my side, the weaving continued. I saw the thin veil of threads thicken over my face, and as it did, my breathing stopped again. This time when I tried to reach up with my hand, the Beast pinned both arms to my sides, and I helplessly watched the black shroud nearly come to completion.

But instead of being fearful of the Beast trying to kill me, I suddenly became angry. I'd had enough. He had messed with my life for too long, and it had to stop. For some reason unbeknownst to me, I screamed (either aloud or in my spirit, I don't know which), "By the Power of His Blood!" My hands suddenly broke free from my sides, and I pulled every last thread of webbing from my face.

I saw the Beast directly in front of me. His body was that of a dragon, and his face was that of a swamp-monster with a cross-shaped tattoo stamped in the center. He was expressionless now, as if bewildered that I had attacked him. I did not fight him in the manner that angels fought, but rather as a simple man who'd had enough. I grabbed him with both *my human arms, and although I felt his awesome strength, I lifted him into the air and slammed him down.*

I felt him flex his powerful muscles beneath the scales of his skin, and I screamed, "By the Power of His Blood!" His muscles went limp and I pinned him to the ground. I was so very, very angry. I grabbed the back of his head and pushed his face into the ground. I recalled how he had once stepped on my back and gloated, "I Beat You! I Beat You!" as his tail dragged back and forth across me. This time, however, I was the one who stood and put my foot on his back. I pressed him further into the ground. I screamed over and again, "By the Power of His Blood! By the Power of His Blood!" It was like a magical phrase that made him frail.

Then the Shroud Man appeared and pulled me from behind and took me away, as a parent would pull a child off the neighborhood bully after an unavoidable fight, to take him home and console him.

It was the best post-ordeal feeling of any journey I had taken. The Beast had no power over me, not even in the flesh. I had learned how to make him feeble and helpless. He wasn't so tough, after all—not since I learned the magical phrase. I felt pretty relaxed when I went back to sleep. "By the Power of His Blood."

***

"By the Power of His Blood," refers to the spilled blood of Jesus Christ on the Cross. That single phrase is the most potent weapon to use against Bad Things. Its effect is complete and immediate. It's as if you are throwing a nuclear spear through the heart of Satan or anyone of his spiritual soldiers.

And that was my last trip to the Dark World. My last fight. My last encounter. To put into your hands the ultimate weapon at your disposal. "By the Power of His Blood!"

***

Now, as I prepare War of the Angels for a third printing, I find that I have grown old. I remember being young when I first encountered the Shroud Man, but somehow a quarter-century has lapsed. My body can no longer endure what once was simple. I even look much older than my years. The homelessness. The battles. Sometimes I feel as if it has all been for nothing. That my life has come and gone. I got word that Patrick died several years ago. And for what? The news rattled me. Is there any point at all to my life? I remember the Shroud Man saying to me, "Well done." But reflecting back, I cannot for the life of me find anything in my resume that would be worthy of such an accolade. Why would an awesome spiritual being care about a feeble old man approaching the twilight of his life?

***

Suddenly, while wide awake reading in bed, I was snatched out of my body and moved to the side of my bed so I could observe. My body was still in bed, sitting up against the headboard. (I finally had furniture.) There was a Living Being inside my body (that it had borrowed from me), and it was speaking in gibberish while looking upward toward the skyline out my window. And I heard a Voice in the Air responding in a two-way conversation that lasted several minutes. I had no idea what was being said for they both spoke a language I did not understand. It was not even a human language. But I do know that it was a loving, romantic conversation.

The Voice in the Air greatly loved the Living Being inside of me. The fluctuations in its voice stirred me. The gentleness overwhelmed me. It was the greatest love story ever told. It was not necessary to understand the words of love, for they carried the same meaning in any language, and the Voice in the Air repeated over and again its love for the Living Being inside my body. I observed, thinking how beautiful was the conversation and the perfect love. The Voice in the Air nearly swept my breath away with its love for the spirit inside my body. I thought about how merciless the Voice in the Air would be if a Bad Thing ever messed with this Living Spirit. The Voice would take no prisoners; it would accept no excuses. It was best to never, ever upset this Living Spirit or else you would be answerable to the Voice in the Air, and surely the punishment would be supernaturally swift and terrifying. I was watching LOVE at its finest hour.

***

Suddenly it was over, and I was returned to my body so quickly I never realized I had been transported back. I sat against the headboard in tears. Happy tears. I had never witnessed such an exhibition of pure love. The emotions were more than I could bear. In my spirit body I had been unable to cry, but now that I was back inside my fleshly body my face was wet. "He loves you!" I said with envy to the spiritual recipient, wondering if it was still inside me sharing my body, or if it had gone.

And the Voice in the Air spoke to me, "I love you, too."

And it overwhelmed me and I knew my life had not been wasted. I could hardly believe that such a powerful, supernatural being had said he loved me. I kept repeating over and over to myself, "He loves me." Good Things were ahead for me.

"Dear Michael," began the unexpected letter from an anonymous person called, *Guided Investigator.* "I found Sharon for you."

TOP SECRET

FROM: US Air Force Patrol Bombing Squadron 152
TO: CINCPAC (Commander-in-Chief, Pacific) Guam
      August 3, 1945:

"ORBITING SURVIVORS INDIANAPOLIS X SEAS ROUGH X ADVISE ON LANDING."
("NEGATIVE ON LANDING X CONTINUE ORBITING.")
"SCENE GRUESOME ... DOWNING PLANE."
("REPEAT X NEGATIVE ON LANDING")
"REPEAT X DOWN FIGHTER PILOT X RESCUES UNDERWAY."

EPILOGUE
Bad Things In The Dark

August 3, 1945
South Pacific Ocean

Bad Things happened in the dark. And at well past midnight, while floating low in an oil-caked sea during a tropical storm, it was very dark. Very bad.

But rain was a Good Thing. Hafford Sharp had not enjoyed a drink since last week aboard the Indianapolis, and the boy now tilted his head and opened his mouth wide as a rain barrel. The few drops he gathered didn't add up to a swallow, and the pain he endured hardly seemed worth the effort. His forehead had burst open earlier, when sun poisoning stretched the skin beyond its limits; now the evening rain pelted his raw face every time he reached with his neck to savor the downpour of fresh water. But as little as he drank, and as thirsty as he was, he refused the temptation of guzzling oily saltwater. He had witnessed the results and he was not ready for that route, no siree, so he sipped what little rain fell between his split and bloodied lips.

In fifteen minutes, the fresh water shut down like a spigot being turned off. Rain clouds parted. The moon came out and shone brightly, enabling Hafford to see quite well; he was thankful, except there was nothing he wanted to see.

A heinous scream from a Loner reminded the men in the group to bunch more closely for protection. Hafford edged toward a Marine floating nearby. It was too cold for *conversations, but talking eased tensions and provided assurances that their ordeal would soon end. For that reason, Hafford endured the trouble of holding his chin steady from the jarring cold, as he mumbled to the Marine, "Wwe ... we'll ... bbb ... bbee ... rrr ... scued ... inin ... the ... mmorn."*

He quit talking when a wave flipped the Marine topsy-turvy. There was no body below the life jacket. The Marine had been eaten from the waist down. Hafford had been talking to a floating head and shoulders. Startled, he swam away to look for someone alive.

Suddenly, a group of men within the circle broke the steady silence of knocking teeth and pneumatic-wheezing. The sharks had been especially active this evening because there were not enough living beings to discourage them. Sharks were now brazen enough to do their feeding in the middle of the (table) circle, and Hafford drew his legs up into a ball and thought about Alabama. He thought about the fun he and best-friend Huie would have, when they went home after the war. He daydreamed about Good Things and not about sharks gobbling him up.

But the current skirmish was not about sharks.

"Japs! There's Japs in the group!" Someone had a knife in a sheath strapped to his leg, and he pulled it out and killed the man next to him. Then he swam after another one to kill.

"He ain't a Jap! He ain't a Jap!"

"Keep out of his way!" said someone. "He's crazy from drinking saltwater!"

"I ain't no ..."

Killed him, anyway. His brain had deteriorated and he did not know what he was doing.

The Saltwater Man swam after Hafford. For a moment, Hafford was mesmerized by the gruesome sight. Saltwater had swollen the man's eyes, until they had popped out of their sockets and dangled from stretched muscle, down to his nose. Hafford barely missed the flailing knife. The Saltwater Man—screaming as tenaciously as the Loner being eaten by a shark a few yards away—swung wildly. He tried to kill Hafford, thinking he was the Japanese enemy.

Hafford tread water, keeping his distance from the blind Saltwater Man. It was only a short minute until the Saltwater Man stopped chasing and gurgled the fluids of Death. Hafford turned his back; he did not want to watch the Saltwater Man die.

But there was soon another and another throughout the night. They had warned them—warned them all—not to drink saltwater! A Civil War erupted between the sane and insane. The Saltwater Men killed everyone unable to keep out of their way: stabbing; drowning; choking; anyway they could kill, they killed. They had gone crazy from the pain, and their minds had altered reality to the point of murder.

Suddenly a new Saltwater Man grabbed Hafford from behind, and they both went below the surface, choking and drowning. Neither could breathe as they wrestled underwater. The Saltwater Man engaged a headlock on him, and Hafford could not break free. He twisted, turned, kicked. But finally, when in a panic from breathing water instead of air, Hafford broke the Saltwater Man's death grip.

They surfaced, both pausing to gulp oxygen and to regurgitate water and oil. "Leave me alone!" screamed Hafford. The Saltwater Man lunged at him again. Hafford dodged. "Leave me be!"

Soon the Saltwater Man stopped moving. Hafford observed carefully, making sure it was safe to drop his guard. Grotesque, that Saltwater Man. A light-colored pus streamed from his nose, from his mouth, and even from the holes in his head that used to house his eyes. His tongue was swollen, so large that it no longer fit inside his mouth, and it split his lips at the side. Hafford had seen enough. Not wanting to rob the man of his dignity, he let him die without an audience.

Hafford turned his back and ...

The Saltwater Man jumped him! He had one last ounce of fight in him before death would claim him. Under they went, again. Hafford had one arm free this time, however, and when they broke water, Hafford punched the Saltwater Man! He hit him hard between the eyes, which by this time was the same as a punch in the nose, because that is where the dangling eyes were located.

Hafford had never heard such a scream from a punch, as when he crushed that poor Saltwater Man's eyeballs. Hafford retreated. He was so sorry. So very, very sorry. "Why didn't you leave me be?" He wondered if he had done the right *thing to hit this poor creature, who hadn't known what he was doing. "I told you to let me alone," he said again.*

Finally before dawn, the battleground quieted when the last of the Saltwater Men died. Beautiful, blessed morning. Morning tranquilized the nightly beasts. "Be rescued today," said Hafford. And he used the last of his energy to help with the morning round-up of survivors.

There were only thirty-seven survivors this morning. There were hundreds last Sunday, thought Hafford. Sumpin' wasn't right, the way Headquarters forgot to rescue their own Flagship. Sumpin's not right at all. They aren't coming! He had avoided that dreadful realization for an horrendous week. But by mid-morning, when one of the thirty-seven said he'd had enough and wanted to kill himself, Hafford bid him farewell, instead of trying to save him with a pep talk of rescue on the horizon.

And Huie? Dear, dear Huie. Huie's dead, he thought, admitting to himself for the first time. Wonder how he died? Hoped it wasn't painful. The luckiest were those who had gone down with the ship.

What about Huie's wife and baby boy? Who would tell them? Who would take care of them? He wished he and Huie would have had the money for a train ticket to Alabama, when the Indianapolis had been dry docked for three months in San Francisco. But they hadn't. And now, way out here, Huie was dead.

Hafford was ready to die now, too. He could not go on. He had tried his best. Good thoughts had been eaten up by Bad thoughts. It was time to let go. He drifted away from the group, and he no longer had the power to fight the waves and swim back. Hafford was a Loner. There was only himself and the nearby fins, cutting the surface of the water.

His mind came to him long enough to converse with the nice Alien Man drifting in the sky above him. He was friendly to Hafford. He held out his hands to comfort him. He looked so fatherly, with his snowy-white hair and his thick white mustache contrasting against the nice tan skin he had gotten out there in the Pacific.

Hafford asked the kind Alien Man if he would be so good as to watch over him, while he took a nap.

"Do not worry," replied the Alien Man.

So Hafford got some sleep. He rested up amongst the sharks, while the Alien Man made them keep their toothy mouths closed.

March, 1976
Jacksonville, Florida

"I thought he had died," Hafford said to me, about Huie. "I didn't see him until we were already spotted, on the last day, just before sundown. I don't know where it came from, but a big, yellow raft fell from the sky and nearly hit me in the head. I pulled myself aboard and when a big wave pitched me up, I saw Huie on a raft, not too far away. We waved to each other.

"A PBY Catalina flew overhead and saw how bad off we were, so it crash-landed and pulled us both aboard its wings. They talked to us like we were *babies*—which we were —we had the *minds* of babies.

"I don't know how I ever made it. I'd drifted away all by myself for I don't know how long. There was somebody who watched over me that wasn't human. I didn't believe in that sort of thing before, but I *became* a believer, let me tell you. We are *not* the only life there is. It was a supernatural being that made me live."

And that's when Hafford leaned forward across his desk and first spouted to me about Bad Things. Introduced me to Evil. Scared me with talk about the rulers of darkness. "A Beast is coming to Earth," he said. "He's going to take over his Antichrist's body and people are going to be nearly terrified to death." He knew it as fact.

"And he's alive. He's here, right now. Not something far, far away, a long, long *time* from now. But *now*. I don't know *who* he is, or *where* he is, but I do know *what* he is. And *what* he is, is Evil, pure and simple. But he'll fool everyone, you see, because all the people who'll remain (*after the Shroud Man shelters believers in the Cloud World to protect them*) will be those who don't know any better. The people who'll have never paid attention to what was going on in the world. The people who thought the whole idea was a joke.

"But the Beast is real. He'll rise to power during your generation. Not *my* generation, but *your* generation. And that's why I believe I was kept alive. To tell you that."

"Behold, I am against thee, O (Russia), the chief prince of (Moscow) and (Siberia). And I will turn thee back, and put hooks into thy jaws ... I will bring thee forth, and ... (Iran and Iraq, Syria and Lebanon, Ethiopia and Sudan), and Libya with them ... Thou shalt come up against my people of Israel ... and in the fire of my wrath ... there shall be a great shaking in the land of Israel; So that the fishes of the sea, and the fowls of the heaven, and the beasts of the field, and all creeping things that creep upon the earth, and all the men that are upon the face of the earth, shall shake in my presence, and the mountains shall be thrown down, and the steep places shall fall, and every wall shall fall ...
And I will send (nuclear) fire on (Moscow) and those that dwell carelessly in the isles (America): and they shall know that I AM ..."
Ezekiel 38, 39

"The truth is coming to pass, whether you're ready or not. And neither you nor I, nor anyone else, can prevent it, no matter what you believe. What you believe, does not necessarily change the truth. It's just too bad you believe, in what you believe."
William Hafford Sharp,
Survivor, U.S.S. Indianapolis

About the Author

Michael Mullen worked in the National Basketball Association for ten years, where he helped pioneer NBA franchises into the computer age. He was the first person to fully automate an NBA franchise. He was first to create a commercial basketball site on the world wide web when he designed and maintained the original site for Prodigy, and he managed an international cyberstaff of more than 200 volunteer reporters. He was recognized as the top computer analyst in professional basketball, and was acknowledged by the White House and the U.S. Senate.

Mullen eventually left computers and ventured into other areas of the sporting industry. He chaired career seminars with numerous professional teams, and with multiple USA Olympic governing bodies. He also authored, *How To Get A Job In Sports* (Masters Press)." He served as General Manager of historic Venice Arena (former headquarters of Ringling Brothers and Barnum&Bailey Circus in Venice, FL), where he hosted international events in Olympic-style boxing for Team USA, and nationally televised professional boxing. He consulted for the newly revised American Basketball Association, then became one of the league's first General Managers. He currently assists emerging authors through AuthorHouse, the largest book publisher in the world.

THE WHITE HOUSE
WASHINGTON
September 6, 1991

"Dear Mr. Mullen:
"You are an example of what can be achieved through hard work and determination. Congratulations on your success, and I hope that you'll continue to share your story and to encourage others. Keep up the good work, and God bless you."
Sincerely,
George H. W. Bush

"Michael Mullen of Indianapolis, Indiana, is a true American success story."
Richard Lugar, United States Senator, Chairman Foreign Relations Committee

"The Indiana Pacers are the most sophisticated computer users in all of sports, and Mike (Mullen) is the reason why."
Bob Perkins, Corporate Program Manager, TicketMaster

"The League (NBA Headquarters) has no comprehension as to the level (you) are at. You are going into areas where no one has ever been."
Seymour Siwoff, President, Elias Sports Bureau

"Michael Mullen is generally regarded as the top computer analyst in professional basketball."
Scholastic Coach Magazine

"We at PRODIGY recognize that you provide invaluable information to our sports board."
Jenny Ambrozek, Manager, Business Communications, Prodigy

CPSIA information can be obtained at www.ICGtesting.com
Printed in the USA
BVOW01s2011291013

334976BV00001B/50/P